FRANCIS FRITH'S
TOWN & CITY
MEMORIES

STAMFORD

GEORGE KEEPING became familiar with Stamford through his work during the 1990s as rights of way and countryside manager for Lincolnshire County Council. He is now a freelance Countryside Access Consultant, specialising in historical research, and has also contributed to books on long-distance and village walks. He has a strong interest in local history and was recently a co-author of 'Heckington a Journey Through Time,' a photographic history of the Lincolnshire village where he lives with his wife and three children.

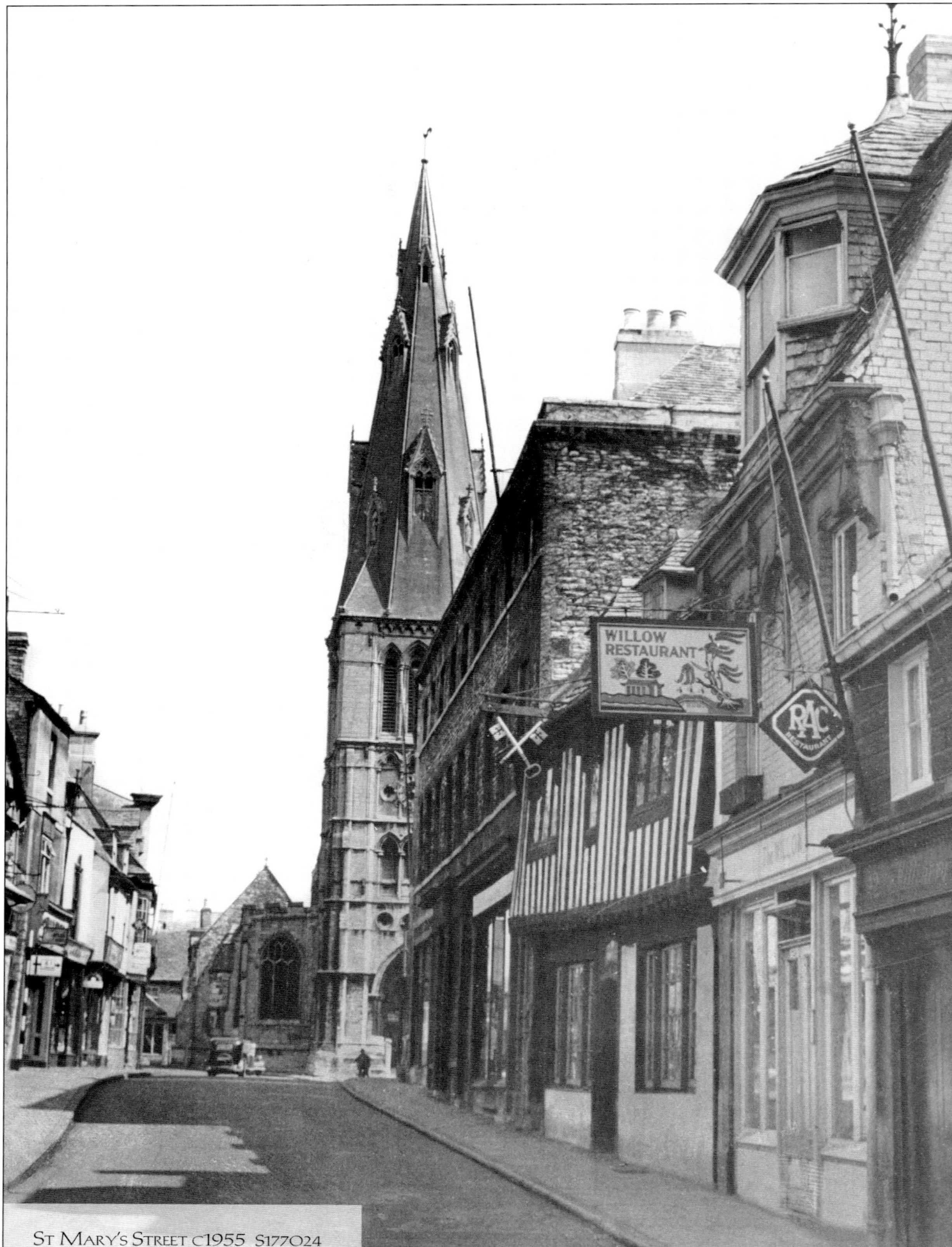

St Mary's Street c1955 S177024

FRANCIS FRITH'S
TOWN & CITY
MEMORIES

STAMFORD

GEORGE KEEPING

FRANCIS FRITH'S

TOWN & CITY

MEMORIES

First published as Stamford, A Photographic History of your Town in 2002 by Black Horse Books, an imprint of The Francis Frith Collection
Revised edition published in the United Kingdom in 2005 by The Francis Frith Collection as Stamford, Town and City Memories

Limited Hardback Edition 2005
ISBN 1-84589-026-4
Paperback Edition 2005
ISBN 1-85937-969-9

British Library Cataloguing in Publication Data

Stamford
Town and City Memories
George Keeping

The Francis Frith Collection
Frith's Barn, Teffont,
Salisbury, Wiltshire SP3 5QP
Tel: +44 (0) 1722 716 376
Email: info@francisfrith.co.uk
www.francisfrith.co.uk

Aerial photographs reproduced under licence from Simmons Aerofilms Limited
Historical Ordnance Survey maps reproduced under licence from Homecheck.co.uk

Printed and bound in England

Front Cover: **STAMFORD, RED LION SQUARE 1922** 72300t
The colour-tinting in this image is for illustrative purposes only, and is not intended to be historically accurate

FRANCIS FRITH'S
TOWN & CITY
MEMORIES

CONTENTS

The Making of an Archive

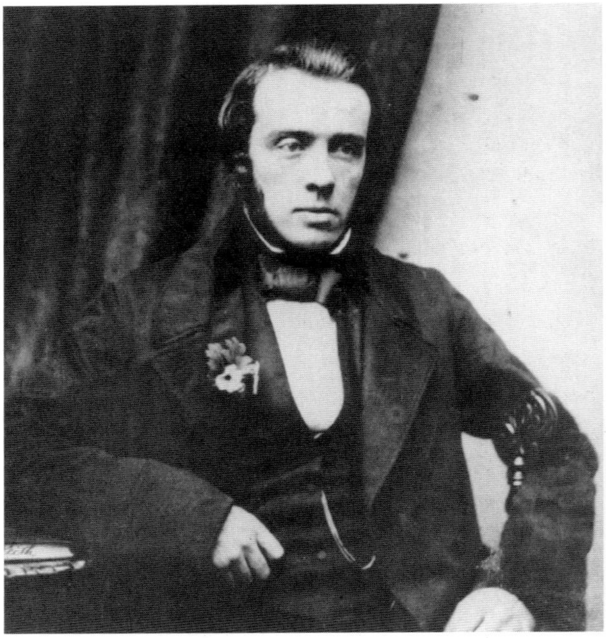

Francis Frith, Victorian founder of the world-famous photographic archive, was a devout Quaker and a highly successful Victorian businessman. By 1860 he was already a multi-millionaire, having established and sold a wholesale grocery business in Liverpool. He had also made a series of pioneering photographic journeys to the Nile region. The images he returned with were the talk of London. An eminent modern historian has likened their impact on the population of the time to that on our own generation of the first photographs taken on the surface of the moon.

Frith had a passion for landscape, and was as equally inspired by the countryside of Britain as he was by the desert regions of the Nile. He resolved to set out on a new career and to use his skills with a camera. He established a business in Reigate as a specialist publisher of topographical photographs.

Frith lived in an era of immense and sometimes violent change. For the poor in the early part of Victoria's reign work was a drudge and the hours long, and ordinary people had precious little free time. Most had not travelled far beyond the boundaries of their own town or village. Mass tourism was in its infancy during the 1860s, but during the next decade the railway network and the establishment of Bank Holidays and half-Saturdays gradually made it possible for the working man and his family to enjoy holidays and to see a little more of the world. With characteristic business acumen, Francis Frith foresaw that these new tourists would enjoy having souvenirs to commemorate their days out. He began selling photo-souvenirs of seaside resorts and beauty spots, which the Victorian public pasted into treasured family albums.

Frith's aim was to photograph every town and village in Britain. For the next thirty years he travelled the country by train and by pony and trap, producing fine photographs of seaside resorts and beauty spots that were keenly bought by millions of Victorians.

The Rise of Frith & Co

Each photograph was taken with tourism in mind, the small team of Frith photographers concentrating on busy shopping streets, beaches, seafronts, picturesque lanes and villages. They also photographed buildings: the Victorian and Edwardian eras were times of huge building activity, and town halls, libraries, post offices, schools and technical colleges were springing up all over the country. They were invariably celebrated by a proud Victorian public, and photo souvenirs – visual records – published by F Frith & Co were sold in their hundreds of thousands. In addition, many new commercial buildings such as hotels, inns and pubs were photographed, often because their owners specifically commissioned Frith postcards or prints of them for re-sale or for publicity purposes.

In order to gain some understanding of the scale of Frith's business one only has to look at the catalogue issued by Frith & Co in 1886: it runs to some 670 pages. By 1890 Frith had created the greatest specialist photographic publishing company in the world, with over 2,000 stockists! The picture on the right shows the Frith & Co display board on the wall of the stockist at Ingleton in the Yorkshire Dales (left of window). Beautifully constructed with a mahogany frame and gilt inserts, it displayed a dozen scenes.

POSTCARD BONANZA

The ever-popular holiday postcard we know today took many years to appear, and F Frith & Co was in the vanguard of its development. Postcards became a hugely popular means of communication and sold in their millions. Frith's company took full advantage of this boom and soon became the major publisher of photographic view postcards.

Francis Frith died in 1898 at his villa in Cannes, his great project still growing. His sons Eustace and Cyril continued their father's monumental task, expanding the number of views offered to the public and recording more and more places in Britain, as the coasts and countryside were opened up to mass travel. The archive Frith created continued in business for another seventy years. By 1970 it contained over a third of a million pictures of 7,000 cities, towns and villages. The massive photographic record Frith has left to us stands as a living monument to a special and very remarkable man.

This book shows your town as it was photographed by this world-famous archive at various periods in its development over the past 150 years. Every photograph was taken for a specific commercial purpose, which explains why the selection may not show every aspect of the town landscape. However, the photographs, compiled from one of the world's most celebrated archives, provide an important and absorbing record of your town.

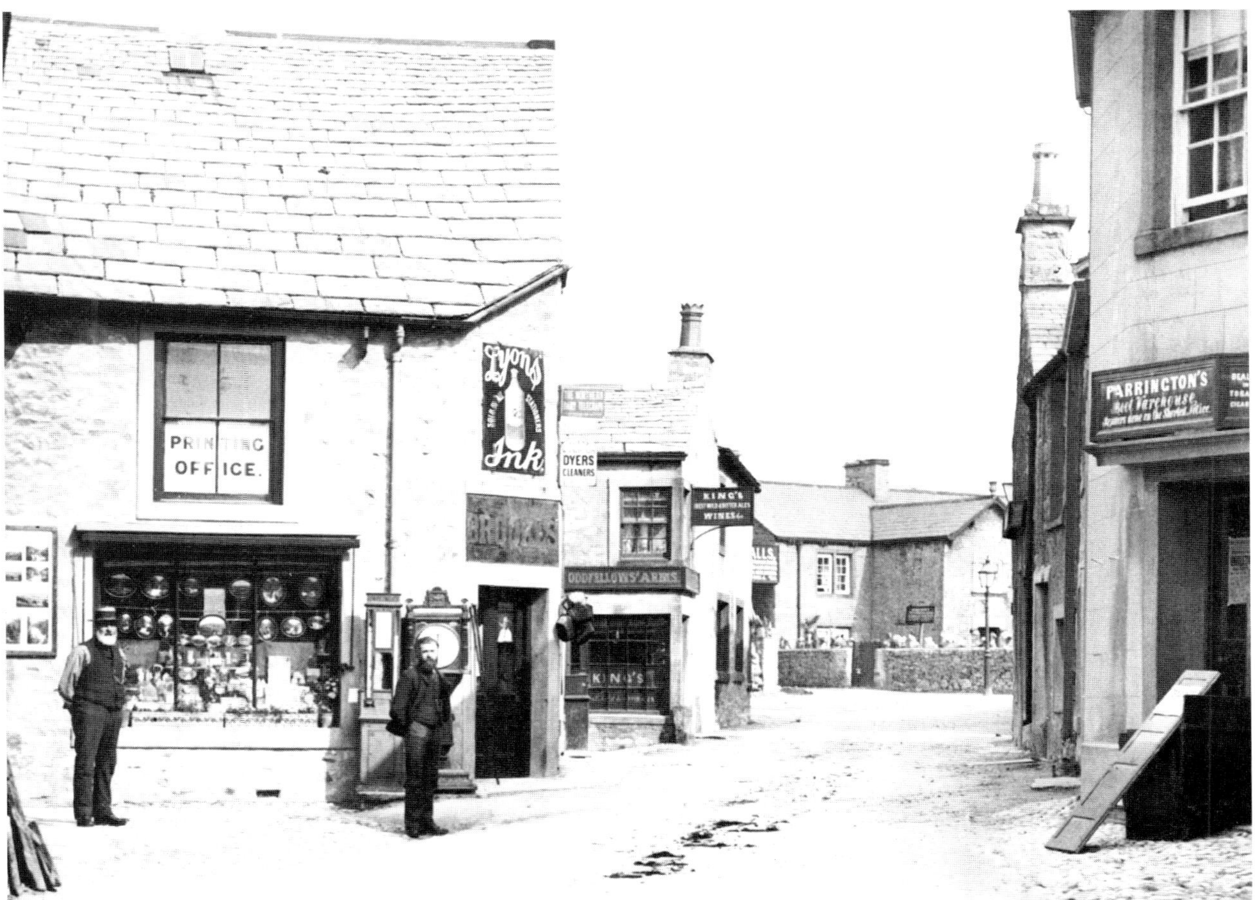

FROM THE AIR

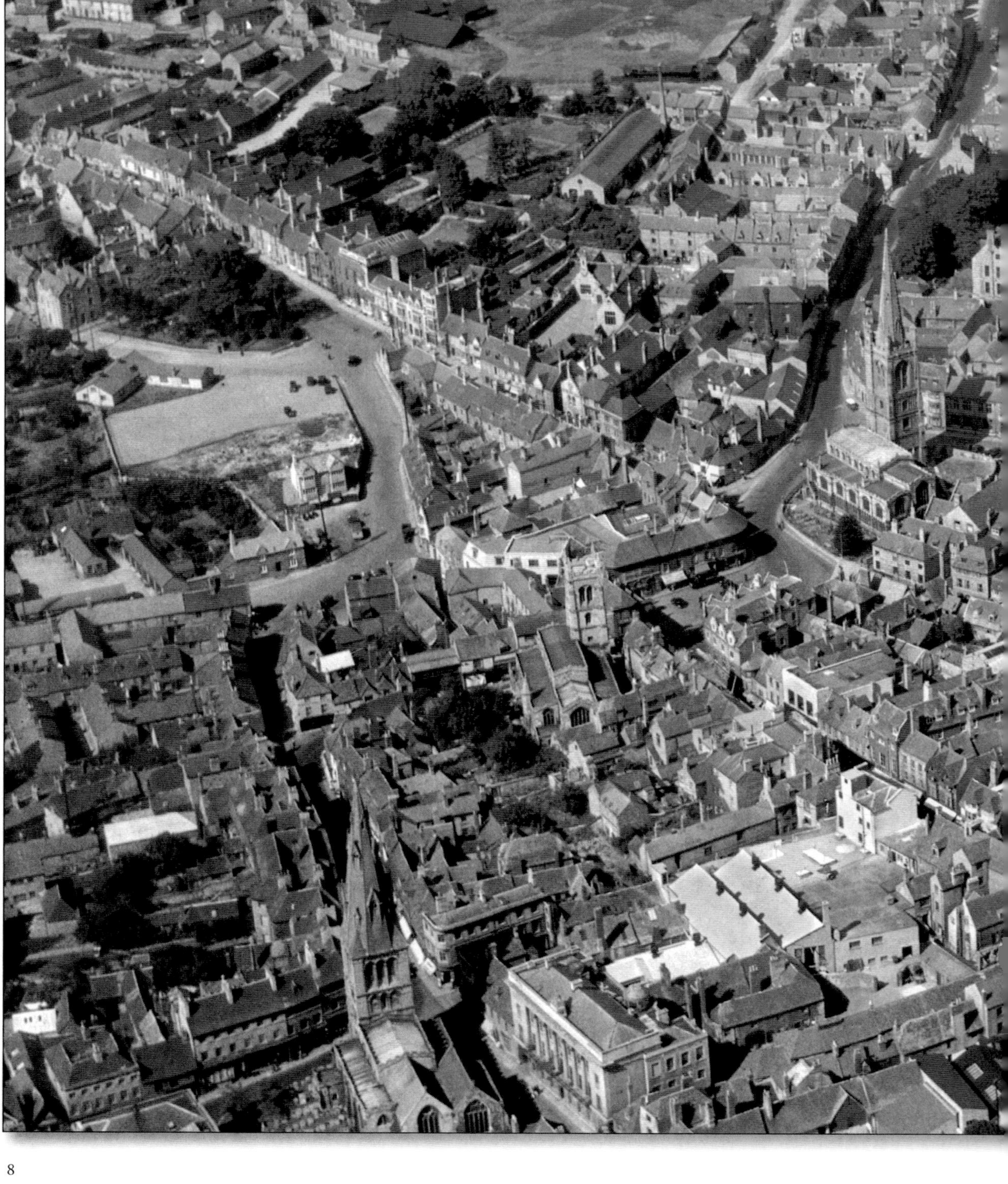

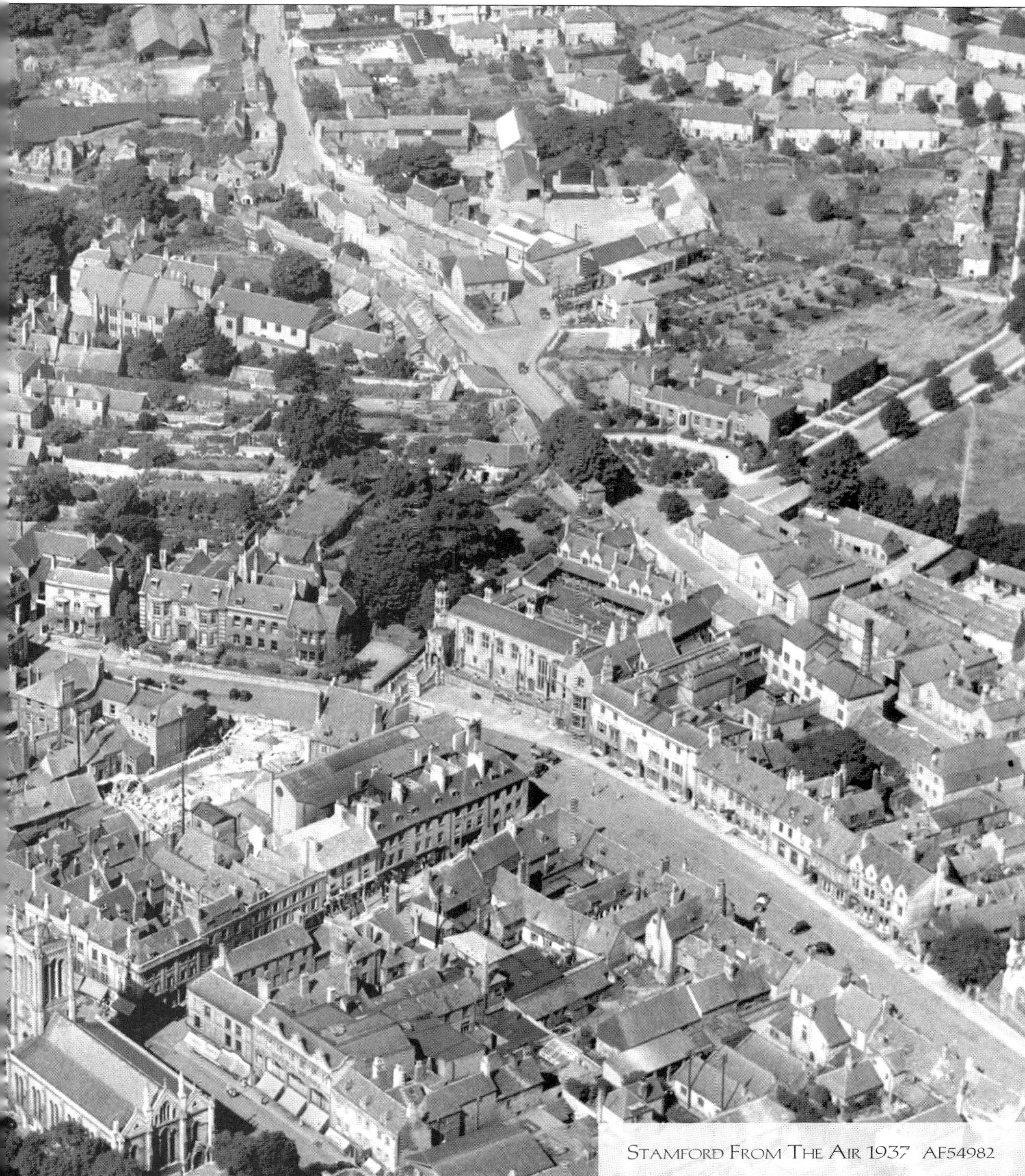

STAMFORD FROM THE AIR 1937 AF54982

EARLY STAMFORD

THE VIEW FROM THE WATER MEADOWS 1922 *72296*

A classic view of the Stamford skyline from the water meadows. From left to right, the four churches are All Saints', St John's, St Michael's and St Mary's. At the far side of the meadows stand the Bath Houses. These were founded by local surgeons in 1722, but were rebuilt a hundred years later. At times the river can spill out across the whole of the meadows, so that the residents of Bath Row are protected behind flood walls. On a sunny day, the meadows are still a magnet for townsfolk and visitors alike.

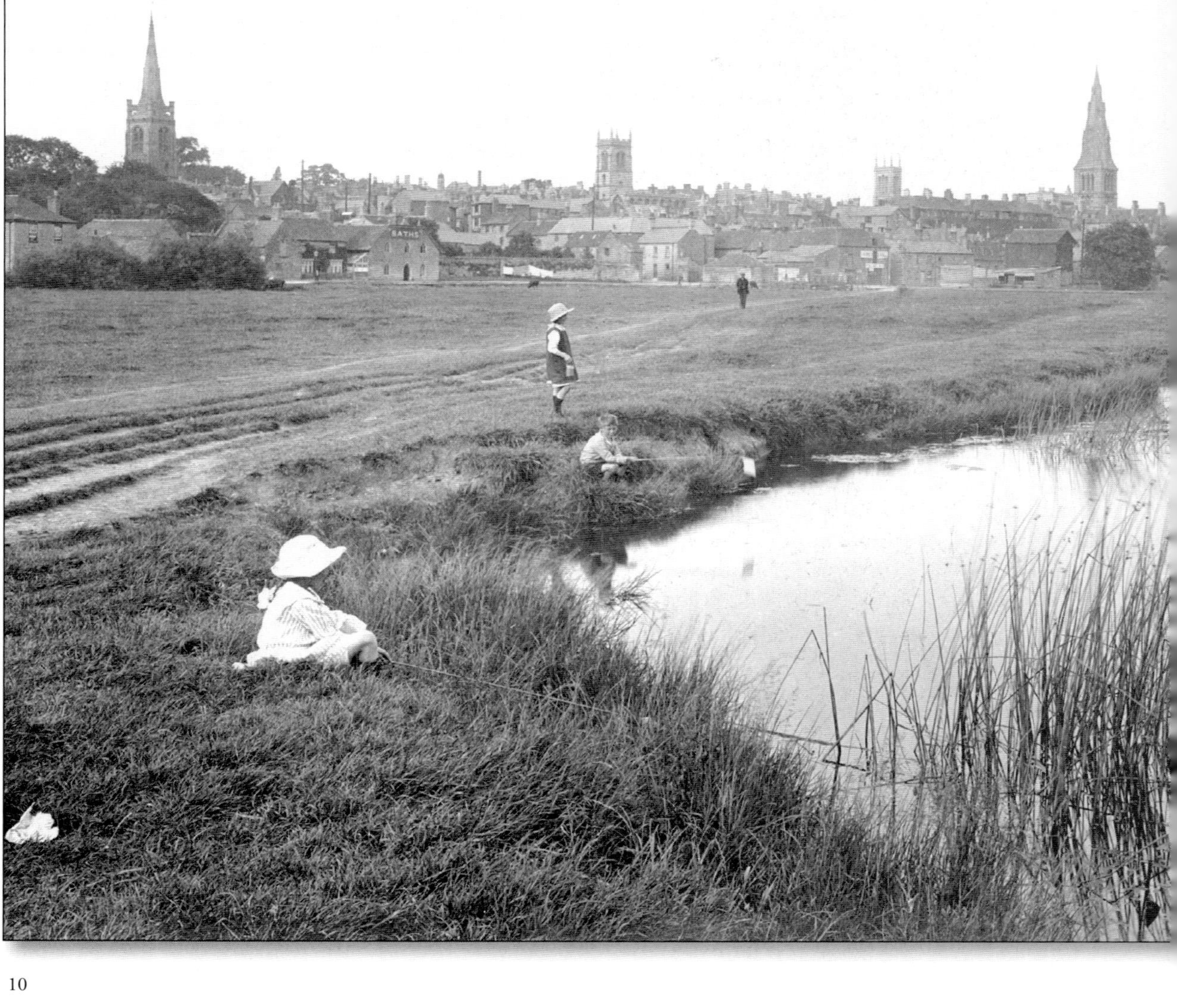

Early Stamford

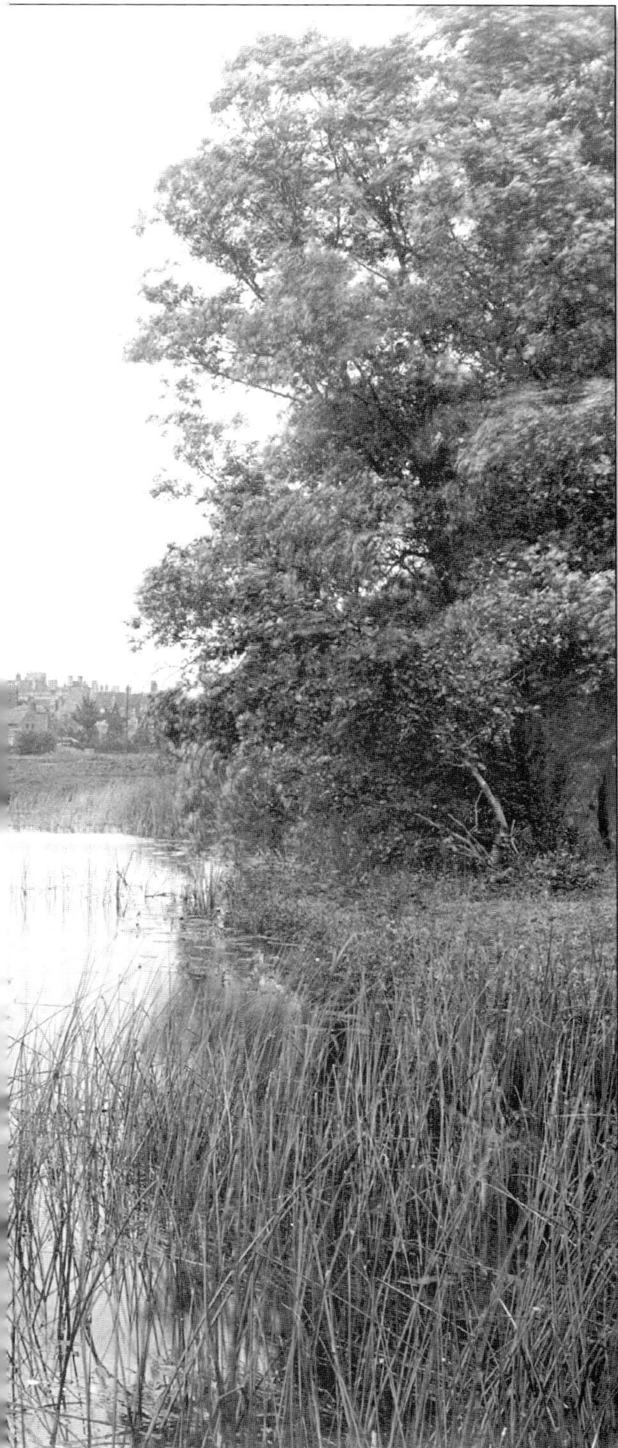

If we are approaching Stamford for the first time on foot, it is interesting to do so from the car park at the end of Station Road, crossing the meadows from the south over George and Lammas Bridges before climbing up along Castle Dyke into one of the market places at the heart of the historic town. The route we take, as well as presenting one of the finest skylines of any town in England, follows the line of an ancient trackway that once crossed the River Welland by the stone ford that gave the town its name.

Almost inevitably, little is known about Stamford in the prehistoric period. Chance finds of stone and bronze objects show that the area was inhabited, but evidence of a permanent settlement on the site has not to date been forthcoming. It is generally accepted, however, that even if there was no coherent settlement on the site at that time, the crossing over the Welland, at a point where the river changed character as it left the higher ground to begin a circuitous, but navigable, journey through the Fens to the sea, lay on an ancient route-way which followed the ridge of Jurassic limestone from the Cotswolds to the Humber.

When they came to build Ermine Street from London to York, the Romans were not interested in the meanderings of old trackways. They chose instead to cross the Welland at a new point, some way upstream of the present town, before going on to place a camp on the River Gwash two miles to the north-west at Great Casterton. Stamford had to wait for its big opportunity until the arrival of another band of overseas adventurers, the Danes, who began to settle the area in the latter part of the ninth century. By that time the stretch of Ermine Street over the Welland had long disappeared, but the old ford was still in use. The Danes settled close to a small Mercian defended enclosure centred on the site of St Peter's church. The rectangular shape of the Danish town is still reflected in the grid pattern and sharp corners of the streets in the upper part of modern Stamford.

Danish rule was not to carry on unchallenged: the early 10th century saw a concerted attempt by King Edward the Elder to restore the area to Anglo-Saxon control. The Danes were defeated, for a while at least, in a series of battles across the Midlands, and Edward built a separate fort at Stamford, to the south of the river, in what is now St Martin's.

Early Stamford

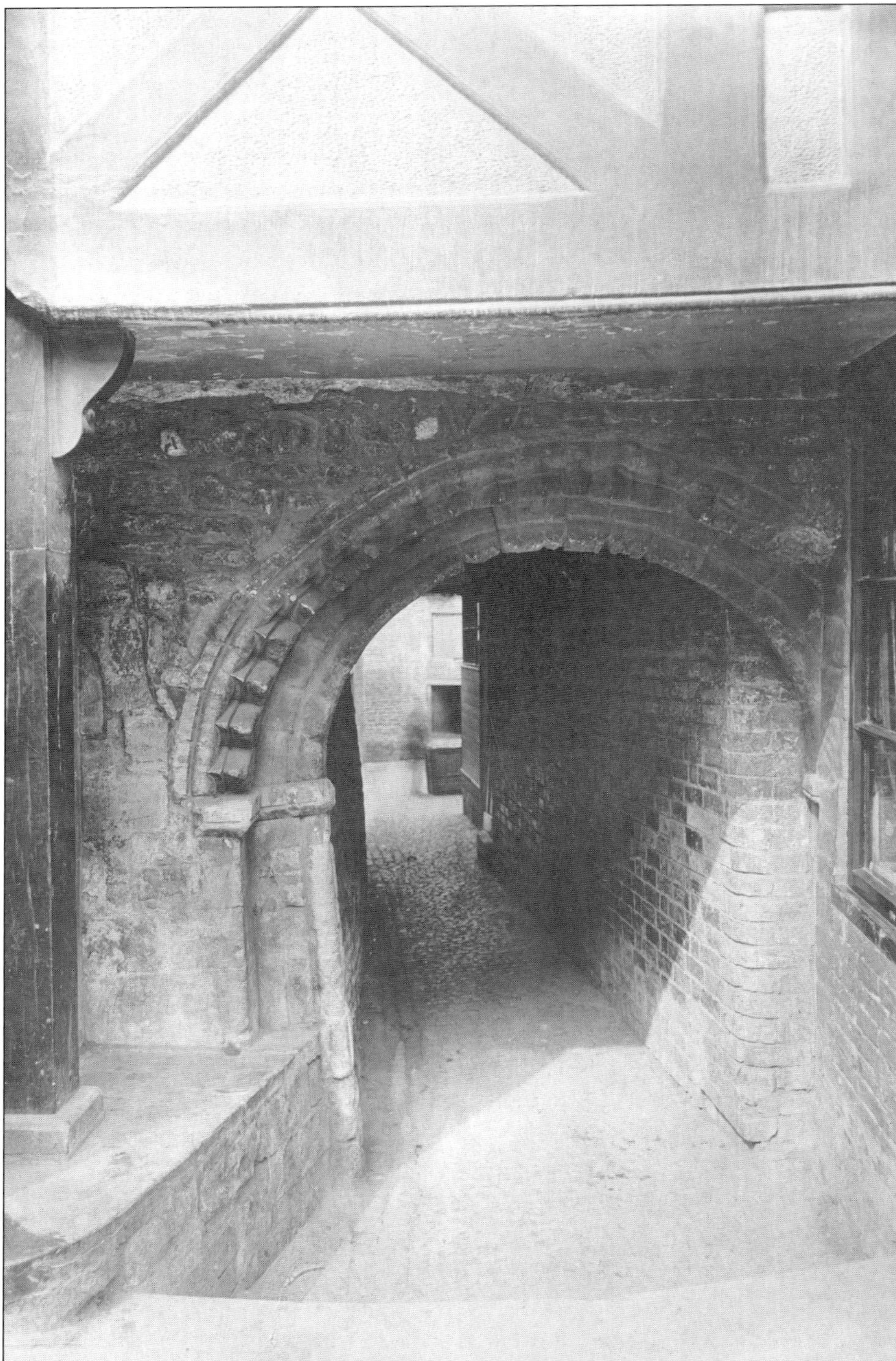

The Norman Arch
1922 *72338*

One of the oldest surviving fragments in the town, this 12th-century arch now forms the entrance to St Mary's Passage, a narrow path running down towards the meadows. The original building above the arch was replaced in the 16th century, going on to become the Packhorse Inn and later still the Queen's Head. Nothing in this photograph has changed, even down to the whitewashed beam-ends just to the left of and above the archway.

EARLY STAMFORD

Stamford prospered, and by the end of the 10th century it was on a par with Lincoln, Nottingham, Leicester and Derby; this grouping was known as the Five Boroughs. In the period leading up to the Norman Conquest, the town became a centre for the trade in a popular type of warm and close-woven cloth known as 'haberget', as well as establishing a pottery industry whose wares graced medieval tables well into the 13th century. It was also the site of one of the major mints of Anglo-Saxon England, striking some 10% of all coins produced in the country.

Objects in museums and street-plans apart, the Normans were the first inhabitants to leave traces that we can still see as we walk around Stamford today. The arch at the entrance into St Mary's Passage on St Mary's Hill is a fine example of 12th-century architecture (72338, left) which may originally have formed the entrance into an undercroft (or cellar) beneath the house of a well-to-do merchant. These undercrofts were used for the storage of materials and also as trading areas. The Normans built a castle in Stamford, based around a circular tower or keep, on top of a mound. Traces of this survived until 1933, when it was levelled to make way for the wide, open spaces of the bus station. The aerial photograph on pages 8 and 9 shows this area soon after work was completed. We know from the Domesday Book that the town had a population of some 4000 people, similar to that recorded in 1801.

By the end of the 13th century, in addition to the castle, Stamford possessed town walls (S177014, pages 14-15) 14 churches and 6 monasteries and friaries. It was exceeded in size by only a handful of other towns in the country, and located as it was at the junction of two important medieval routes, the Great North Road and the present A43, it was even the site of parliaments. Although graced with later facades, a number of the houses in town have their origins in the medieval period. Stamford's fairs had come to be of national importance, and brought wealth if not to the whole community, then at least to the merchants, who responded by giving the town some of its most important and enduring buildings.

But the period of prosperity was drawing to an end. The fortunes of Stamford fell into decline during the 15th century, a state which continued through the 16th, despite the personal rise to eminence of the Cecil family; William Cecil, secretary of state to Queen Elizabeth I, built the magnificent Burghley House at this time. The process of decay was accelerated by the silting up of the River Welland, which cut the town off from the lucrative foreign markets. By the approach of the Civil War, which began in 1642, Stamford had been diminished by recession and plague. Even one hundred years before, it had been described as decayed; now areas within the walls lay empty, and the town found itself begging to be excused from paying taxes. The Civil War did not affect the town greatly. Burghley House was besieged (for all of one day), and in 1646 King Charles spent one of his final days as a free man here, before going on to surrender to the Scots army, who promptly handed him over to the forces of Parliament.

After the war, efforts were made to revive the town. In 1664 a local entrepreneur sponsored the construction of the Welland Canal. Although the canal never linked into the Midlands canal system, Stamford once more had access to the ports to the east. The turn of the 18th century saw matching improvements in road communications, which heralded a period of great prosperity, as the town became a major service centre for the coaching trade. With the coming of the railway age, however, Stamford gave away its opportunity to be on the main Great Northern line to Peterborough. The coaching trade collapsed, and the town slid back into relative obscurity, avoiding the worst effects of industrialisation which the mainline railway would have brought, and preserving the extraordinary richness of its domestic architecture, which forms the backdrop for many of the photographs in this book.

EARLY STAMFORD

OLD ST PETER'S GATE BASTION c1955 S177014

Although isolated fragments of Stamford's 13th-century town walls can still be found around the town, often incorporated into later buildings, St Peter's Gate bastion or angle tower is the only recognisable structure which survives today. St Peter's Gate (demolished in 1770) stood a few yards further down the hill, near the end of Rutland Terrace.

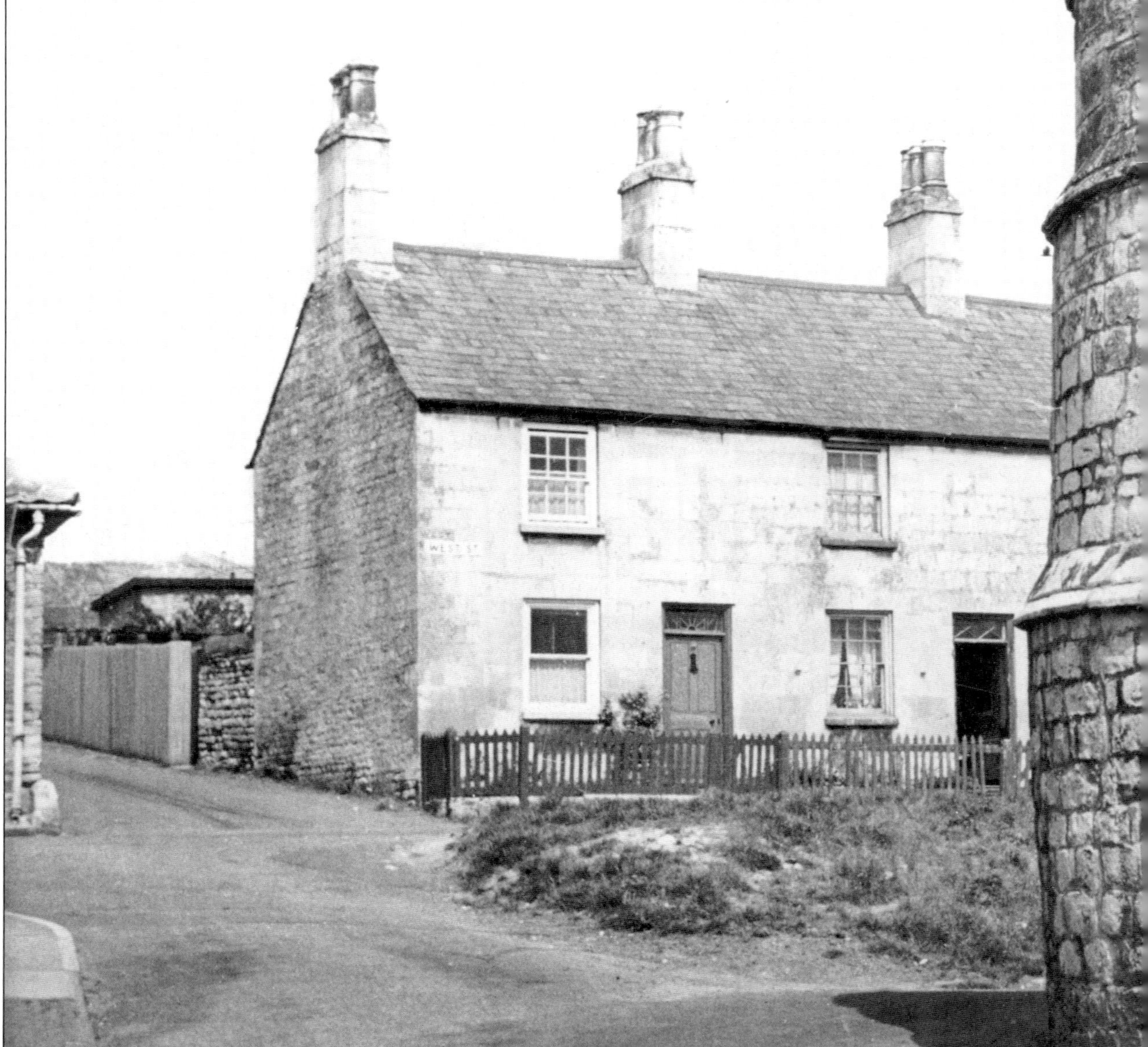

EARLY STAMFORD

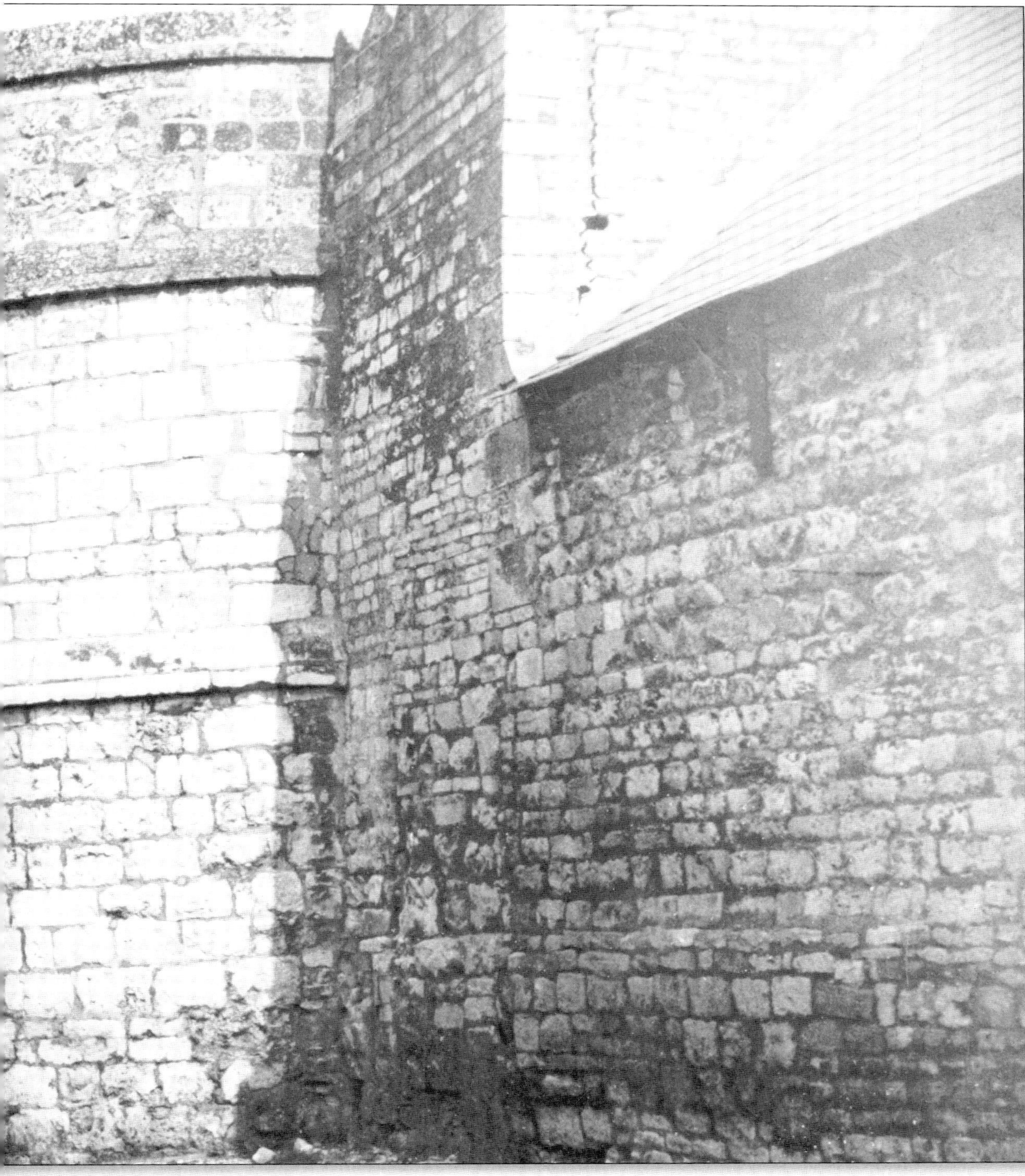

HIGH STREET AND ST PAUL'S STREET

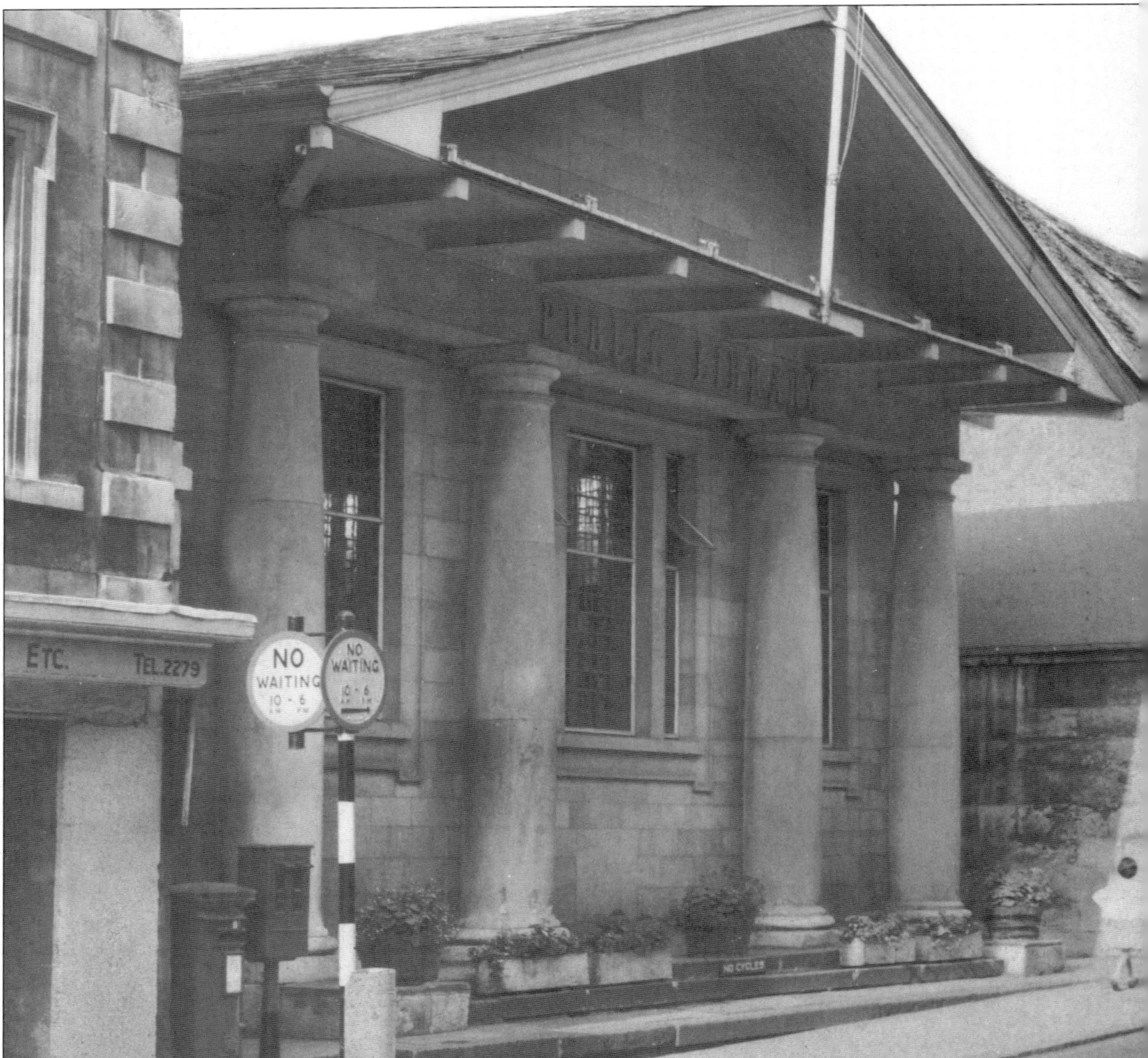

High Street developed from the main route through the Danish fortified settlement or burgh, and has been the commercial centre of Stamford for three hundred years. Although it has been shielded from the flow of traffic along the Great North Road, which passed its west end, commercial bustle and traffic from the east made it a busy enough place. Along with Ironmonger Street, it was in 1972 an early candidate for pedestrianisation.

Since the medieval period High Street (or St Michael's Street, as it was then known) has had strong links with the butchery trade. On the left of S177063 is the present library building, which originally opened in 1808 as a covered portico giving access to the shambles, or

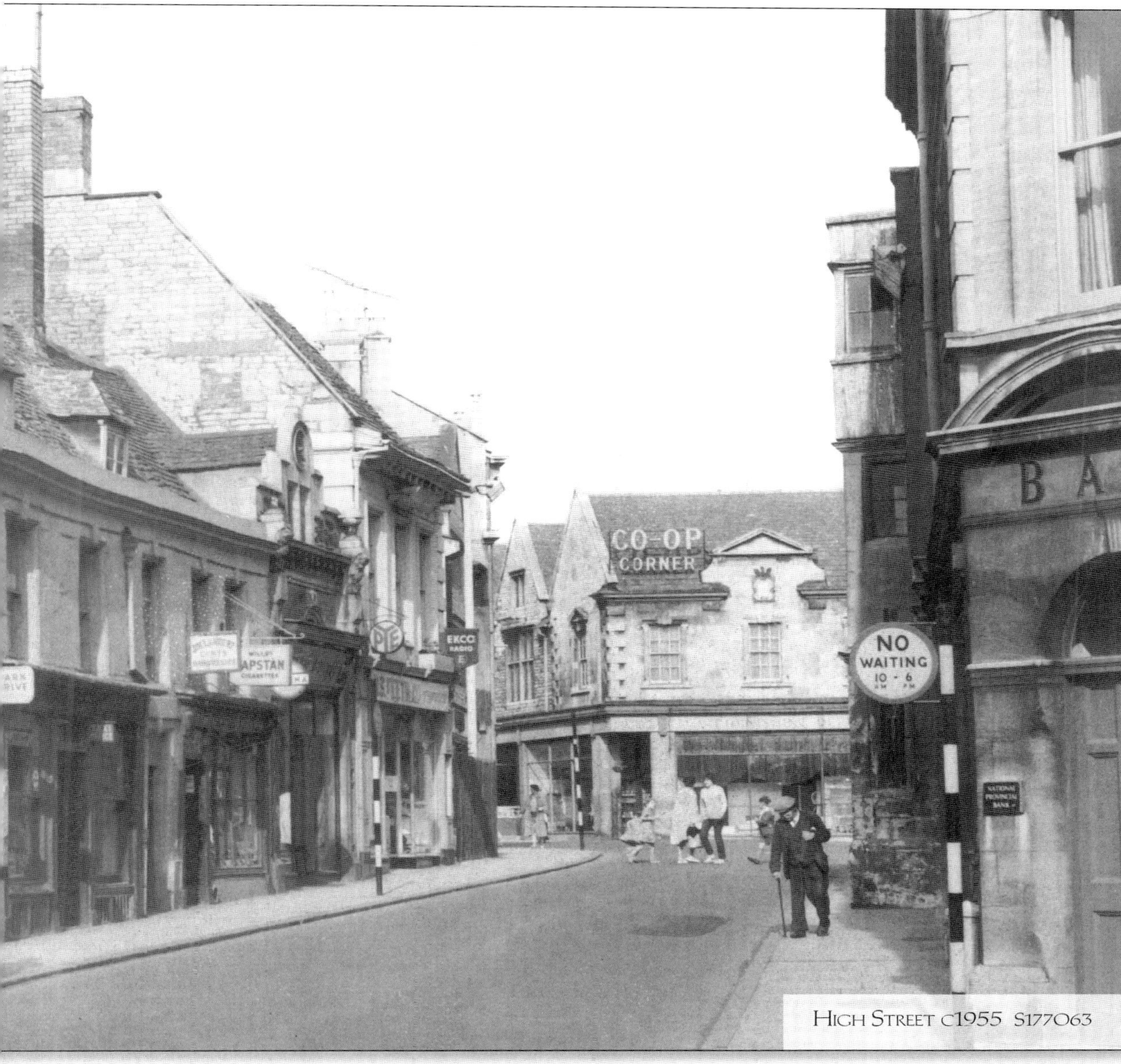

HIGH STREET C1955 S177063

butchers' shops, behind. The old meat market had originally carried on outside St Michael's church, before moving, along with the St Mary's Place Monday market, in its purpose-built accommodation. The grand portico was designed by William Legg, a local architect also responsible for the Bottle Lodges at Burghley Park (72323, page 80); it was based upon an Inigo Jones design in Covent Garden, London. Until 1847 the portico also housed the town beadle, who according to a late 19th-century guide, 'trod with pompous step in cocked hat and gold lace, scarlet coat, and green plush breeches' — a startling sight no doubt. The building was converted into a library in 1906. The Co-op, right, moved to this site on the corner of St George's and St Paul's Streets in 1909, refashioning the buildings that stood there before. On the right, by the then National Provincial Bank, is the entrance to Maiden Lane (72306, right). Beyond this we can see the projecting windows of No 51 High Street, medieval in origin, which in 1966 was demolished along with its neighbours to make way for an unworthy replacement.

As well as the library, the High Street has another connection with the printed word through the pages of the Stamford Mercury, which moved its office here from Maiden Lane around 1785. The Lincoln, Rutland and Stamford Mercury was founded in 1710 as the Stamford Post, and lays claim to being the oldest provincial newspaper in Britain. Under the ownership of Richard Newcomb the paper flourished, and by 1852 it enjoyed the highest circulation of any local newspaper of the day, including the Manchester Guardian. The Mercury kept its office at Nos 61-62 High Street until 1971. During this period there had been a number of changes to the building, chiefly tied in with the expansion of Woolworth's next door.

View 72303 (pages 20-21) was taken just outside the steps to the Library; a shopkeeper is struggling to attach a side awning to keep the sun from his window. Beyond are the grand roof pediments of Oates and Musson's department store; both the pediments and the shop have now gone. The chief change in this view, however, involves the High Street's church, St Michael's, which has had an eventful life architecturally. In 1832 the rector set alterations in progress to lighten the inside of the medieval church, an effect which was spectacularly achieved when the building collapsed following the removal of a few too many pillars. The church was rebuilt in 1836, when it was described by the Stamford Mercury as 'one of the most beautiful buildings in the Kingdom'. By the mid 1960s, however, the church was redundant, and in 1982 it suffered the indignity of being gutted and converted into a row of shops and offices.

We have another view of St Michael's church, taken from the top of Ironmonger Street, in 72312 (page 25). On the right beyond the lamppost is the furniture emporium of Joseph Woods, 'cabinet maker and upholsterer' — he could also provide customers with mangling machines and mail carts. The building now serves as shops and offices. The sign on the left, 'Cycle Works', just above the pedestrian's head, may refer to T H Dickinson, who is listed in 1900 as running an ironmongery, cycle and lawnmower business on this site.

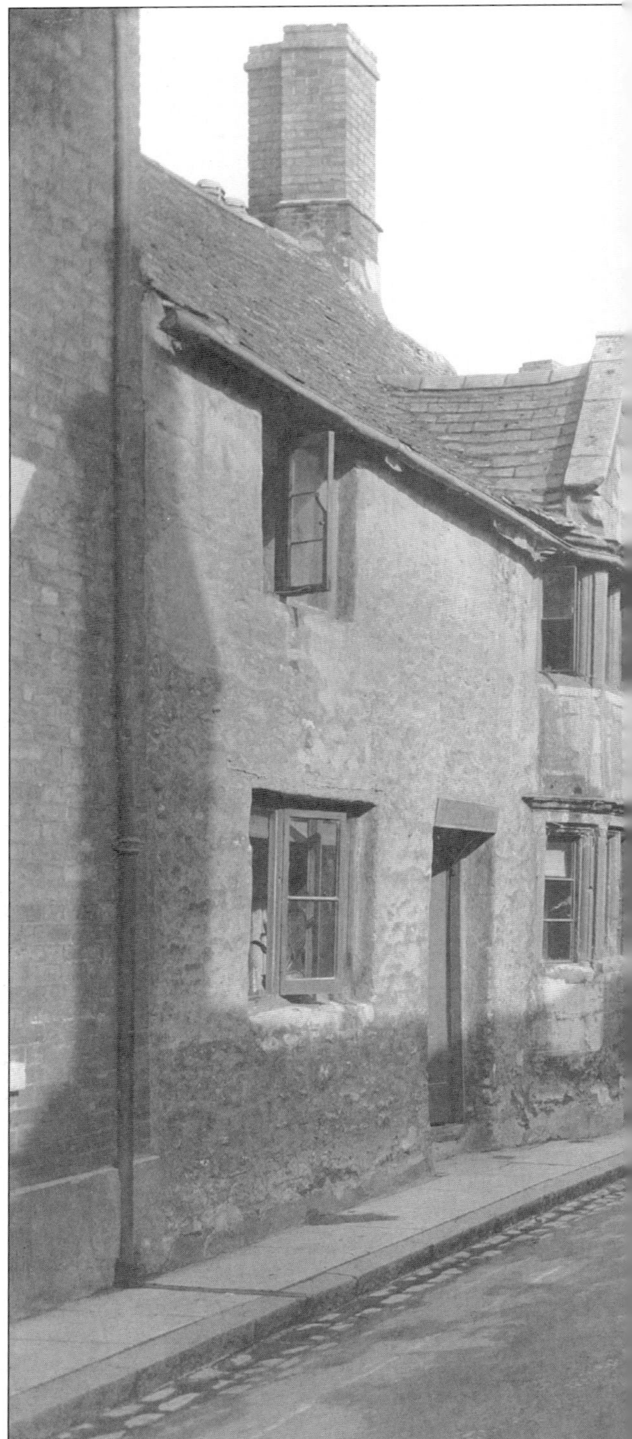

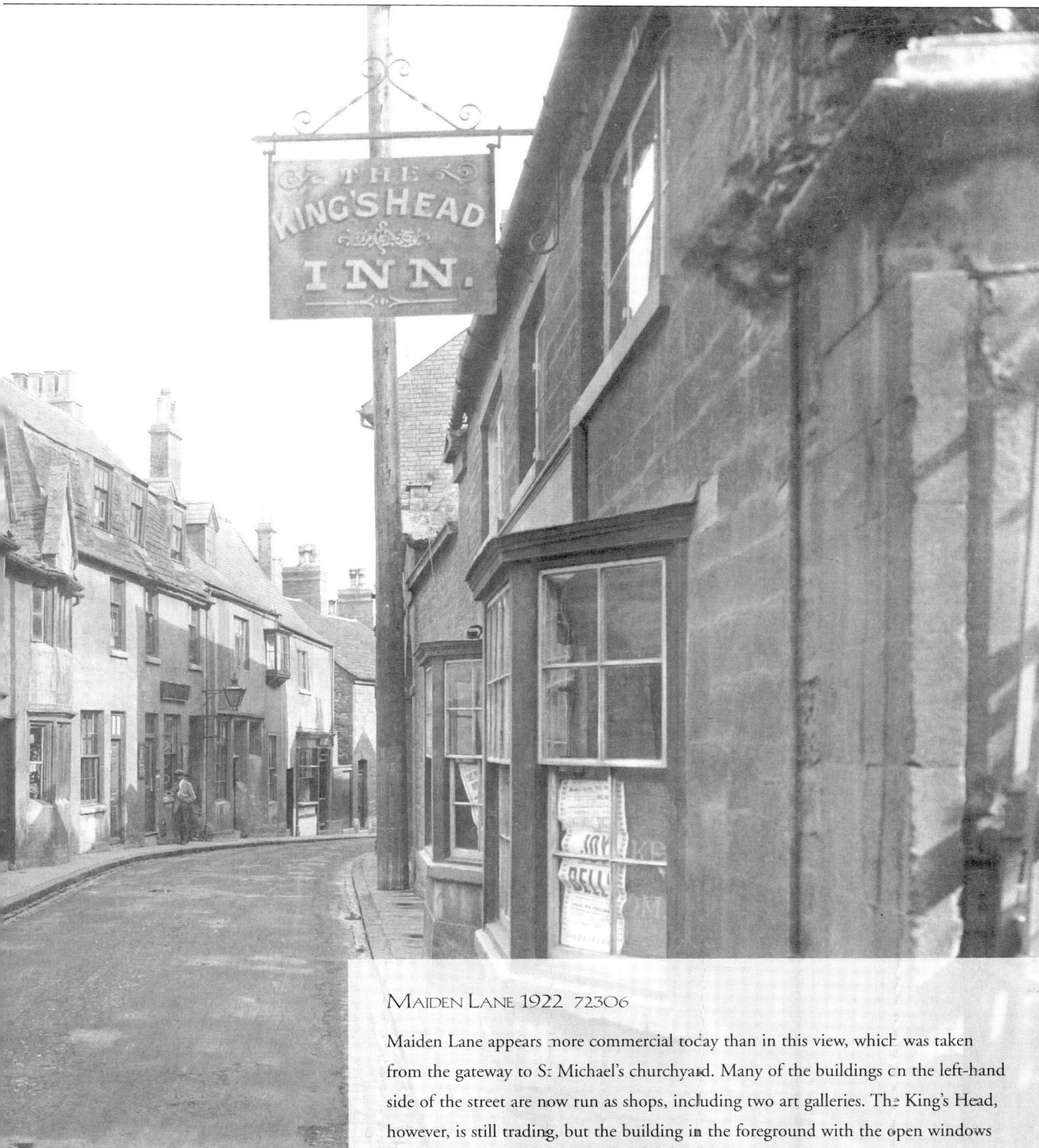

MAIDEN LANE 1922 72306

Maiden Lane appears more commercial today than in this view, which was taken from the gateway to St Michael's churchyard. Many of the buildings on the left-hand side of the street are now run as shops, including two art galleries. The King's Head, however, is still trading, but the building in the foreground with the open windows has been demolished to create a service entrance for shops on the High Street.

High Street and St Paul's Street

High Street 1922 72303

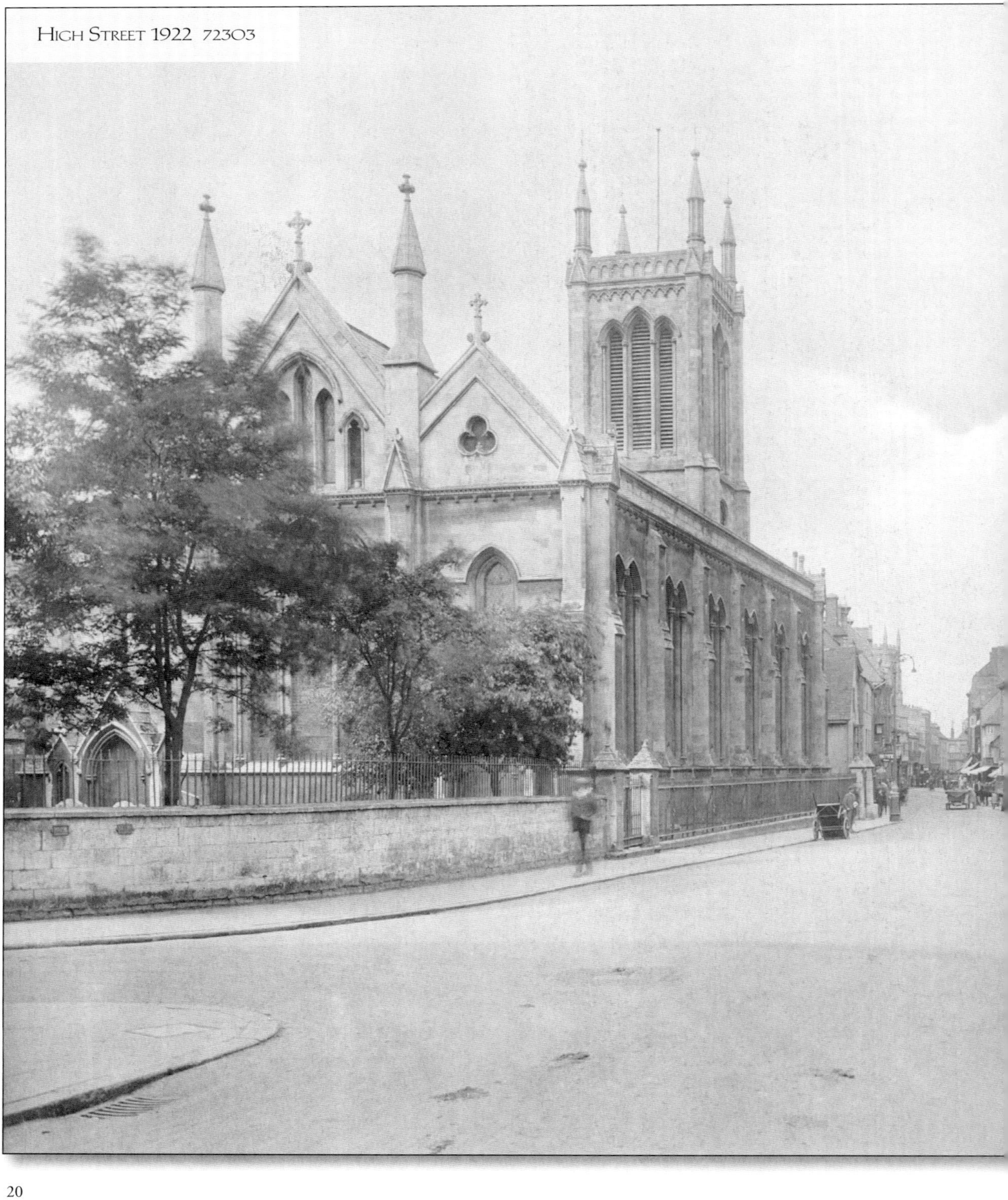

High Street and St Paul's Street

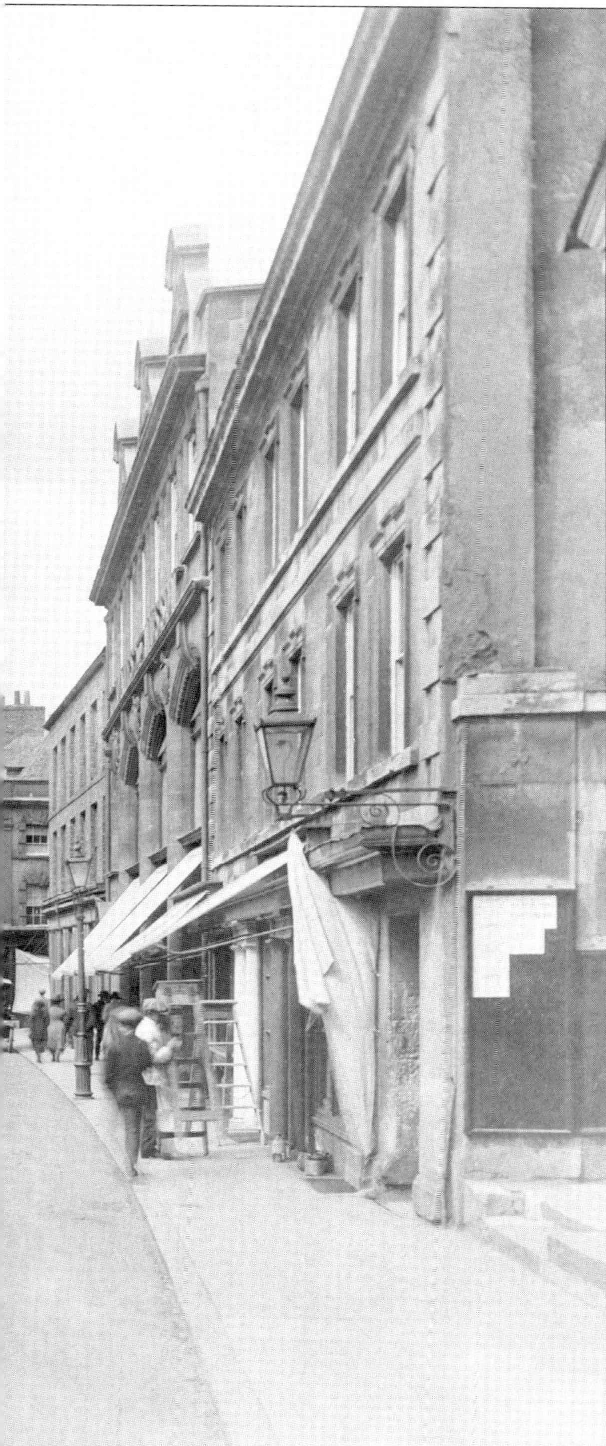

The Pineapple Inn (72302, page 22) operated on this site from 1859 until its closure in 1961, when it was altered to form part of Woolworth's. Its neighbour, Grant's the butchers in 1922 (although in 1900 it was Brown's, another butchers), was dismantled in 1936 and moved to the York Castle Museum, where it can be seen in the famous street scene. Further down the street are the roof pediments (now gone) of a building that has a long banking pedigree: it has accommodated the Northamptonshire Bank (1836), the Capital & Counties Bank Ltd (1900) and today is Lloyds TSB. The building beyond the bank was demolished in 1935, and after a further rebuild, it is now Boots the chemists.

Photograph S177118 (page 25) was taken looking east along High Street on a busy day. The front of Gothic House, left, dates from 1849, although the building, as can be seen inside, is considerably older. It has in the past been a clockmaker's, a post office, and a ladies' clothier, but it now houses Walkers Book Shop. The building next to Gothic House (the Star Tea Company in 1922) collapsed in 1981 during alterations, and the current Halifax Building Society building was designed to reflect its original appearance to some degree. Further down the street the roof pediments of Oates and Musson's stand out, and the library portico can just be made out beyond. Although the new Woolworth's building is in evidence next to the Stamford Mercury Office on the right of the street, the Pineapple Inn just beyond it has yet to be incorporated into the store.

Given its importance to the commercial life of the town, the High Street has been under more pressure from development than any other street in the historic part of the town, especially in relation to the alteration of shop fronts and interiors. To a degree the traditional appearance of the street has been maintained, but there are some notable exceptions, especially at the eastern end between Maiden Lane and St George's Street, where a fine row of mainly 18th-century buildings (but including at least two of medieval origin) was demolished as late as 1967. However, St Paul's Street (S177064, page 27), which runs eastward from the end of the High Street, retains a greater proportion of its ancient buildings.

Although many of the houses in St Paul's Street look as though they date from the 18th century, this is largely owing to their being re-fronted at that time. Behind these facades lie traces of medieval houses built in the traditional design of that time with a large open

High Street and St Paul's Street

central hall. In fact, the history of the street goes further back than the medieval period: the large quantity of pottery waste found here suggests that it was an industrial area at the time of the Norman Conquest. The street has been home to two religious houses. The White Friary is known to have stood to the south of the street, although there are no remains visible today. The Franciscan Grey Friary situated at the east end of the street does still at least have its gateway to show, which has been incorporated into the porter's lodge for the Stamford and Rutland Infirmary (72322 and S177001, page 60). The Grey Friary was of considerable size, accommodating up to 46 brethren, and it is reputed to have had a church with a steeple fine enough to rival that of All Saints'. William Cecil entertained Queen Elizabeth here in 1566 when she was unable to stay at Burghley.

The 13th-century archway we see in 72336 (page 26) is a reminder of one of the stranger episodes in the town's history. In 1333 students from Oxford, dissatisfied with the conditions there, set up a rival institution in Stamford, allegedly bringing with them the brass door knocker from Brasenose College. The break-away university was quashed by order of Edward III and the students trooped back south, leaving the knocker behind them. It adorned this gateway until 1890, when Brasenose College bought the property and returned the knocker to Oxford. A replica was finally provided, which is in position today, but the Frith photograph clearly dates from before its reinstatement.

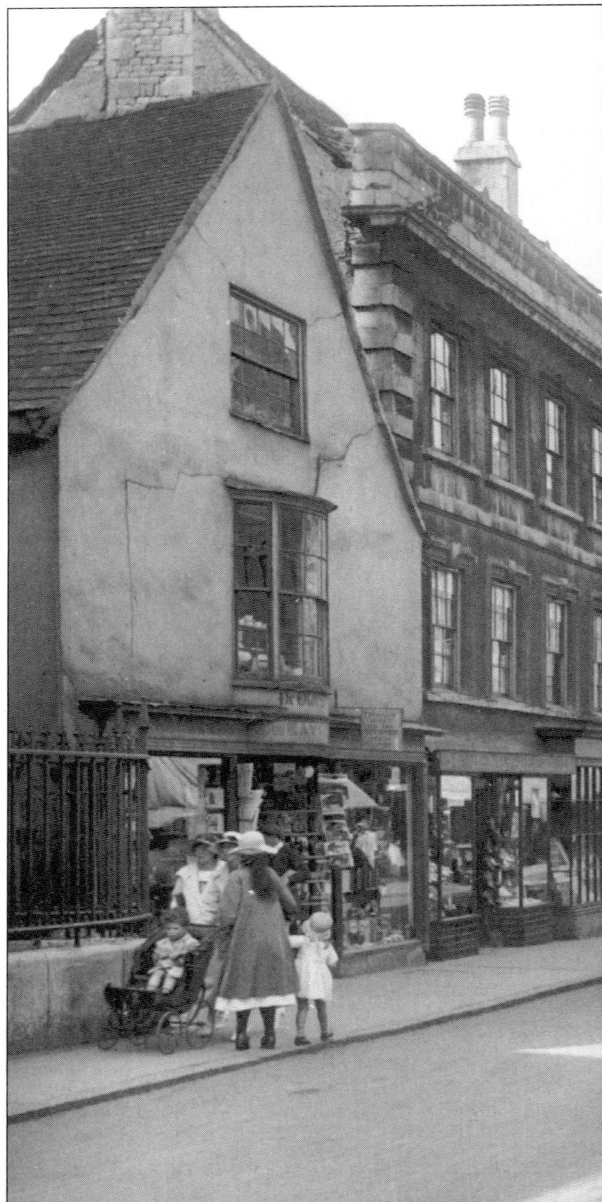

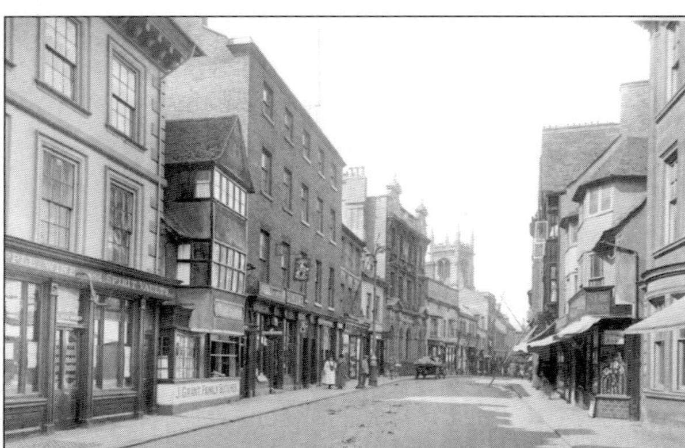

LEFT: HIGH STREET 1922 72302

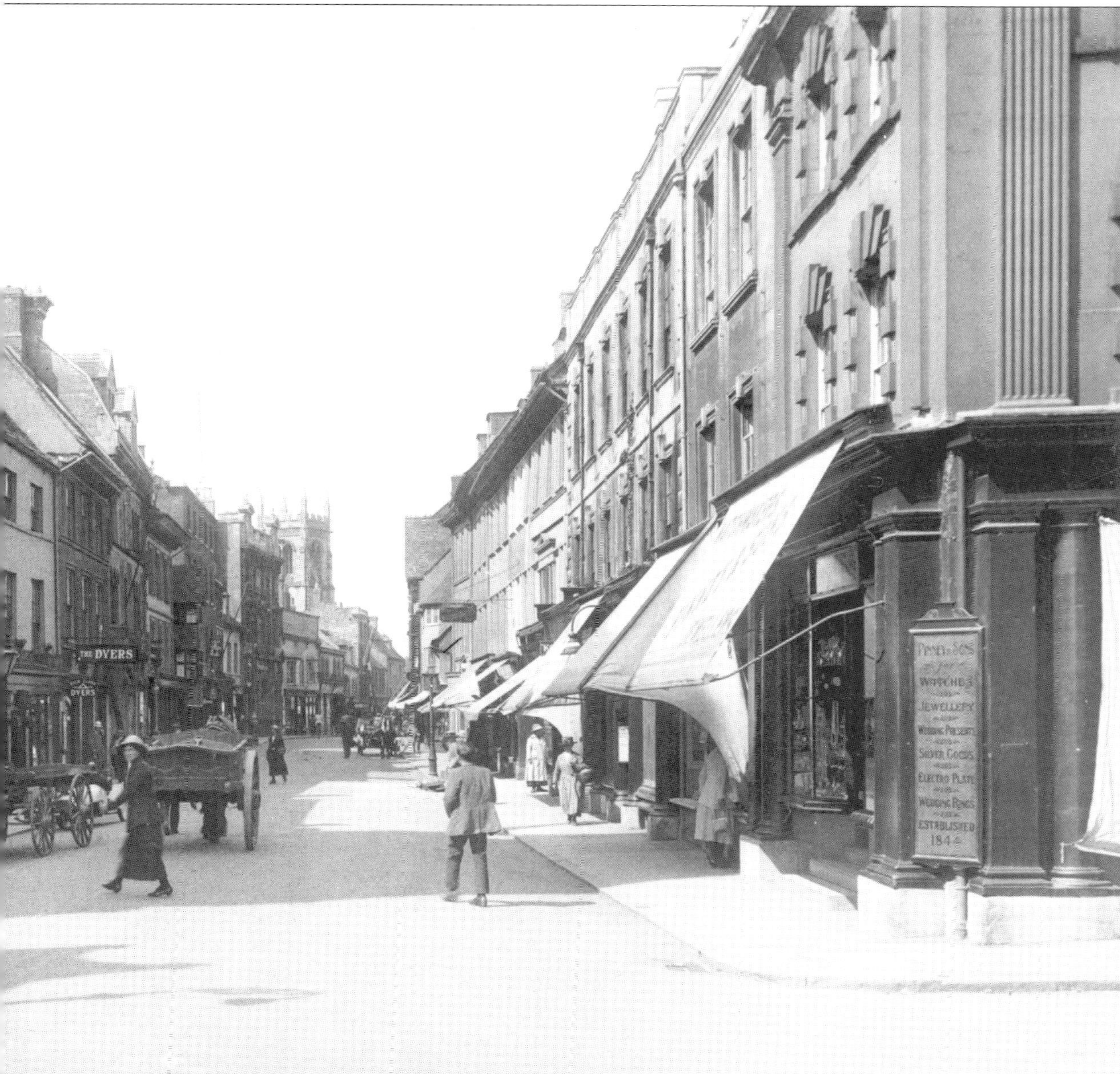

ABOVE: HIGH STREET 1922 72301

This photograph and 72302 (left) show the bustling main street of Stamford at a time when people could still safely share the road with the traffic of the day. The quaint shop in the foreground on the left has undergone some changes since this photograph was taken, and now has a concrete front. Just above the horse's back is the narrow entrance to Cheyne Lane (S177062, page 24). On the right, Pinney & Sons, jewellers, had already been established on this site for over twenty years, although they were later to open a shop in Red Lion Square.

High Street and St Paul's Street

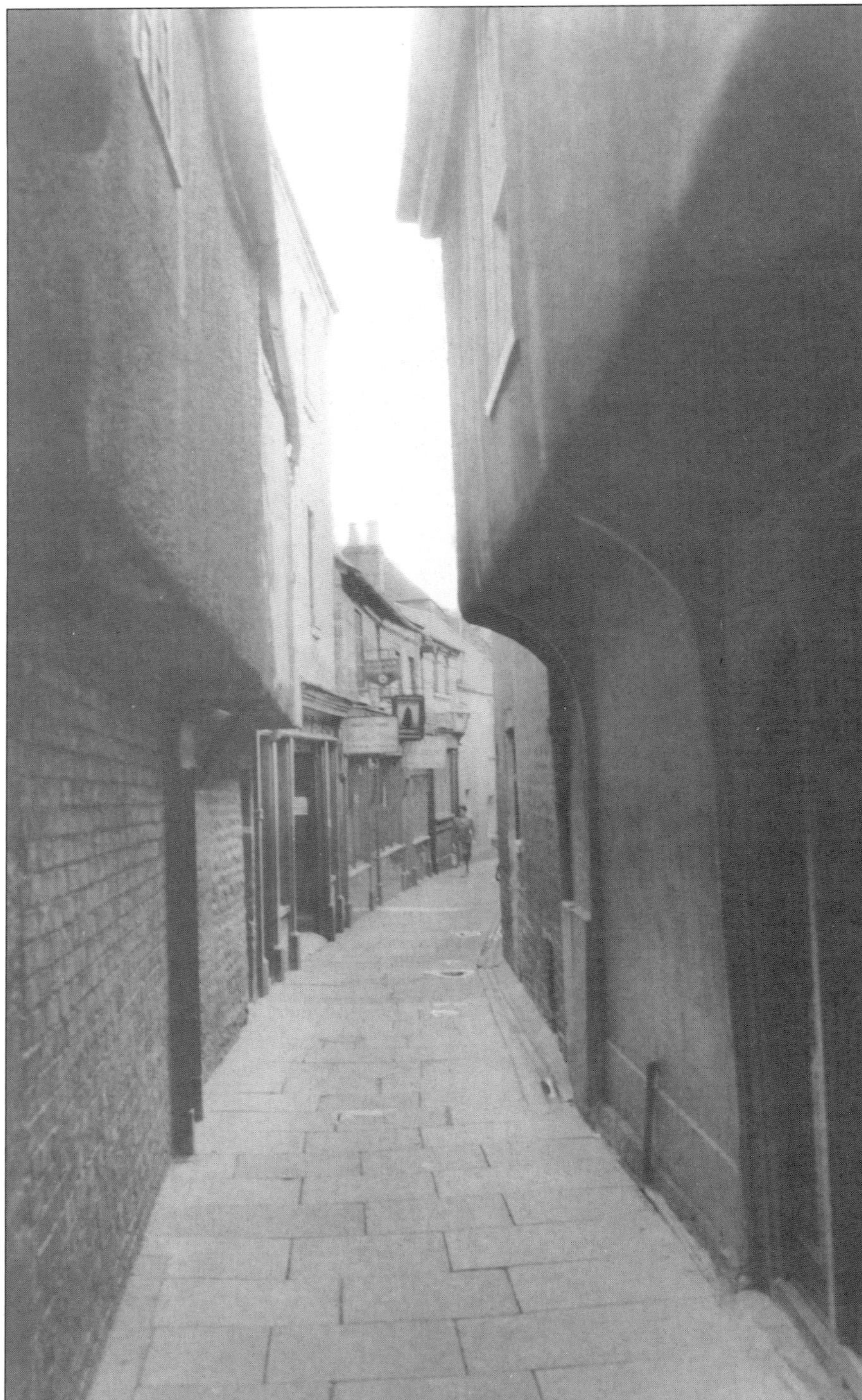

Cheyne Lane c1955
S177062

This narrow passage leading down to St Mary's Street was home in 1900 to a fishmonger and hairdresser, as well as the Hole in the Wall Inn, previously the Coach and Horses (although it is hard to imagine being able to reach it in one). The jetties in the foreground are still there, hanging out over the lane so that the upper storeys of the two buildings almost meet.

High Street and St Paul's Street

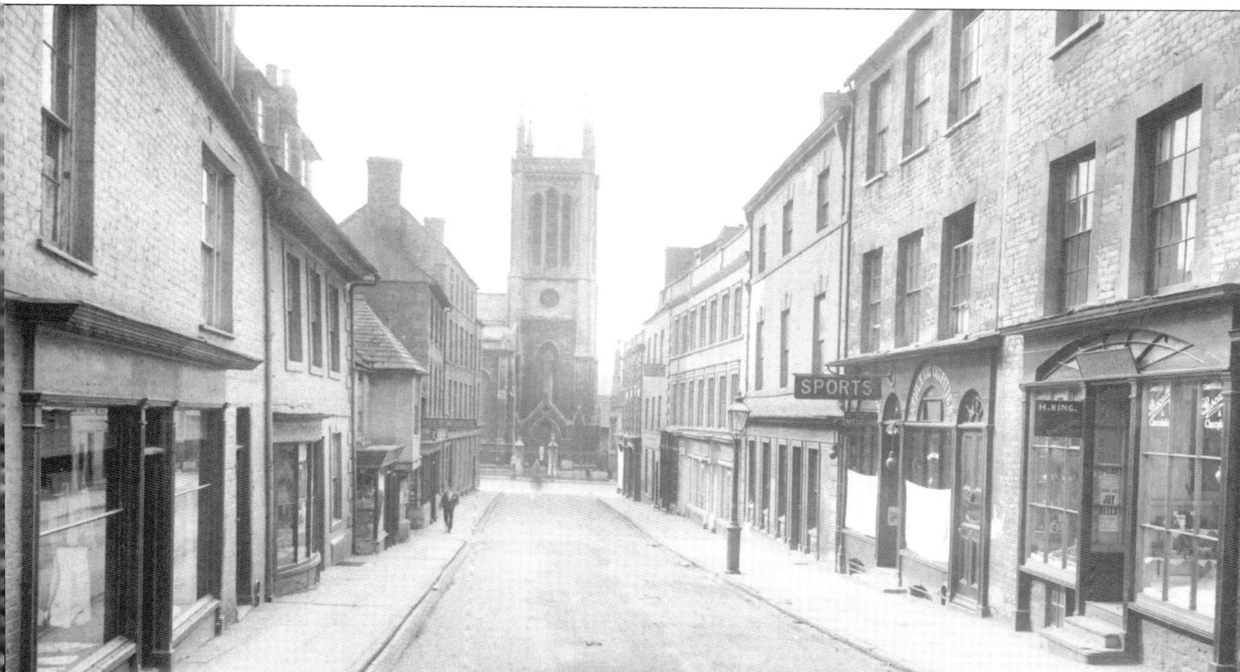

Above: Ironmonger Street 1922 72312

Below: High Street c1960 S177118

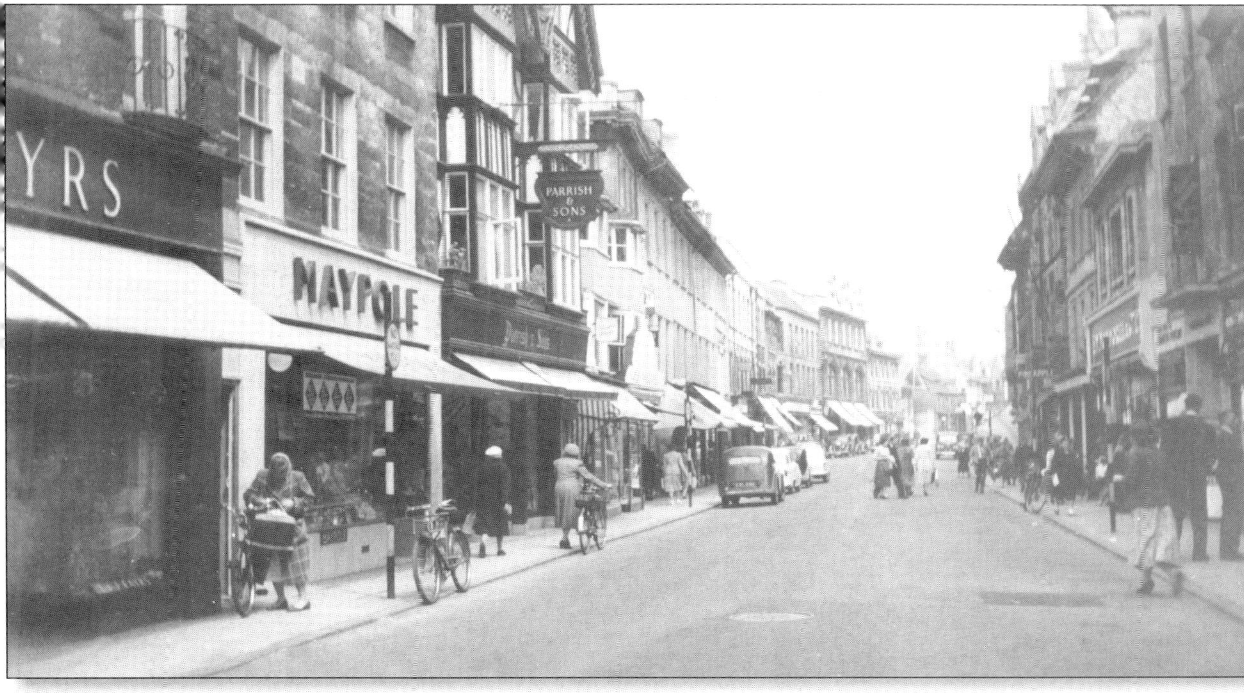

High Street and St Paul's Street

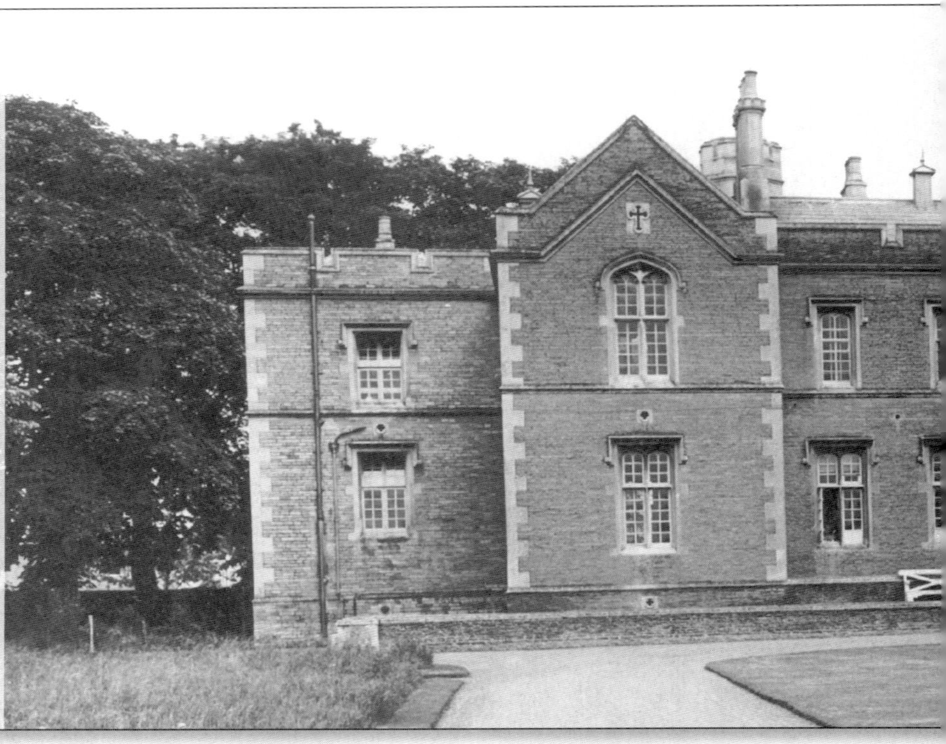

The Infirmary 1922
72321

Following a bequest by a local surgeon in 1828, the Infirmary was built in Tudor-Gothic style on the historic Greyfriars site. Clearly health care was a more peaceful business in the 1920s; today the gardens have disappeared under a mass of wards and car parking belonging to the Stamford and Rutland Infirmary.

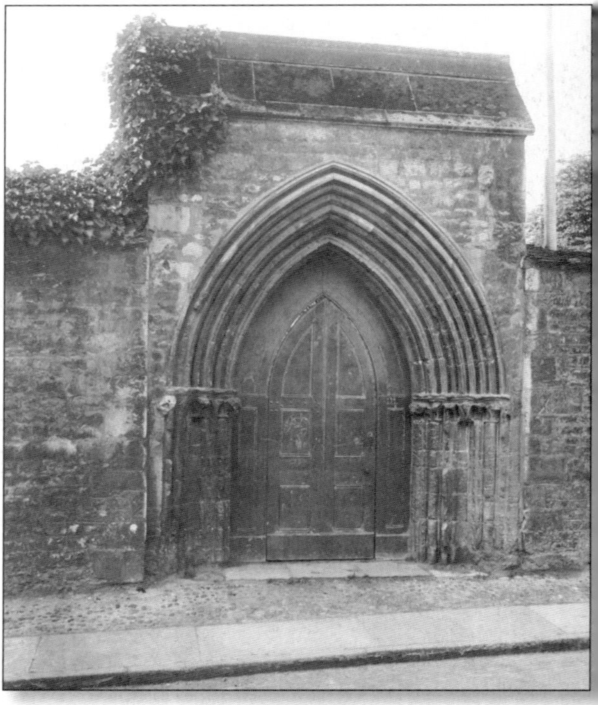

Right: Brazenose Archway 1922 72336

Far Right: St Paul's Street c1955 S177064

Many of the delightful houses in this photograph of the north side of St Paul's Street originated in the 13th century, but their fronts were rebuilt later. The house occupied by the courageous window-cleaner (centre) bears a 1716 datestone, and its neighbour (then, as now, housing the Royal Air Force Association) a datestone for 1663. The trees in the distance mark the site of Stamford School (note the old-fashioned school warning sign), which was rebuilt in 1874 set back from the road. The Shell garage is now a car wash.

HIGH STREET AND ST PAUL'S STREET

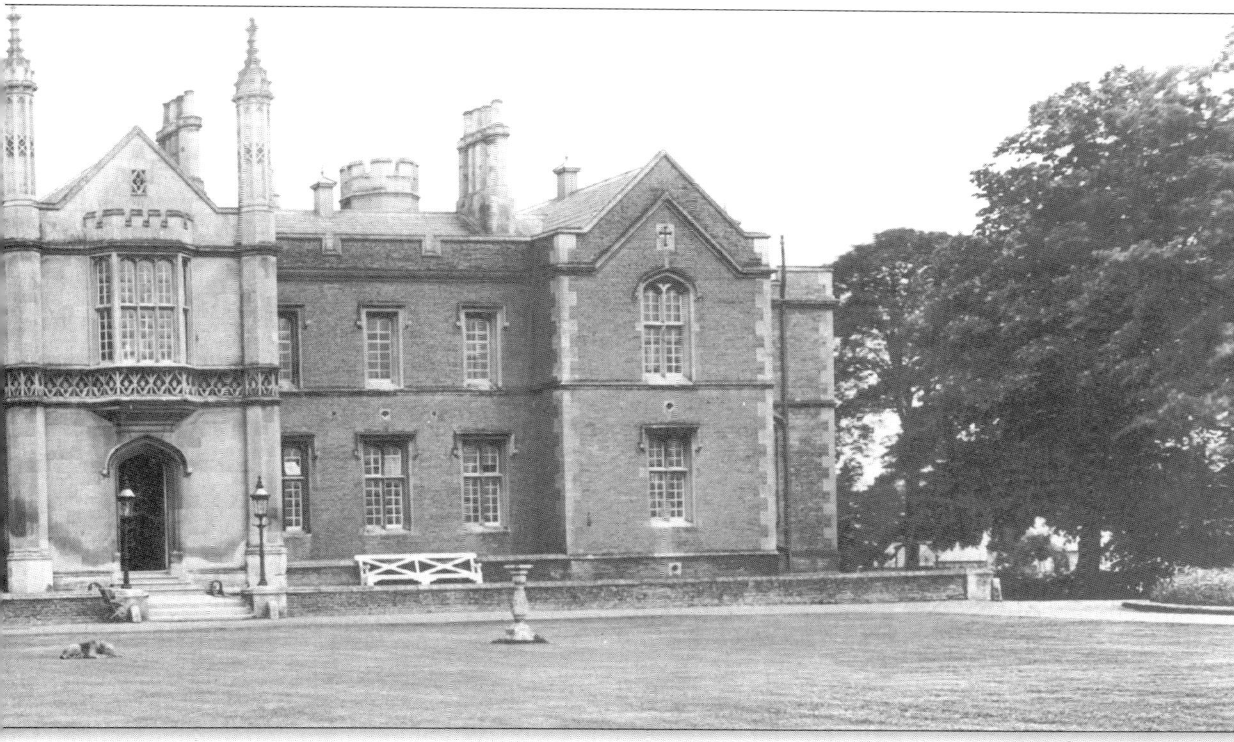

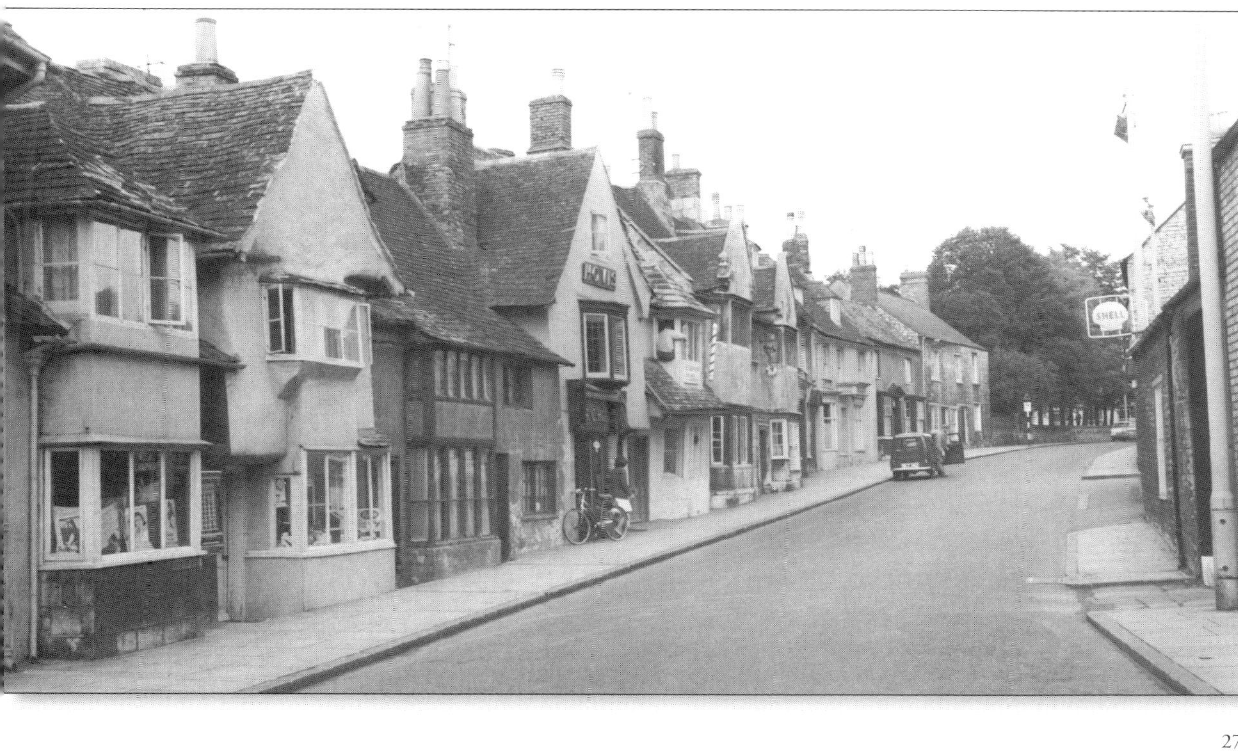

Red Lion Square and Broad Street

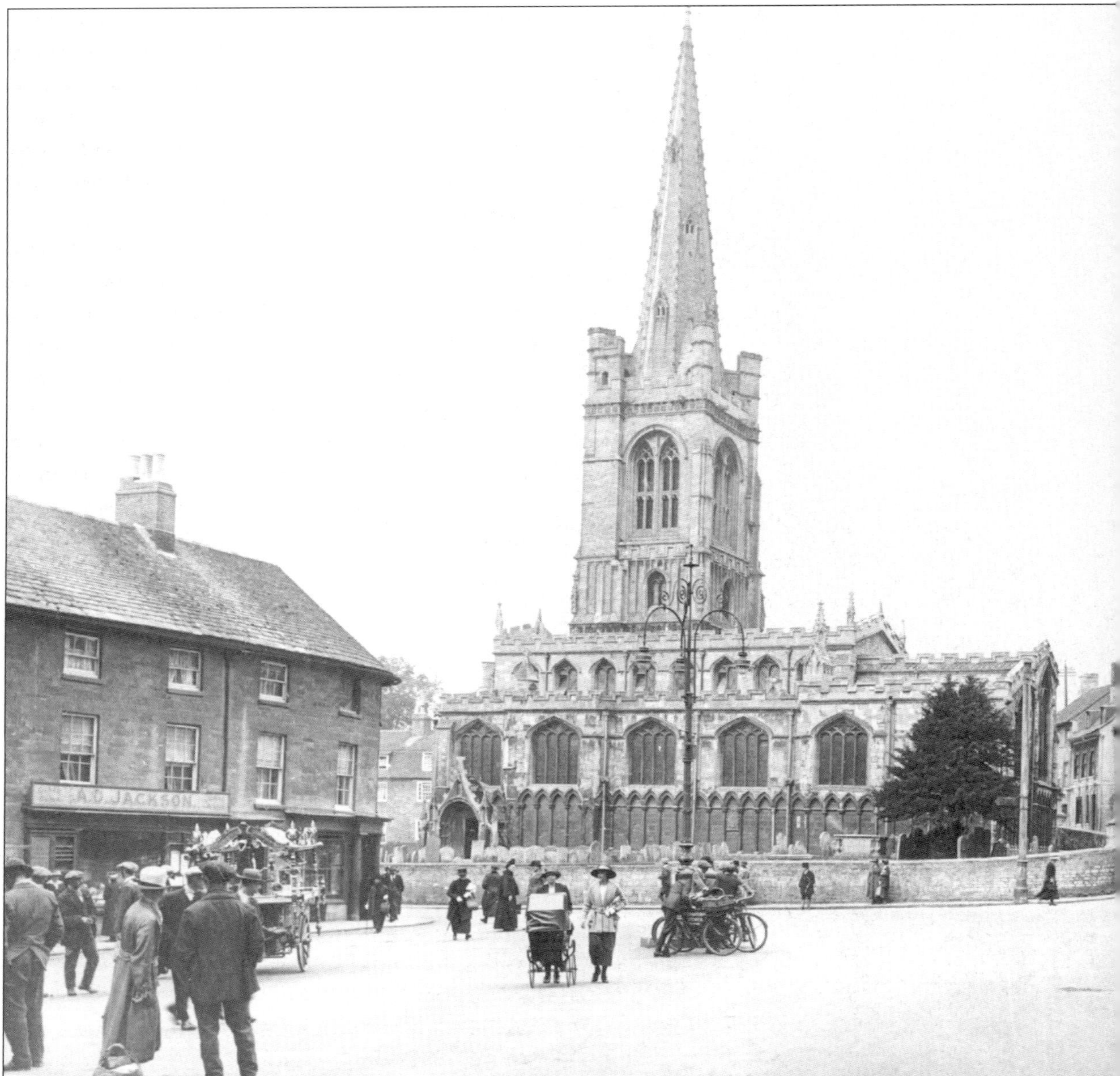

Red Lion Square 1922 72299

The Square, one of the ancient market places of Stamford, appears as a pleasant pedestrian area before the dominance of the motorcar; a convention of delivery boys is taking place around the gaslight. The shop on the right is occupied by Finlay's shoe shop, as is attested by the display outside — today it is the HSBC Bank. On the wall above the shop we can see the old sign from the long-closed Red Lion Inn from which the square takes its name. On the left is Andrew Dale Jackson's glass, china and general stores, with a butcher's shop beside it.

RED LION SQUARE AND BROAD STREET

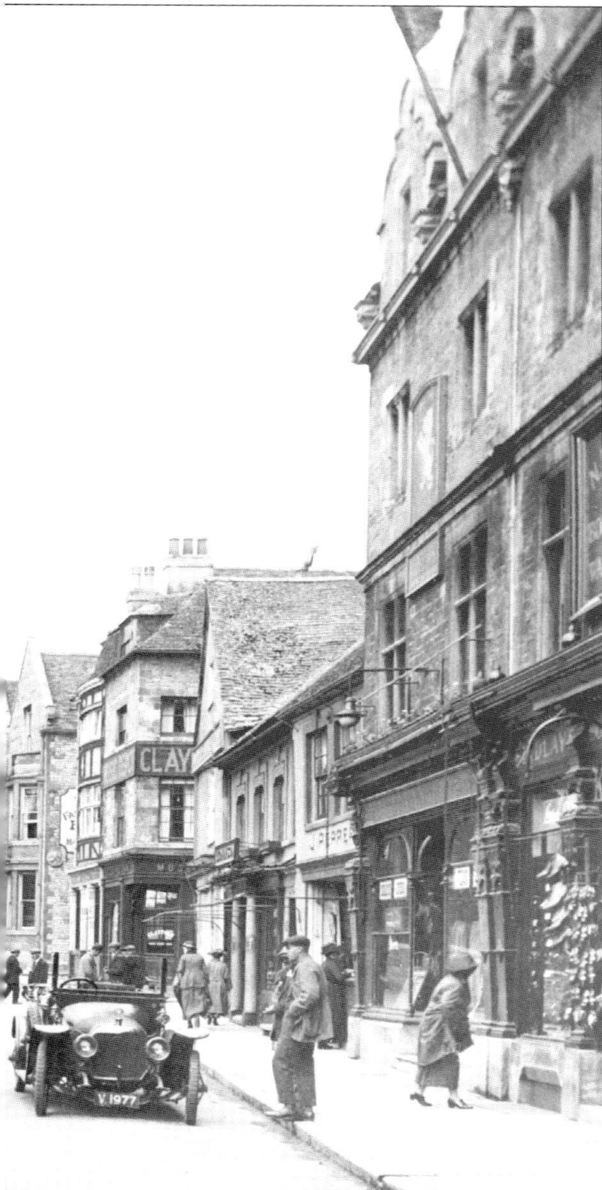

Red Lion Square has always been at the heart of Stamford's commercial life; indeed, seven roads radiate out from the square, including until recently, the Great North Road itself . The square lies between the earliest Mercian settlement, centred on St John's church to the west, and the Danish burgh to the east. It is a natural market site, and by medieval times it had developed into the site of the town's sheep market. The large building which features prominently in photograph 72300 (pages 30-31) as the Freeman Hardy and Willis shoe shop is known to contain elements of a large 14th-century timber-framed building. It has been suggested that this may be the wool house of the Brownes, one of the town's most successful families of wool merchants.

Coaching and the Great North Road aside, the location of Stamford on the boundary between grazing and grain-producing land has always ensured that it has had an important role as a market town. By the 18th century the town enjoyed 6 fairs and 4 cattle markets each year, and the 1895 edition of Brabner's 'Gazetteer of Britain' gives an idea of the busy life centred around the town's markets and fairs: 'The town carries on a good trade in corn, malt, coal, timber, stone and slates, and there are breweries, agricultural implement and machine factories, and cart and wagon works. The market is held on Friday for corn, meat poultry and provisions. The fairs are Candlemas for horses about 8 Feb, for beasts and sheep about 19 Feb, Mid-Lent for horses about 21 March, Town fair about 23 March, Spring fair about 11 April, May fair about 9 May, Corpus Christi fair about 20 June, St James fair about 25 July, St Simon and St Jude fair for horses and sheep about 8 Nov, and for beasts, cheese, and onions the day following. There are also markets for cattle in the early part of January, September, October, and December'.

The holding of markets extended into streets which are today peaceful residential areas. Barn Hill (72308, page 34), running northwards from Red Lion Square, was until 1781 the location of a sheep market. This street was also the home in the 18th century to the antiquary William Stukeley, whom we have to thank for recording many antiquities, both in Stamford and the rest of the country, which have since been lost. It seems to have been Stukeley who was responsible for popularising the tale that it was in his house that King Charles had stayed in May 1646 before his surrender to the Scottish army. Although this story is perpetuated in a plaque attached to the wall of a building near the site of Stukeley's house, there appears to be no truth in it — it is likely that the King in fact stayed in Blackfriar's House, off St Leonard's Street.

We can see a number of these plaques around the town; although somewhat erratic in their content, they are of interest in themselves, as they date from the early 1920s, soon after many of the photographs

Red Lion Square and Broad Street

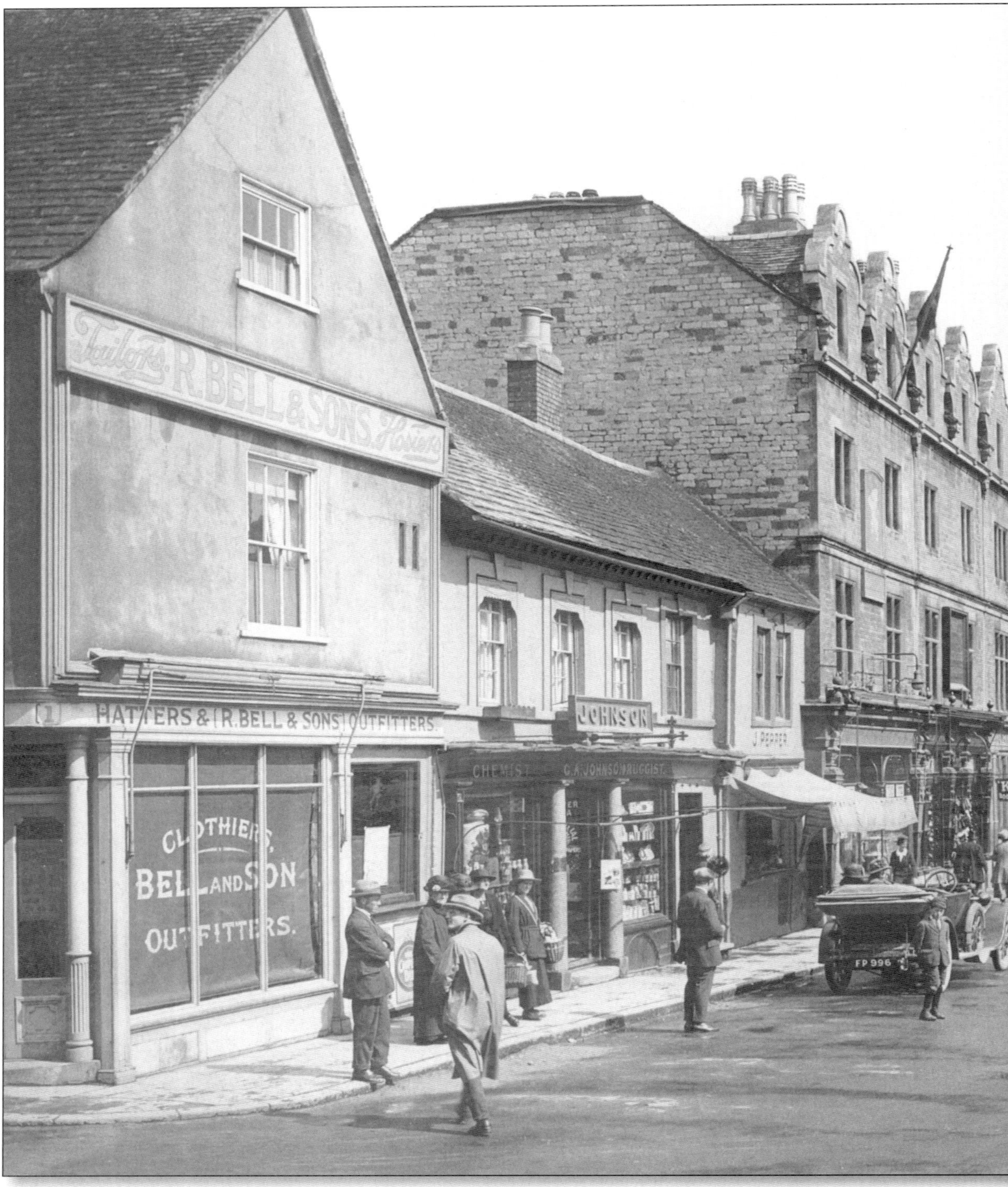

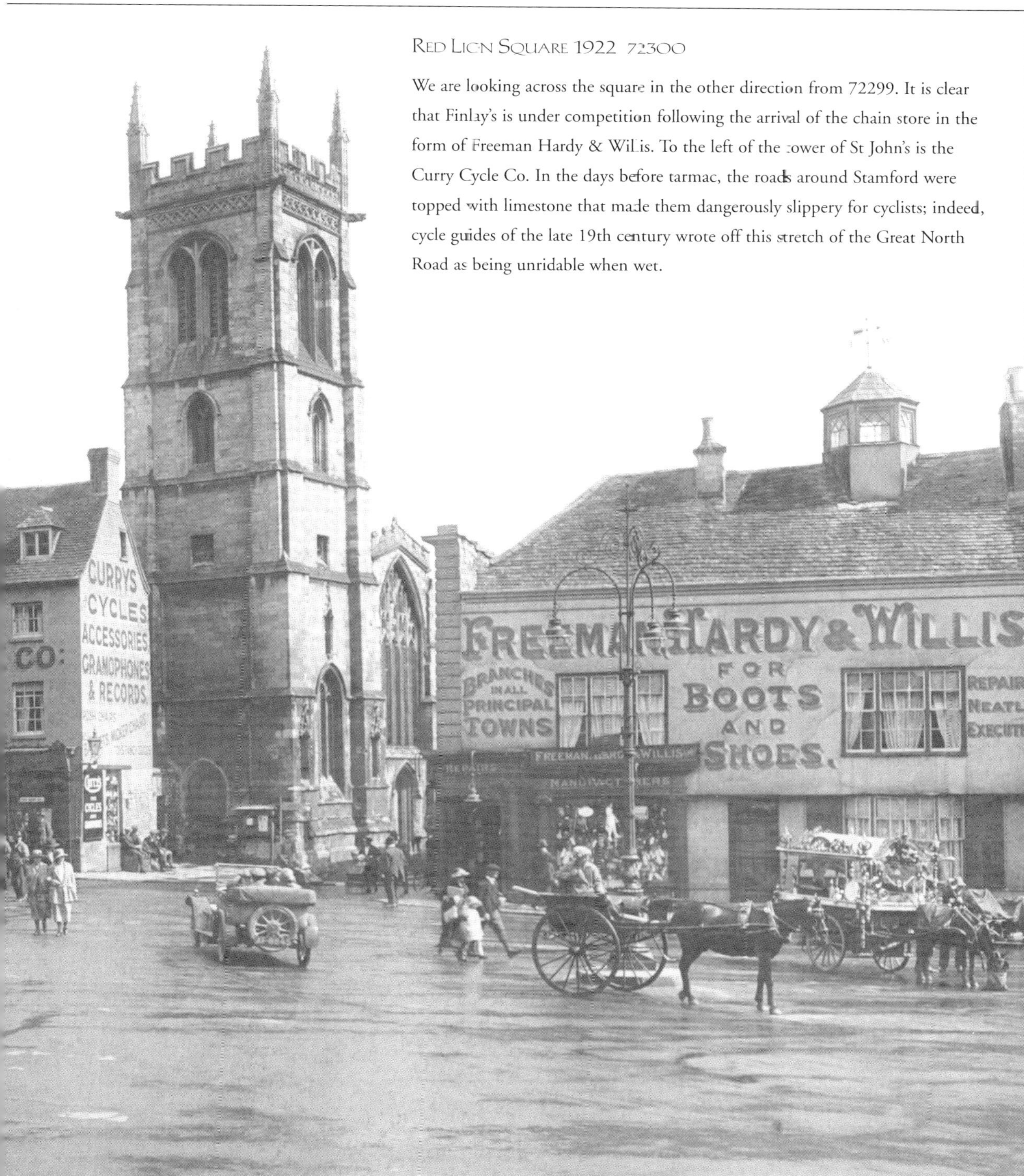

RED LION SQUARE 1922 72300

We are looking across the square in the other direction from 72299. It is clear that Finlay's is under competition following the arrival of the chain store in the form of Freeman Hardy & Willis. To the left of the tower of St John's is the Curry Cycle Co. In the days before tarmac, the roads around Stamford were topped with limestone that made them dangerously slippery for cyclists; indeed, cycle guides of the late 19th century wrote off this stretch of the Great North Road as being unridable when wet.

Red Lion Square and Broad Street

RED LION SQUARE c1955 S177058

On the eve of the 60s, the bicycle shop has gone and the car now reigns supreme in the square, which is signed as the A1. Coca Cola and snack bars have arrived too. Freeman Hardy & Willis have trendily abbreviated their name and put up new signage. On the architectural side, Pinney's the jewellers have replaced their more traditional building with a 1930s structure (left). The ornate gas lamp has gone. Today a wonderfully complicated tourist sign stands here, with arms pointing down each of the seven roads that leave the square.

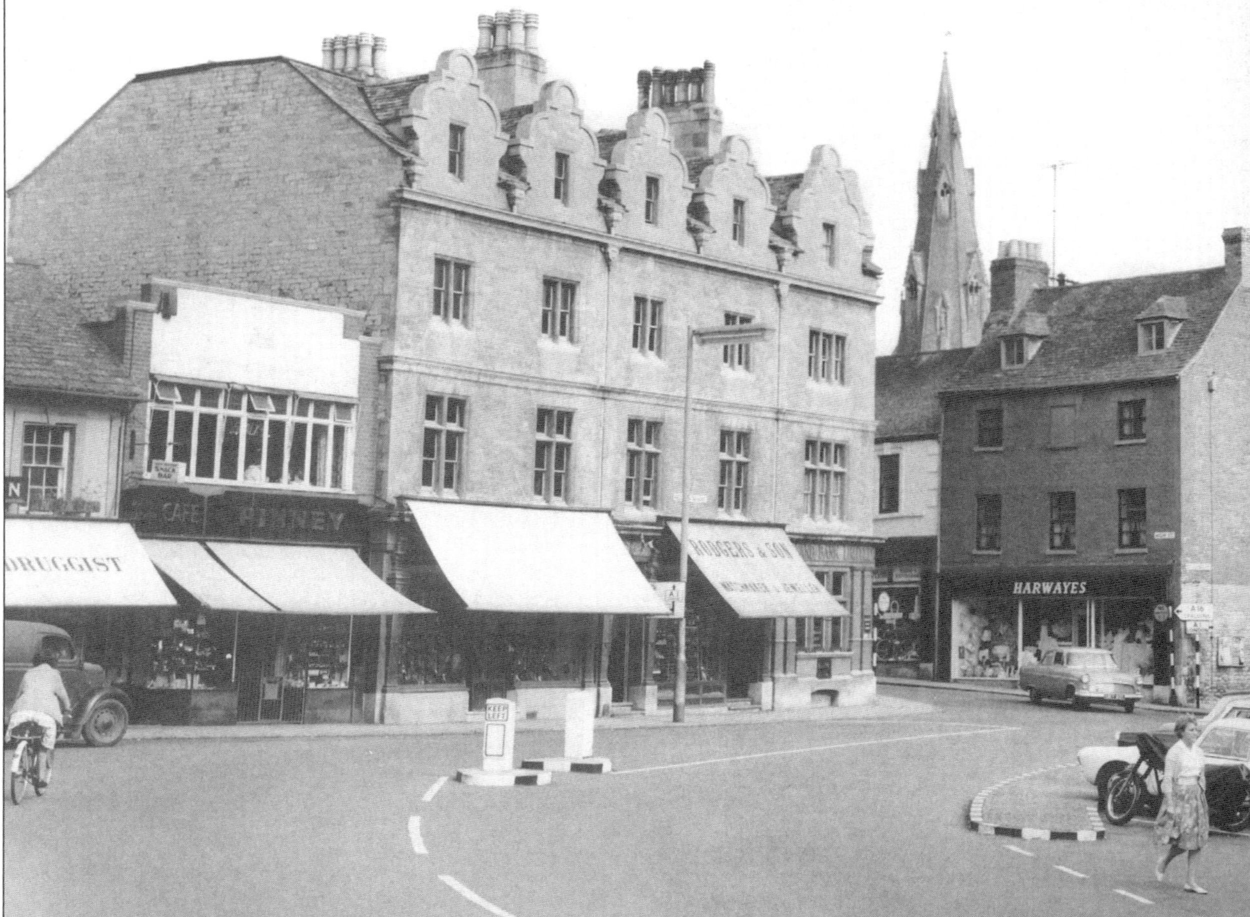

in this book were taken. This was a time when, thanks to the motor car, Stamford was becoming a tourist attraction in its own right for travellers along the A1, or Great North Road.

Broad Street (72311, page 33) formed the northern boundary of the Danish settlement. For a long time it was one of the main markets in the town, holding at various times the beast, leather, hay, corn and Friday markets. It is still home to the Mid-Lent Fair, an event with a long pedigree stretching back to the Middle Ages. At that time the fair, in the words of Alan Rogers in his 'Book of Stamford', 'lasted for two or three weeks and was a trading occasion of some importance to the nation as a whole. The King sent his servants to Stamford fair to buy ... cloth for himself, his Queen and his household'.

But the inhabitants of Stamford did not have to rely upon the fairs as their sole means of entertainment. In 1698 the town was one

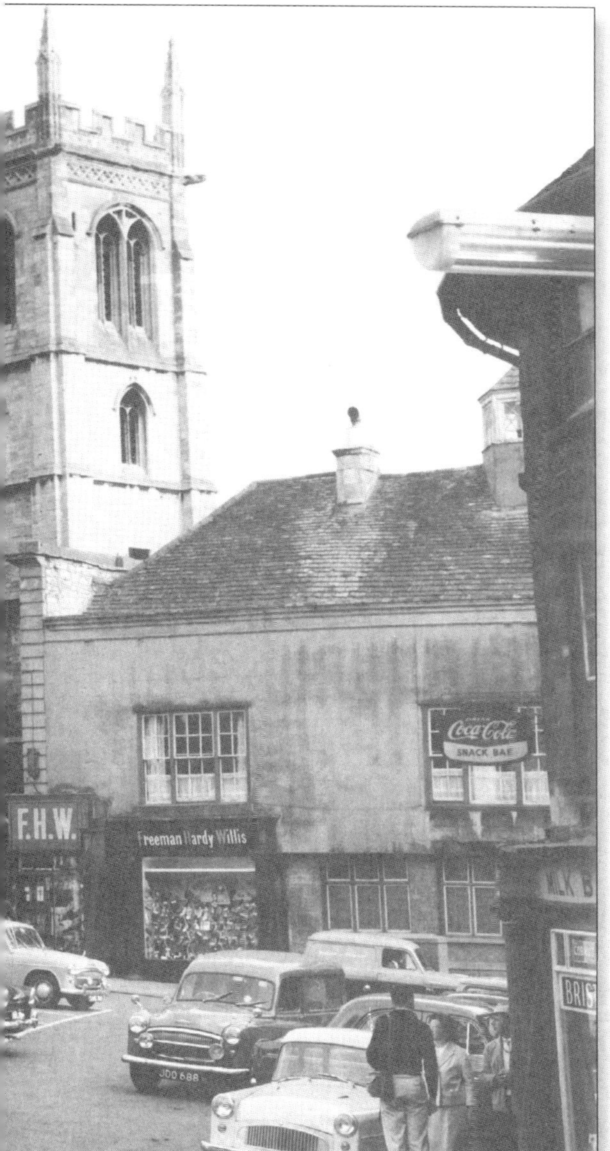

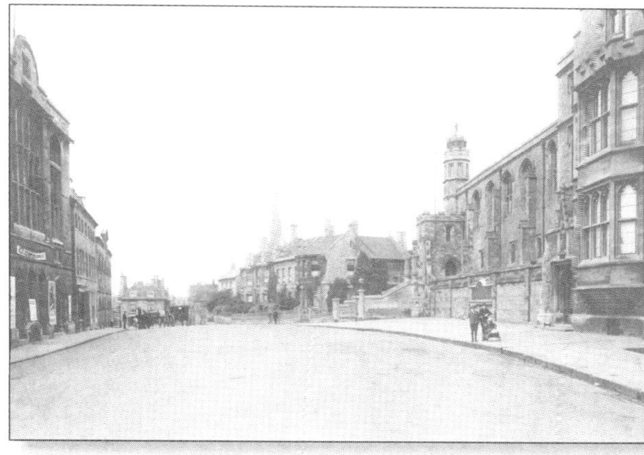

BROAD STREET 1922 72311

The building on the left, with the large window facing the street, is the Corn Exchange, then acting as a cinema — we see it as it was before the alterations that were made following a 1925 fire. The horse and cart are standing outside the showrooms and warehouse of the local engineering firm of Blackstone & Co. This building too became a cinema before being destroyed by fire in 1937. The scar left by its demolition can be seen in AF54982 on page 9. Over the street stands Browne's Hospital.

of the first provincial towns to stage plays and hold dances, and by 1717 it boasted a racecourse, which was popular with the surrounding gentry. The corn exchange building (72311, above), which stands at the highest point on Broad Street, opposite the almshouse of Browne's Hospital, dates from the period when the street's importance as a market was waning. It was built in 1858 on the site of the Black Swan Inn for the sum of £3,600, and was fitted out with stalls for salesmen. The building was also used for public meetings and concerts. In the end, providing entertainment took over, and by the time of the Frith photographer's visit in 1922 the building was in use as the Electric Cinema.

Three years later it was to suffer a disastrous fire; the building required extensive restoration before it could be reopened as the Picturedrome.

RED LION SQUARE AND BROAD STREET

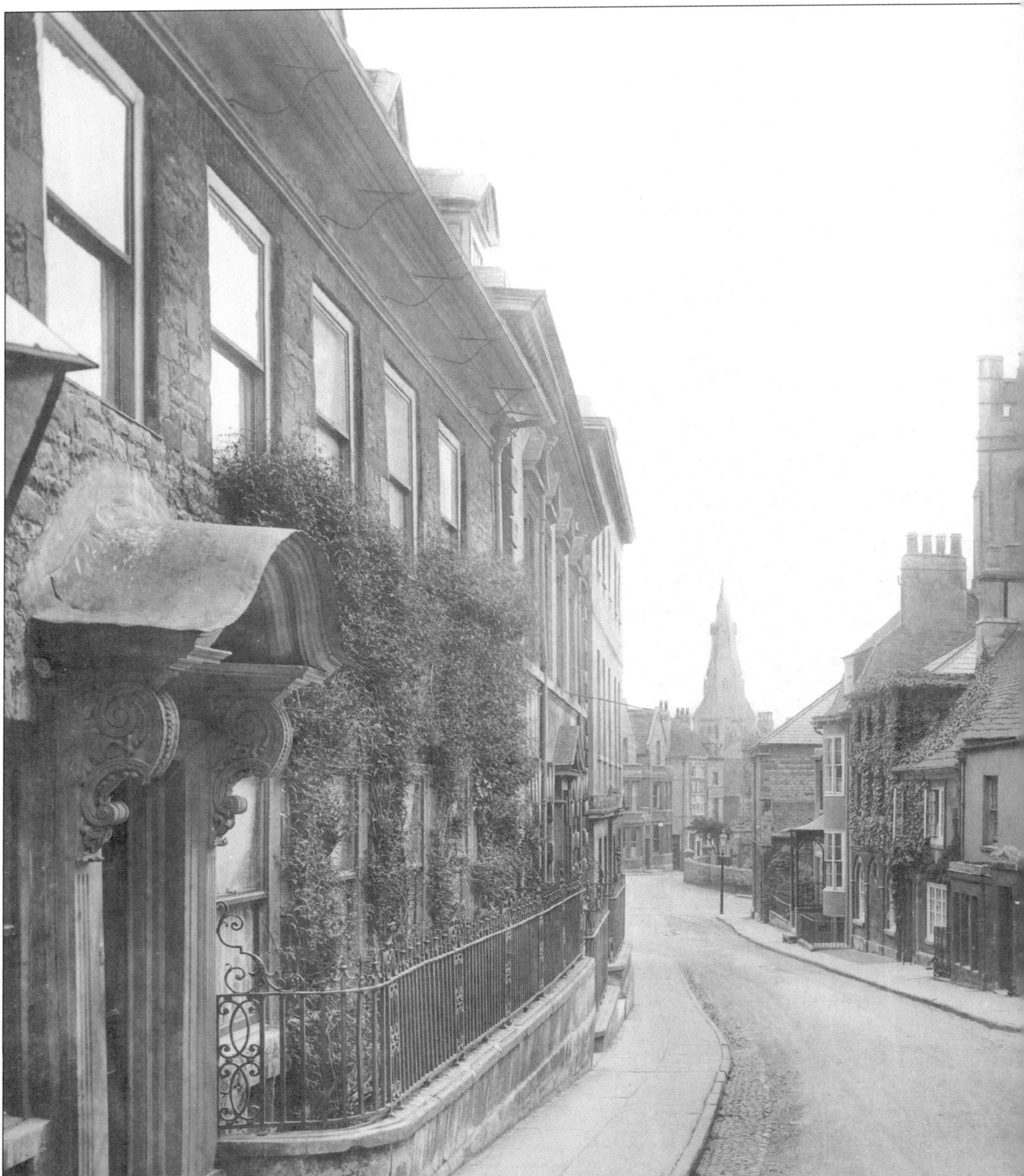

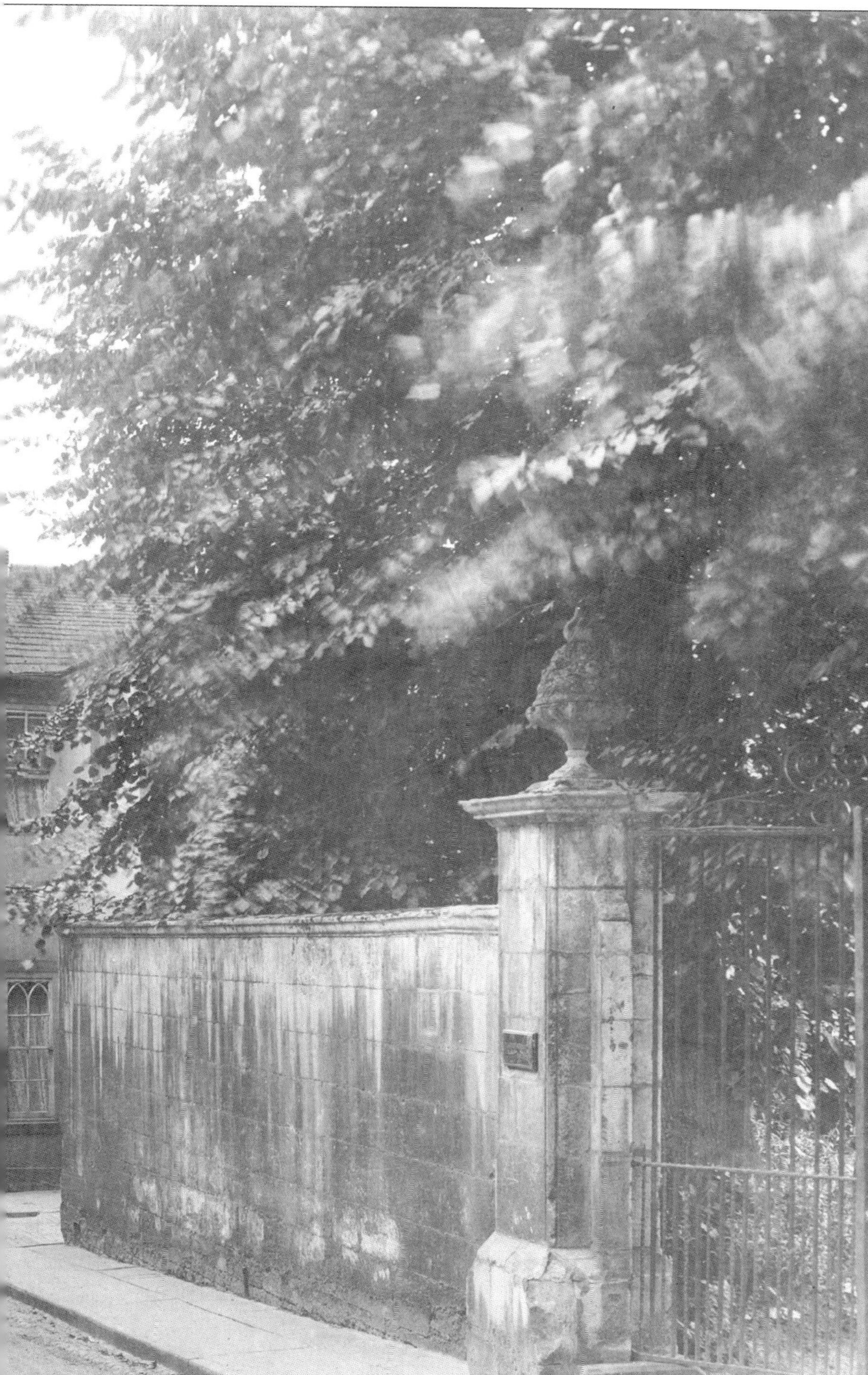

BARN HILL 1922 72308

Just a few yards up the hill from All Saints' Church, Barn Hill is a far cry from the commercial bustle of Red Lion Square. The photograph is taken from outside the Trinity Methodists Church (opened 1886). The gates on the right lead to Barn Hill House, which was fitted out at a cost of more than £3,000 as lodgings for Sir Robert Peel and other ministers during Queen Victoria's visit to Burghley House in 1844. More recently it was used as the setting of the New Fever Hospital in the BBC production of 'Middlemarch'. This scene has remained virtually unchanged over the last eighty years, except for the arrival of a set of double yellow lines.

Red Lion Square and Broad Street

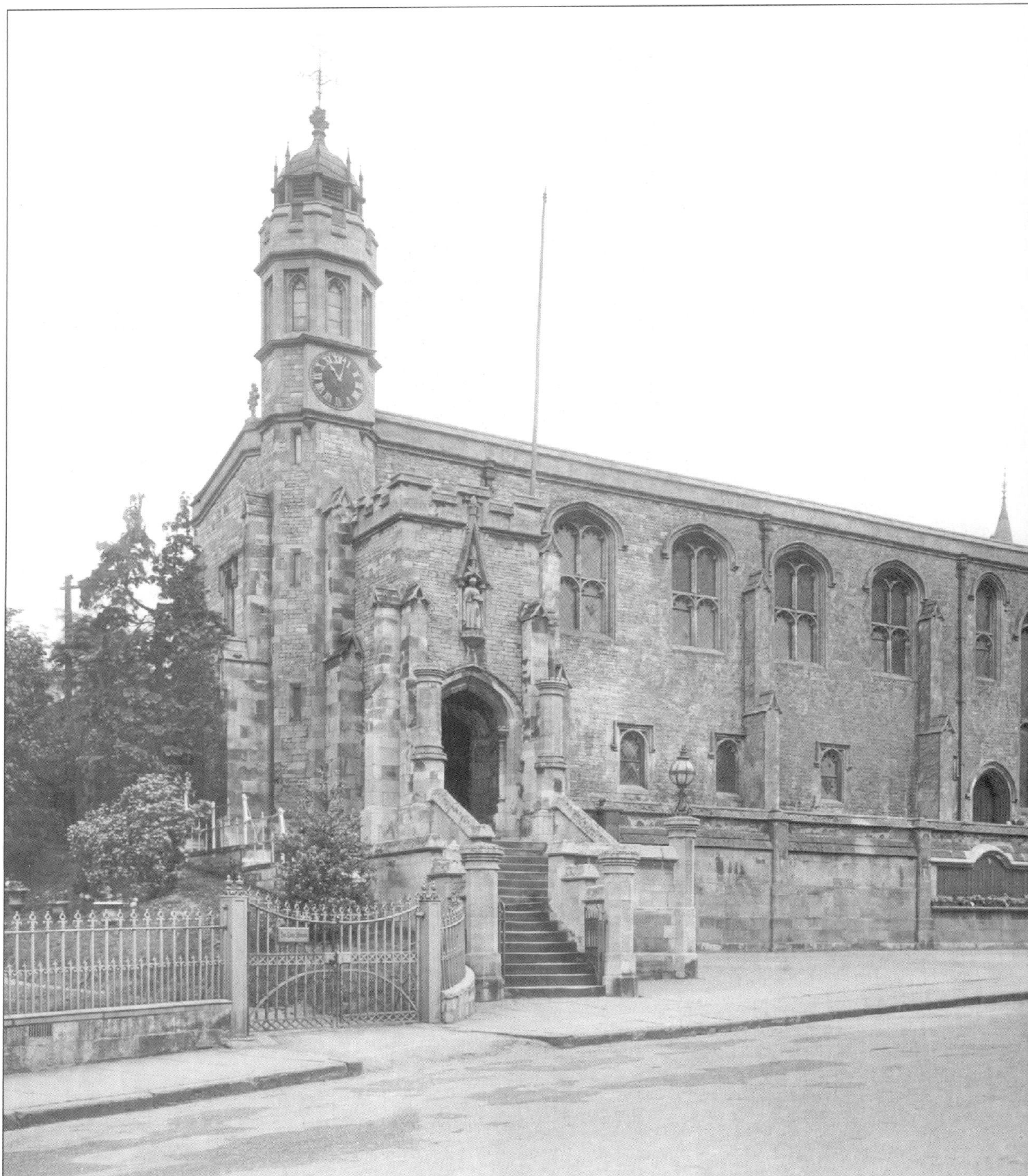

Red Lion Square and Broad Street

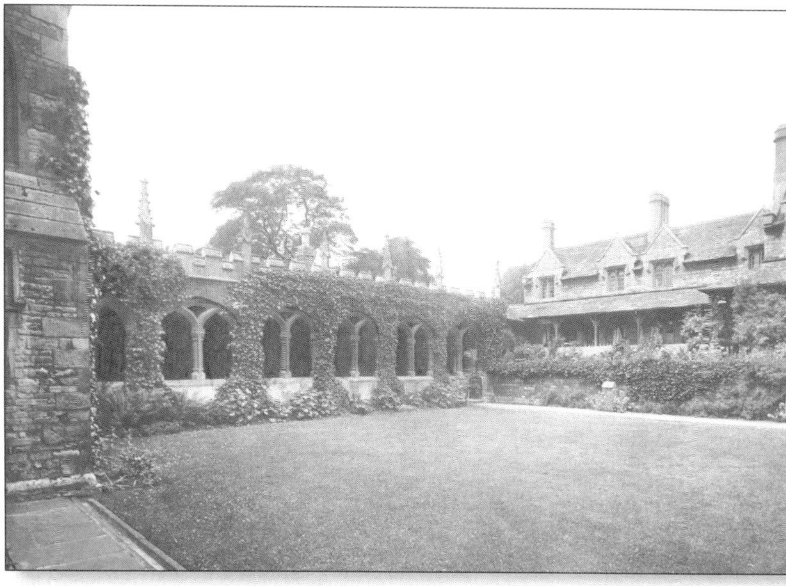

Browne's Hospital, the Cloisters 1922 72319

Browne's Hospital (72317 and 72319, these pages) is one of the most important medieval almshouses in England, dating from 1475 when it was founded by the wool merchant William Browne. The Hospital, which was restored by James Fowler of Louth in 1870-71, includes a common room for the ten poor men (who were accommodated in cubicles), a chapel and an upstairs audit room, which may have doubled as a guildhall. The cloisters and court form a beautiful centrepiece to the complex.

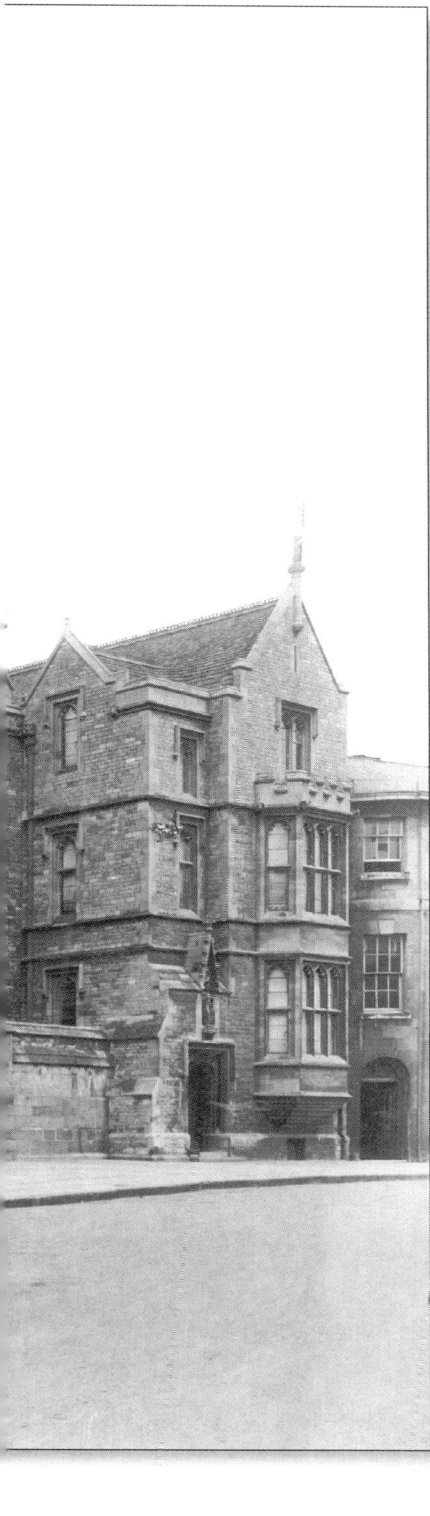

Browne's Hospital 1922 72317

The external view shows the war memorial, which now has the inevitable extension beneath it to include those who died in the Second World War. The site of the memorial had from 1839 to 1858 been occupied by a glass-roofed corn market — it was then transferred to its new location on the other side of Broad Street.

St Peter's Street, St Mary's Street

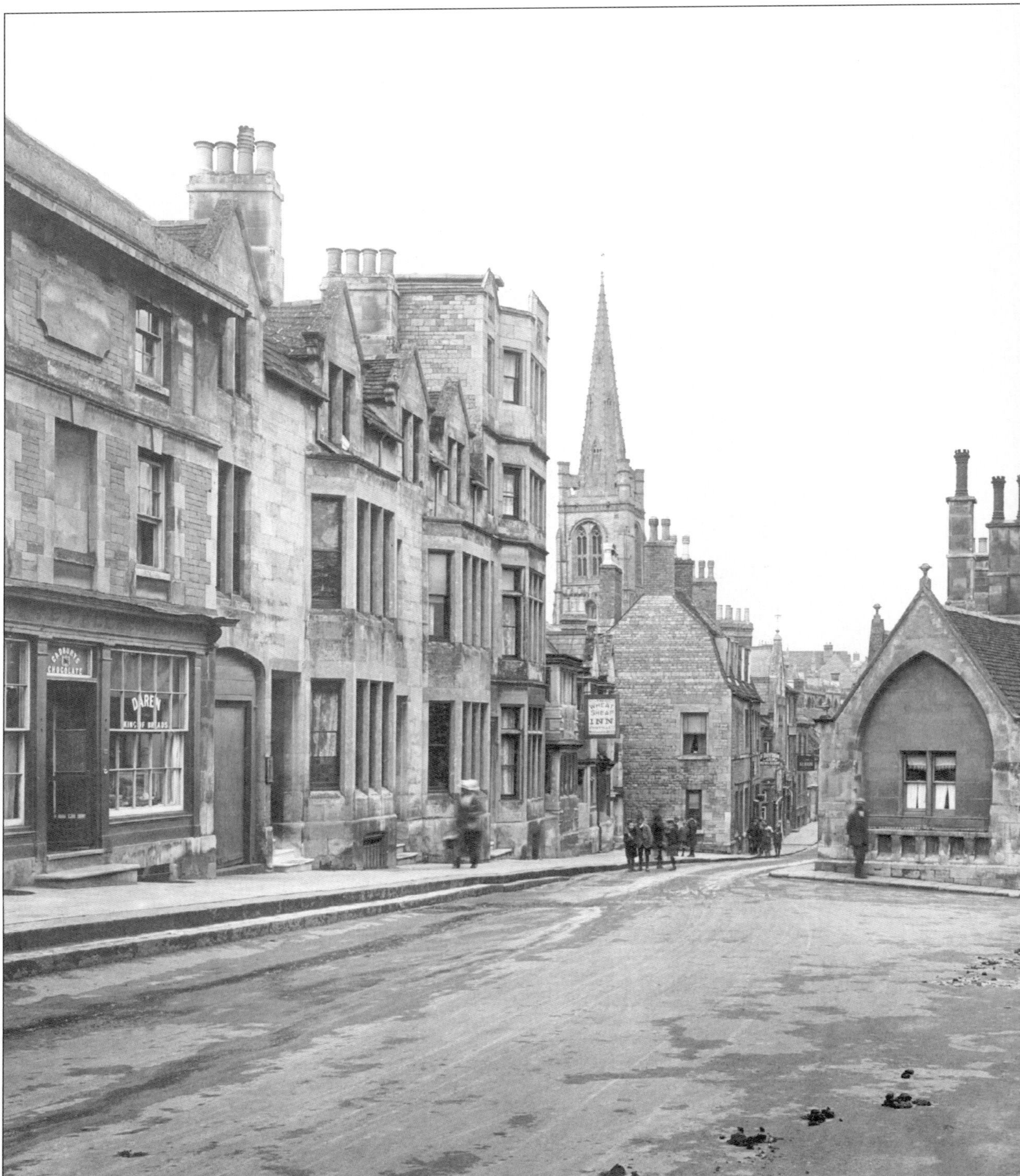

AND HIGH STREET, ST MARTINS

ST PETER'S HILL 1922 72307

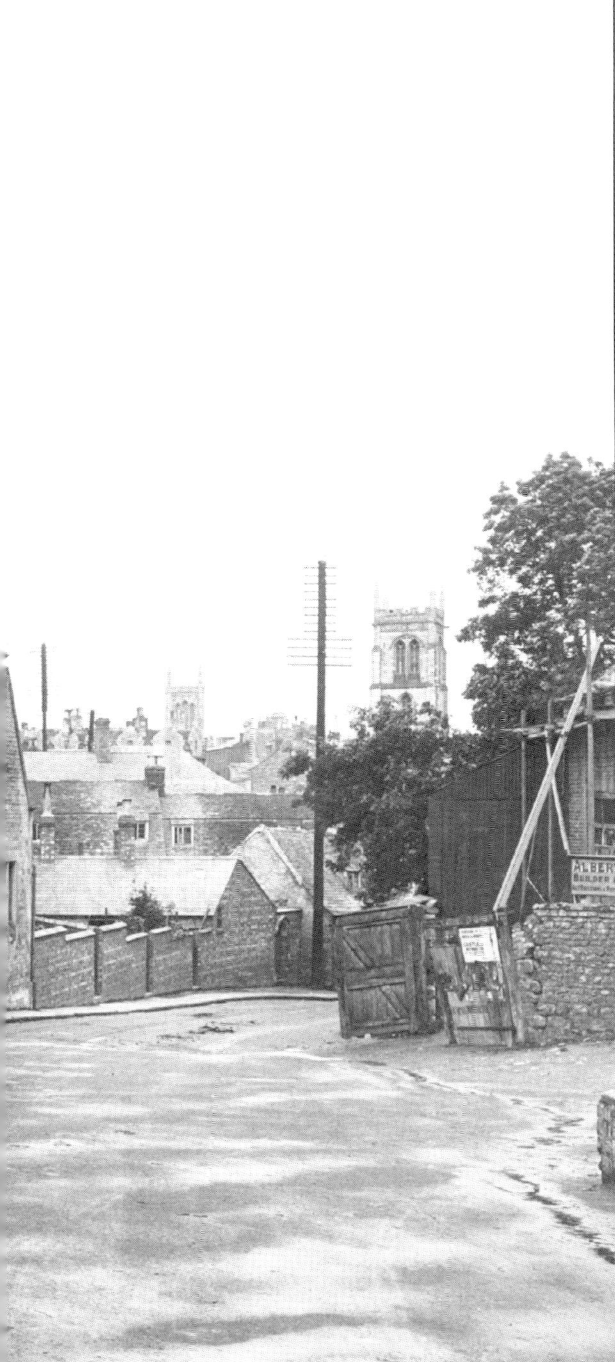

Leading from a gate in the town walls towards the castle and the commercial centre, St Peter's Street has been the main entrance to Stamford from the west since the days of the Danish burgh. One of the most impressive buildings in the street was constructed in 1842 to house the Stamford Institution (the last building on the left on the brow of the hill in S177021, page 40), which was founded in 1838 'for the dissemination of literature, philosophical, scientific, mechanical and other useful knowledge'. The building cost £1,200, with financial support coming from the Cecils. The Institution housed a concert and lecture hall, a museum, a 8000-volume library and a reading room. It also boasted a unique attraction, which an 1896 guide to the town described thus: 'at the summit is an observatory with camera obscura, where the visitor may for a few pence obtain fine views of the neighbourhood'. The observatory was removed in 1910.

Photograph S177021 was taken close to the entrance to Williamson's Callis, which was adapted as an almshouse in 1762. Further down the street, is St Peter's Callis. Photograph 72307 (left) gives us a closer view of St Peter's Callis, the building in the centre of the photograph. An almshouse was recorded on the site in 1466; in the late 18th century, it is known to have housed twelve poor women. The present structure, however, dates from 1859, when accommodation was reduced to three people. To the left, at the entrance to All Saints' Street, we can see the sign for the Wheatsheaf Inn, which welcomed customers from the latter part of the 18th century until 1960; the building currently houses a firm of chartered accountants. To the right of the callis is a sign advertising 'Albert Peasegood builder and undertaker' on the site of what was soon to become a car park.

St Mary's Street, in contrast, has always been more commercial in nature, and the area between it and the River Welland shows signs of the overcrowding which occurred within the town during the late 18th century. At this time the population of Stamford was growing, but there was nowhere outside the ancient town where new development could take place: common fields encircled the town to the north, and southwards the Cecil estates certainly offered no opportunities for development. What little land did become available was taken, as at Rutland Terrace, for middle class developments (S177015, pages 42-43). The only solution, as in other Midlands

St Peter's Street, St Mary's Street

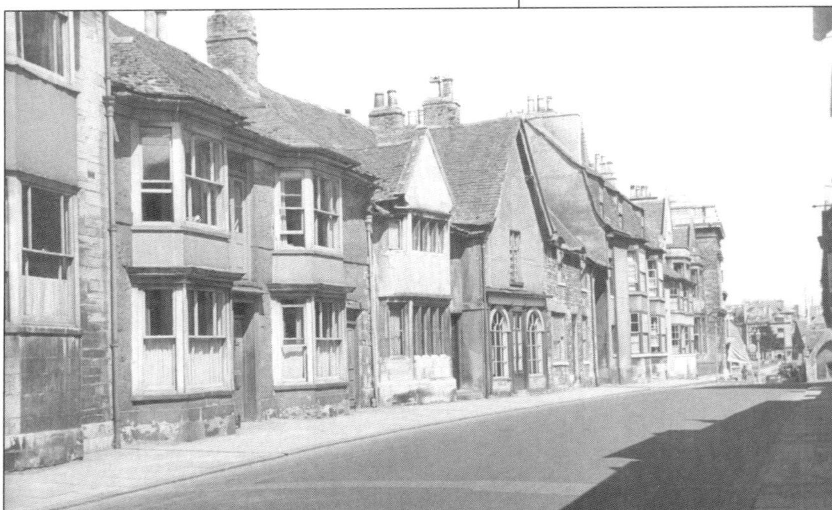

Above: St Peter's Street c1955 S177021

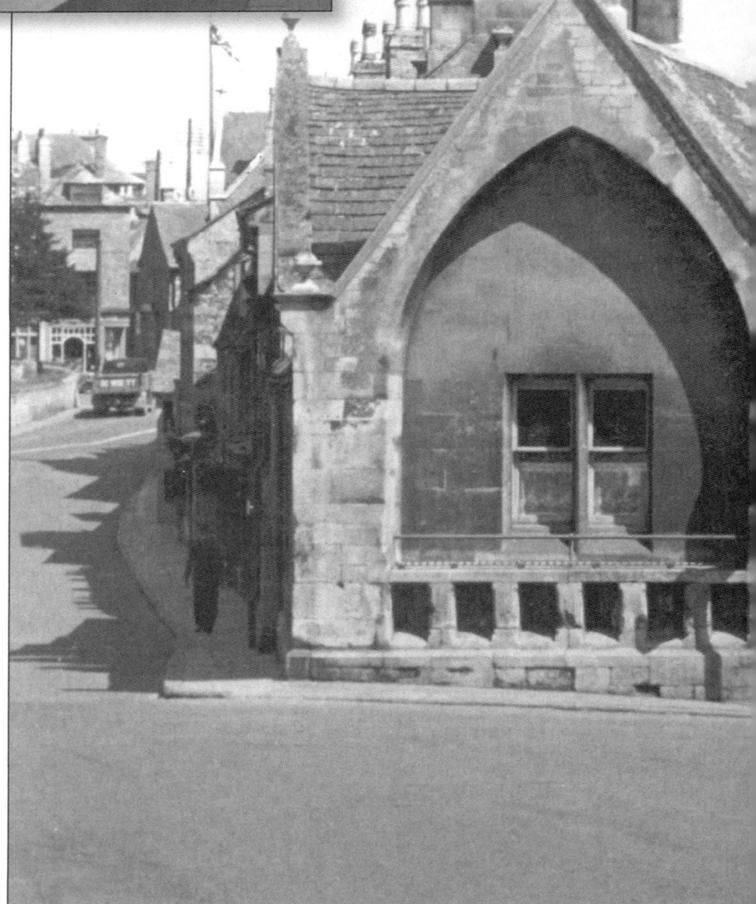

towns (although not to the same extent) was to pack the growing population ever more tightly in the land which was available.

The result was that there sprang up 'many useless shabby places', in the words of a contemporary writer. In Brooke's Court alone (72313, page 42) a narrow alley that ran off St Mary's Street, there were sixteen tenements by the 1890s — these were only demolished in the 1950s.

In the foreground on the right of 72309 (page 44) a lady is animatedly studying the contents of the 'English & Foreign Fruitier', a business run at the turn of the century by Valentine Hibbins. Just beyond her is the entrance to Brooke's Court, and one shop up the hill is the bakers and confectioners of Charles Wade & Son. The children on the left are standing at the corner of the old London Inn, which was rebuilt when the building line was moved back to ease traffic problems on the tight corner (S177047, page 69). Above them are the premises of Eayrs, 'tailors, hatters and gents' outfitters'.

ST PETER'S CALLIS C1955 S177022

The thirty years since photograph 72307 (page 38-39) have left the Callis unchanged, but the area on the right of the photograph, which included the remains of the castle mound, has been levelled and developed into a car park and bus station. Just over the parked cars we can see what is today the café and taxi office. The front of this building was moved here following alterations to the Stamford Mercury Offices on High Street. Since the photograph was taken, there have been changes along the approach to Sheep Market: the building with the mansard roof, end on to the photographer, has been replaced with an incongruous group of shops.

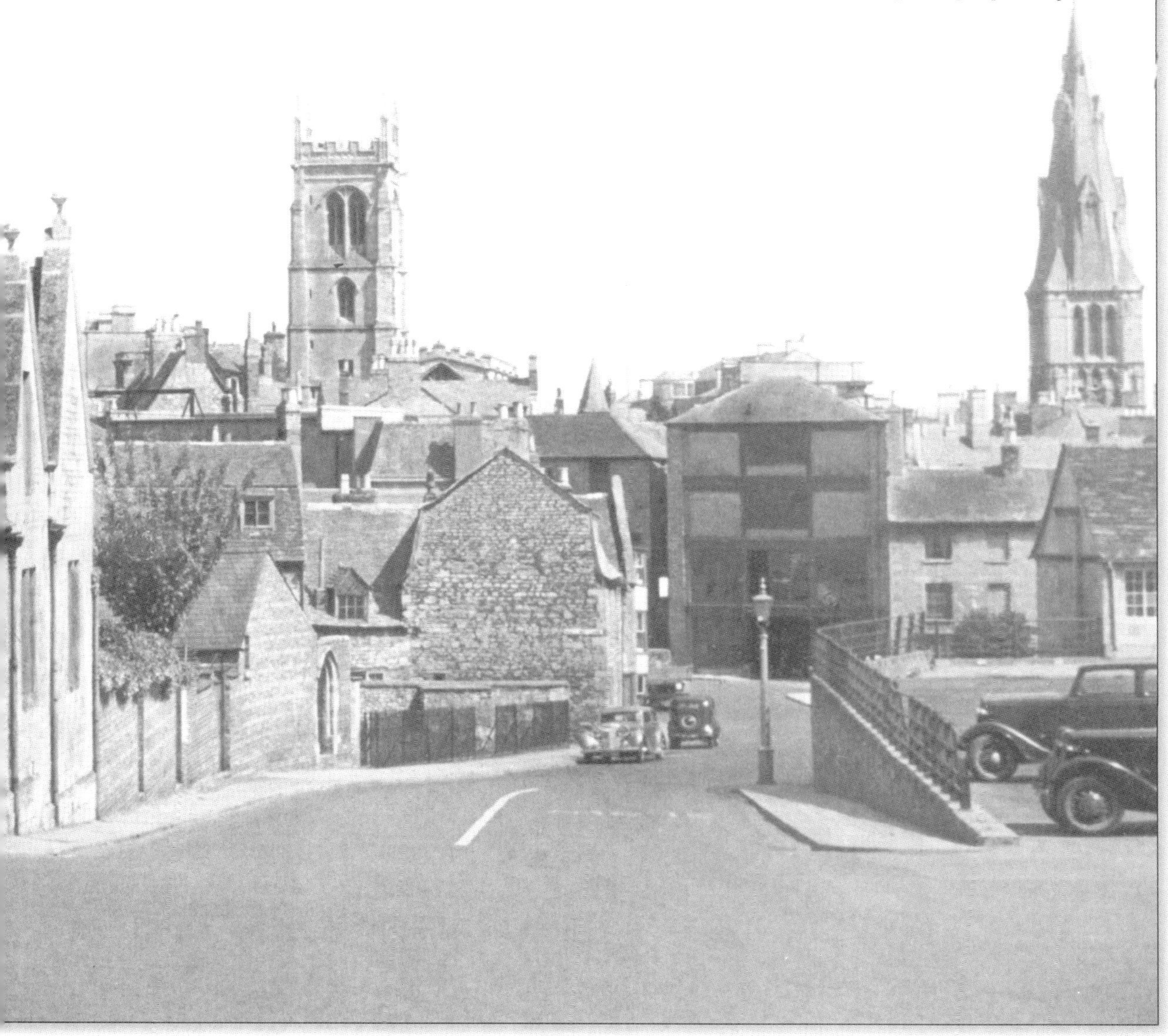

ST PETER'S STREET, ST MARY'S STREET

BELOW: BROOKE'S COURT 1922 72313

This passageway, which now runs from St Mary's Street down into the car park beside the meadows, formed one of a tight network of passages and closes which provided cramped tenement accommodation in this part of the town (see bottom left-hand corner of AF54982, page 8). Most were demolished in the late 1950s, but part of Brookes Court survives. The establishment on the right is Barton's Restaurant, an offshoot from the bakers shop on St Mary's Street (72309, page 44, right). By the 1950s it had become Ye Olde Barn, and it is still a restaurant today.

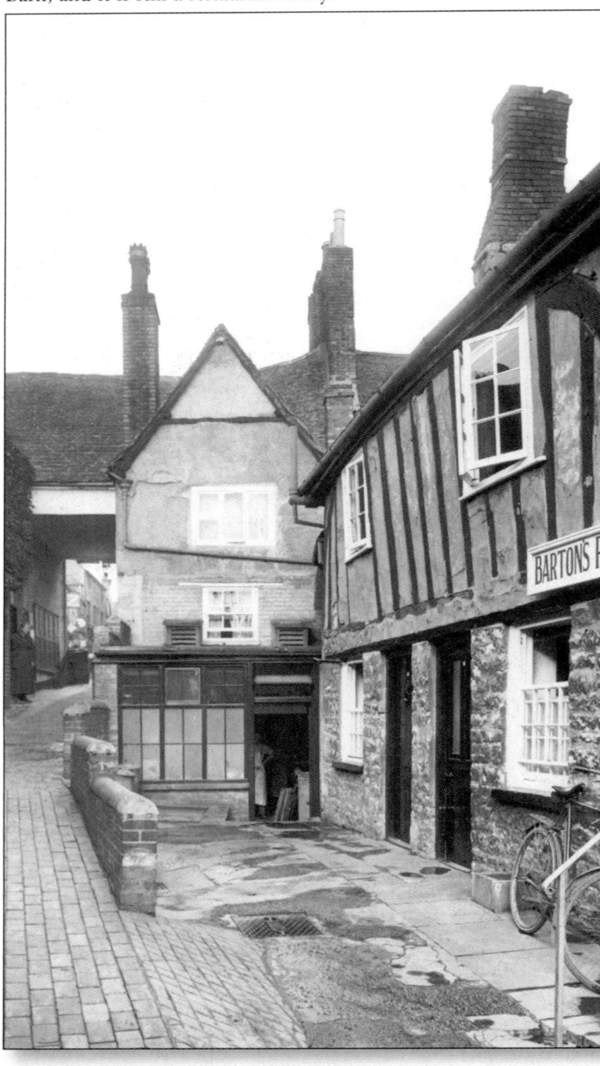

RIGHT: RUTLAND TERRACE C1955 S177015

Situated at the west of end of St Peter's Street, this fine Regency terrace was constructed between 1827 and 1831 on the site of the bowling green to provide houses for 20 middle-class families. The view is little changed today, except for the sprouting of television aerials and an unpleasant lamppost which interrupts the line of the terrace.

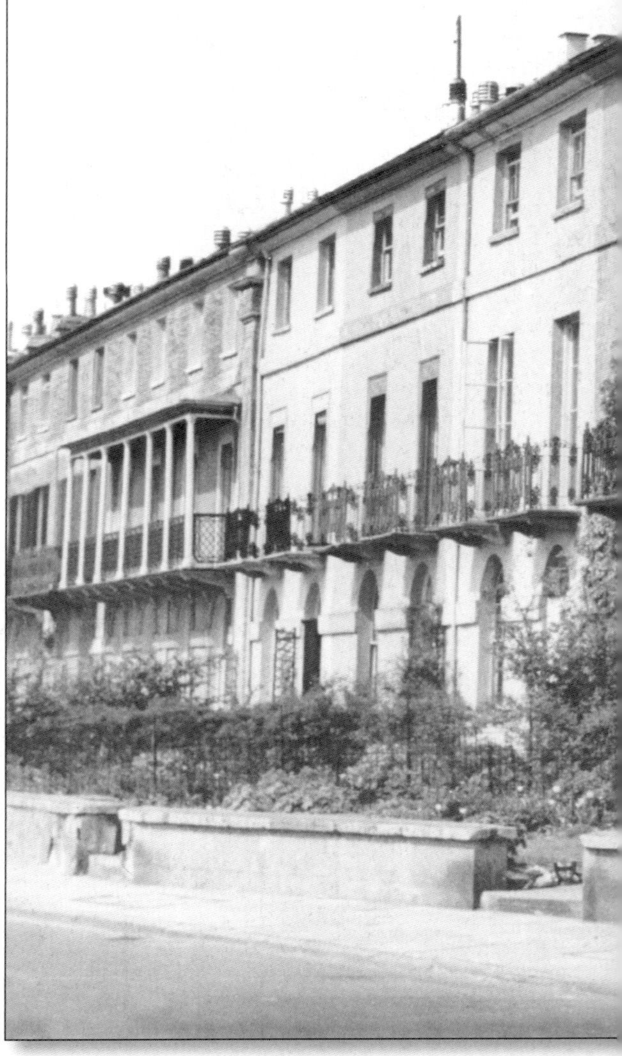

AND HIGH STREET, ST MARTINS

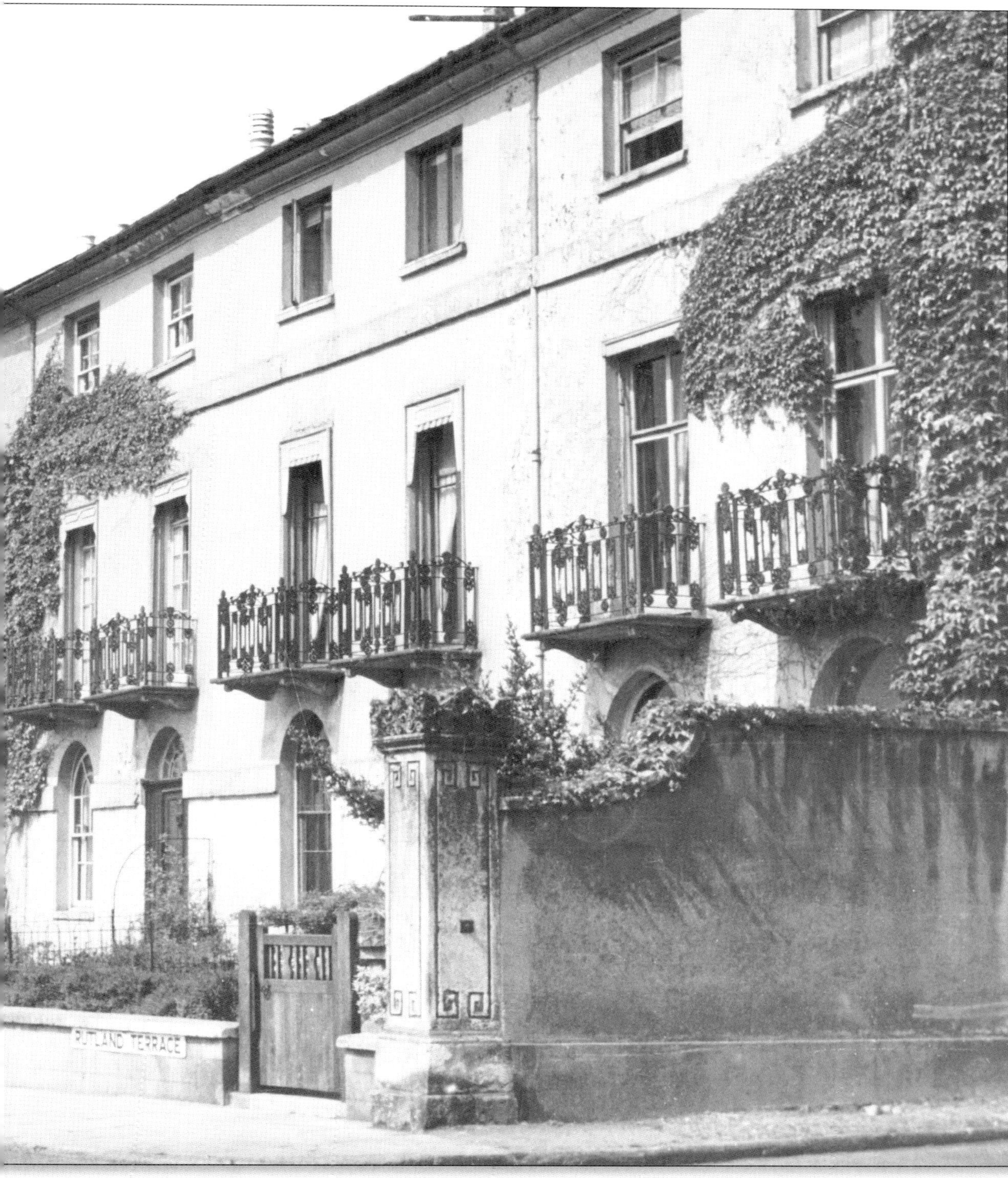

St Peter's Street, St Mary's Street

Right:
St Mary's Street 1922
72309

Below:
St Mary's Street c1955
S177024

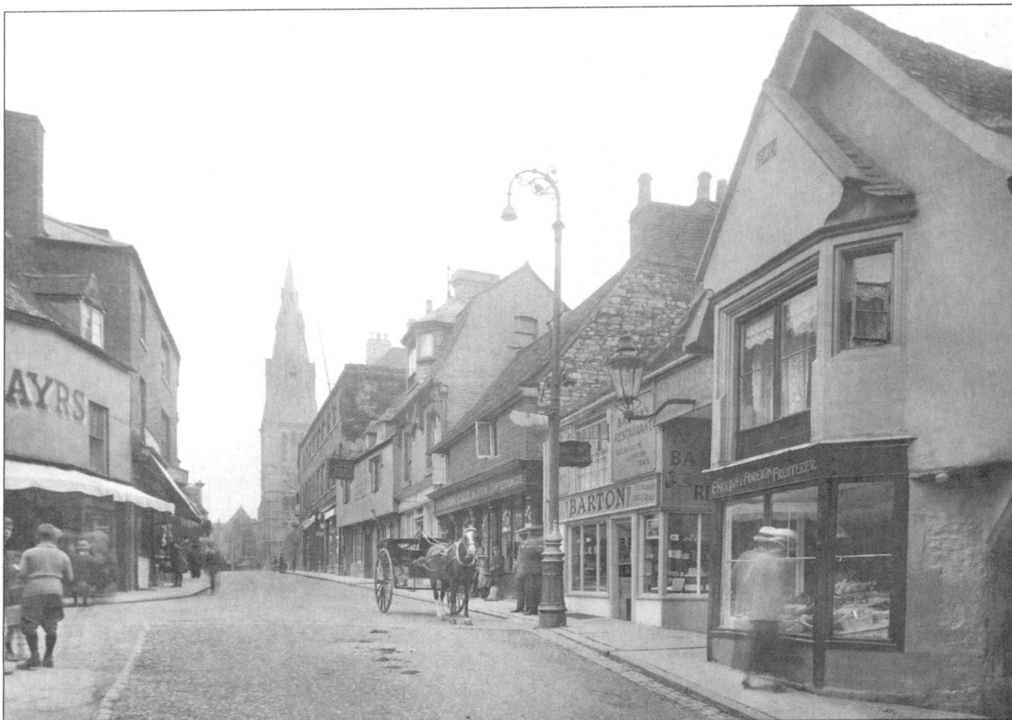

In the 1947 official handbook for Stamford, the Willow Restaurant (S177024, right) boasted that it provided 'the finest meal in Stamford', with a three-course luncheon for 2s 3d. Next-door is one of the most notable timber-framed buildings in the town — until 1931 it was the Cross Keys Inn (the sign remained for some years after). It appears to have had its black and white frontage restored since the 1920s.

No 14 St Mary's Street on the left of 72316 (far right) occupies the site of the George and Angel Inn, one of Stamford's most important coaching inns. The present building was constructed in 1849. For the first half of the 20th century it housed ironmongers, first Willcock's and later Allen's (home perhaps to the child who is watching the photographer from an upstairs window). Just off the picture to the left were the premises of Frederick Dickinson, who in the 1896 town guide was noted as offering darkroom facilities for the use of photographers visiting the town. The hanging baskets under the balcony of the Stamford Hotel go some way towards brightening a rather dull day.

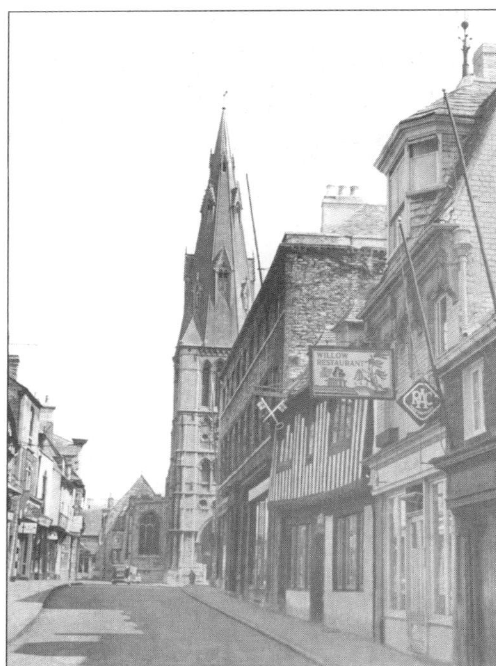

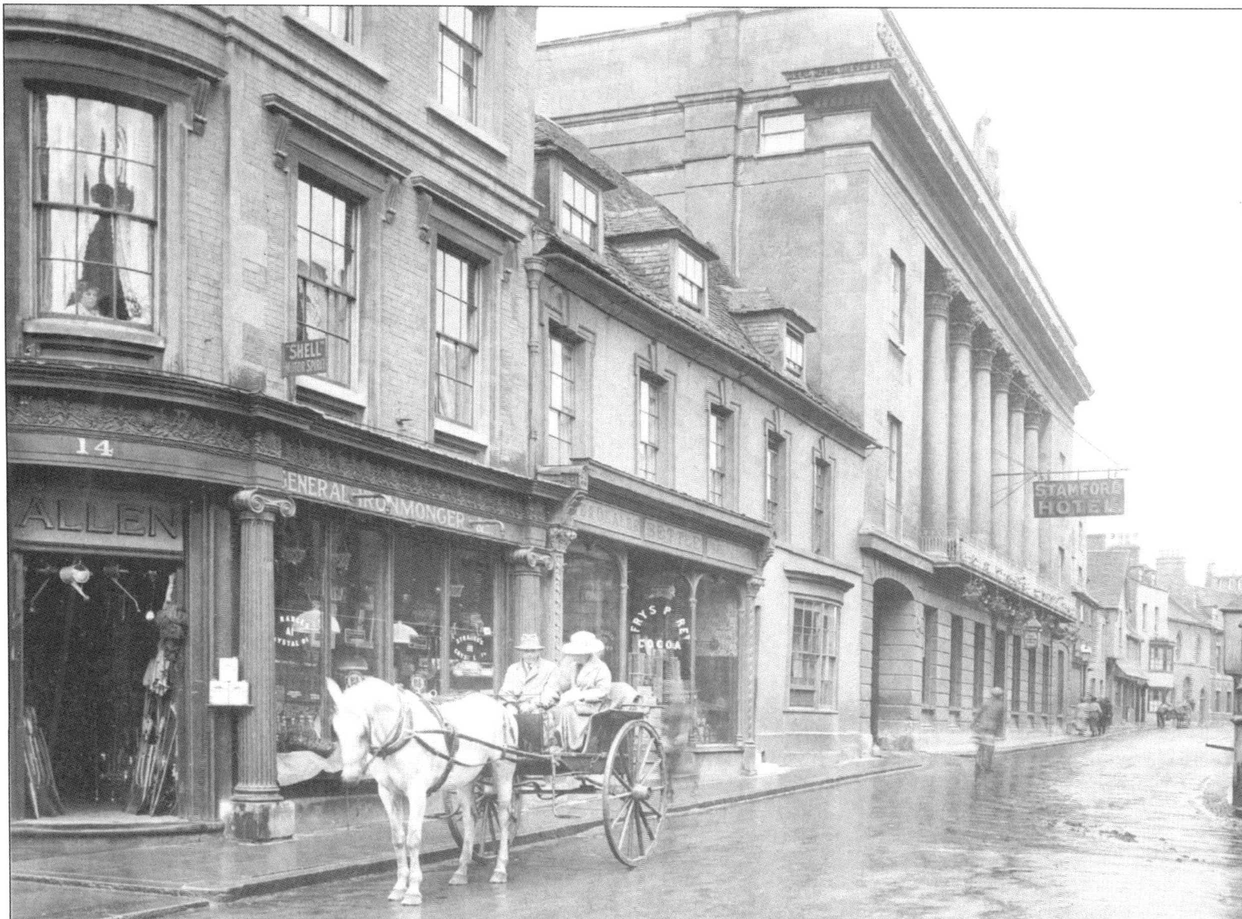

THE STAMFORD HOTEL 1922 72316

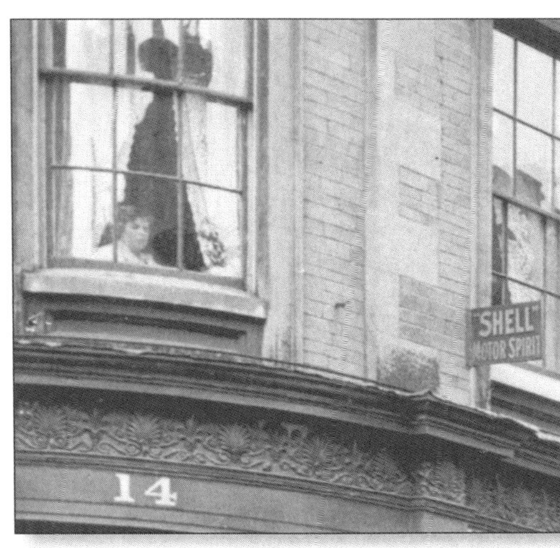

RIGHT: DETAIL FROM 72316

St Peter's Street, St Mary's Street

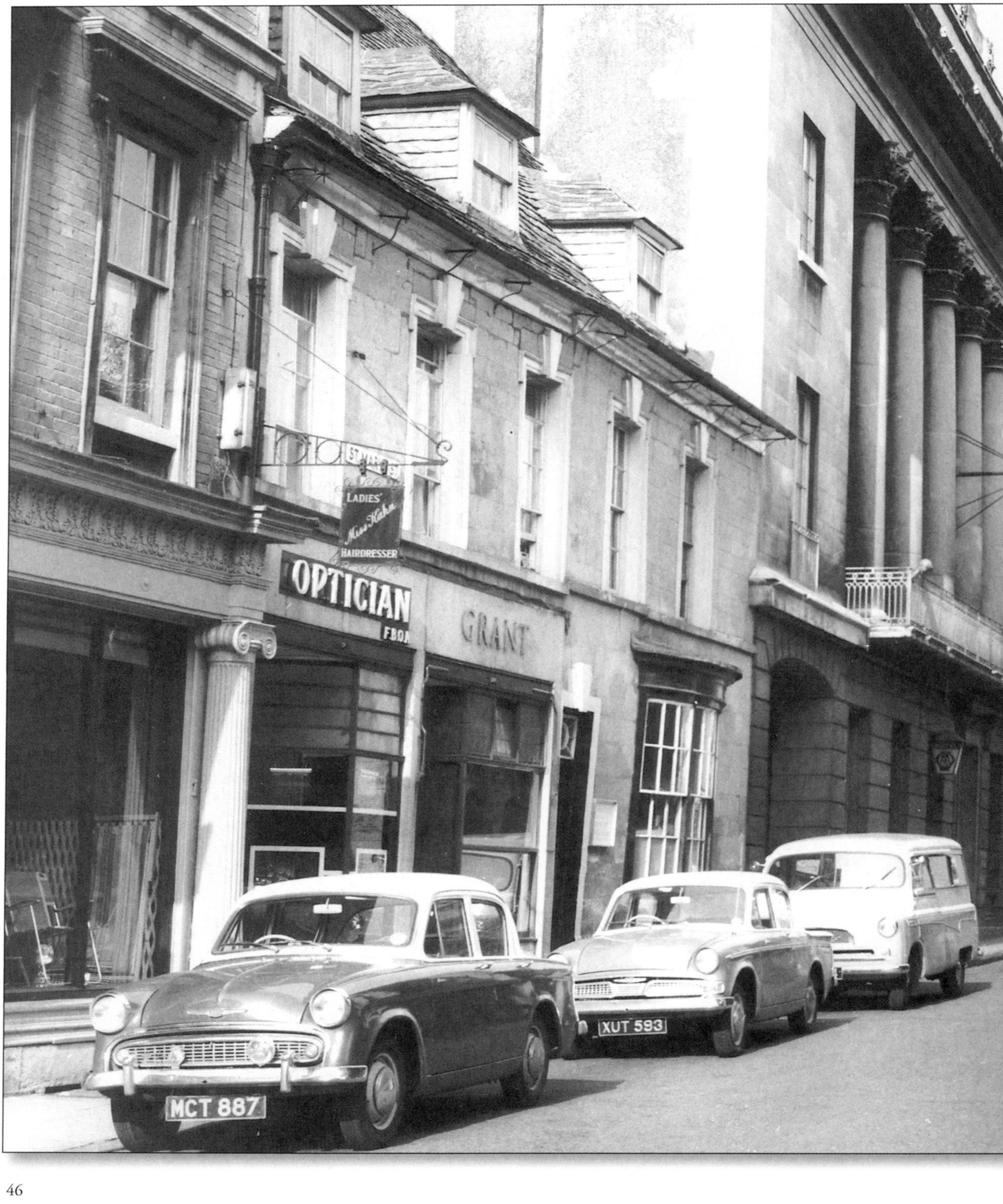

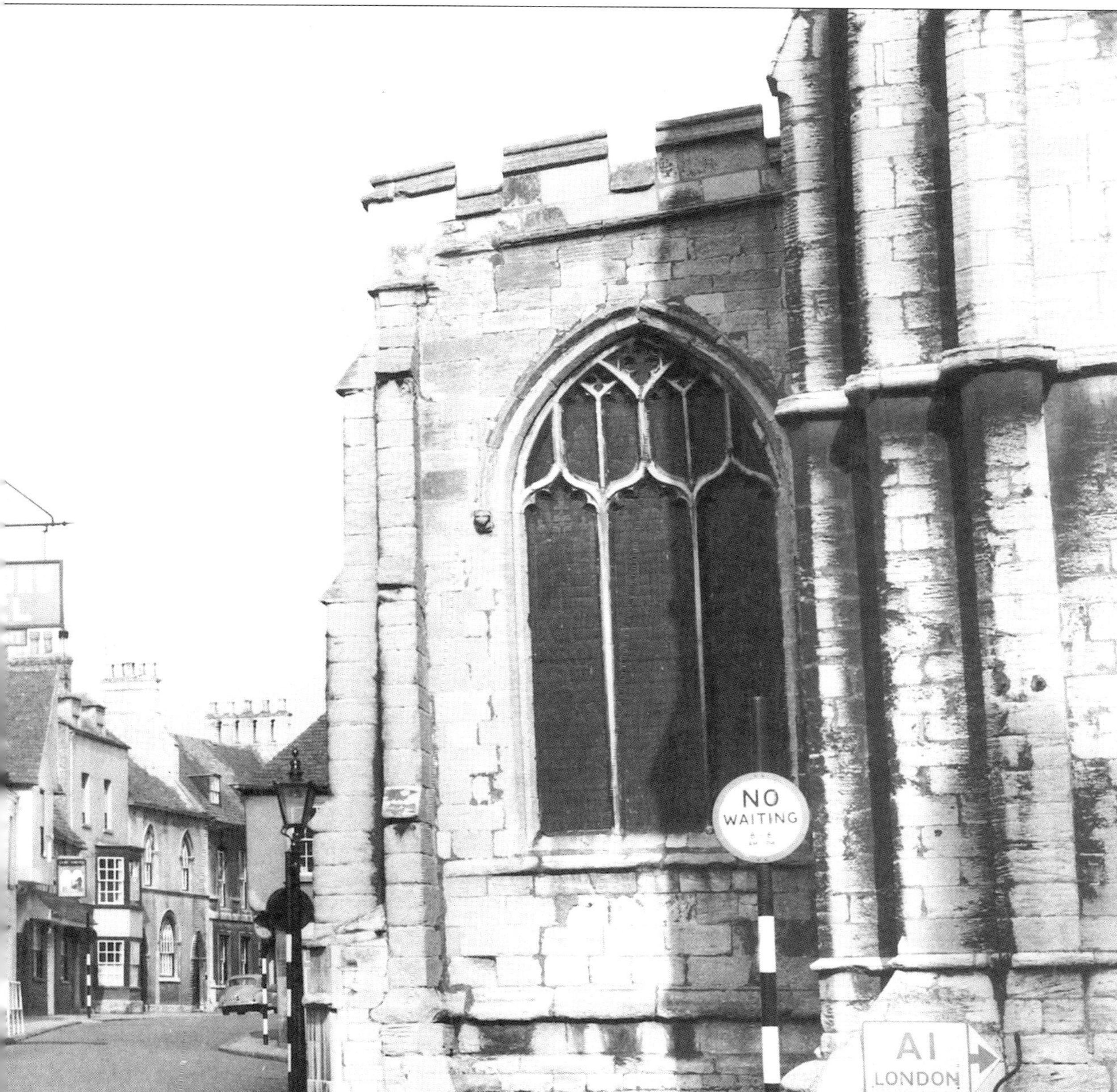

ST MARY'S CHURCH C1955 S177061

By the time that this photograph was taken, Bettle's family grocers, together with its shop front, has gone to make way for two shops. The 'No Waiting' sign suggests that car parking has become something of a problem. In the middle distance that other scourge of modern life, the television aerial, is beginning to make an appearance.

ST PETER'S STREET, ST MARY'S STREET

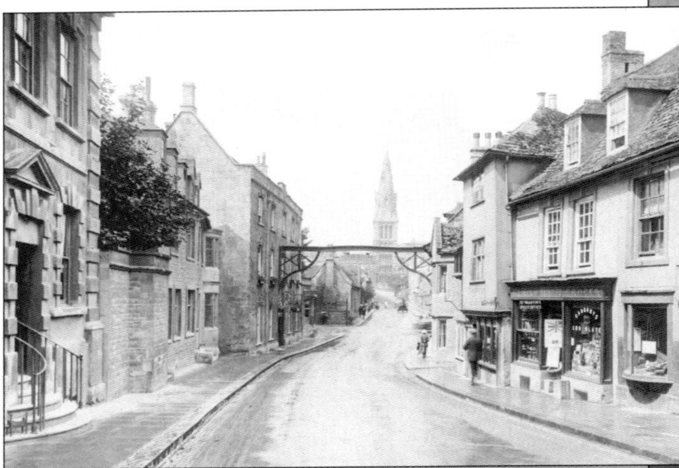

HIGH STREET, ST MARTIN'S 1922 72304

St Martin's, or Stamford Baron, lying beyond the River Welland at the intersection of two important medieval roads, has long been the focus of the town's communications with the outside world. It was also the point of embarkation for access to the coast via the river. Indeed, in the mid 19th century, while other areas in Stamford were suffering from overcrowding, those parts of St Mary's Hill and High Street, St Martin's which face southwards towards London and Burghley Park were being made more presentable, as befits the approach to an important provincial town. When the railway made it appearance in 1846, it too was brought into the town via St Martin's, albeit by means of a tunnel.

On the left of 72304 (above) is the entrance to the fine Georgian house at No 67 High Street which dates from c1740; even the railings and boot scraper remain today. On the other side of the street, however, things have changed more: the range of small shops, including Charles Dodman's and the St Martin's Post Office, were demolished in 1969, sad to say, and replaced by flats. Chapman's is no longer a shop either. Beyond the sign for the George Hotel that stretches over the street, the broach spire of St Mary's church gives a wonderful welcome to the upper part of the town. Like many views in the Frith collection, the photographer appears to have wandered out into the road to get his shot — not something that one could recommend at this point today.

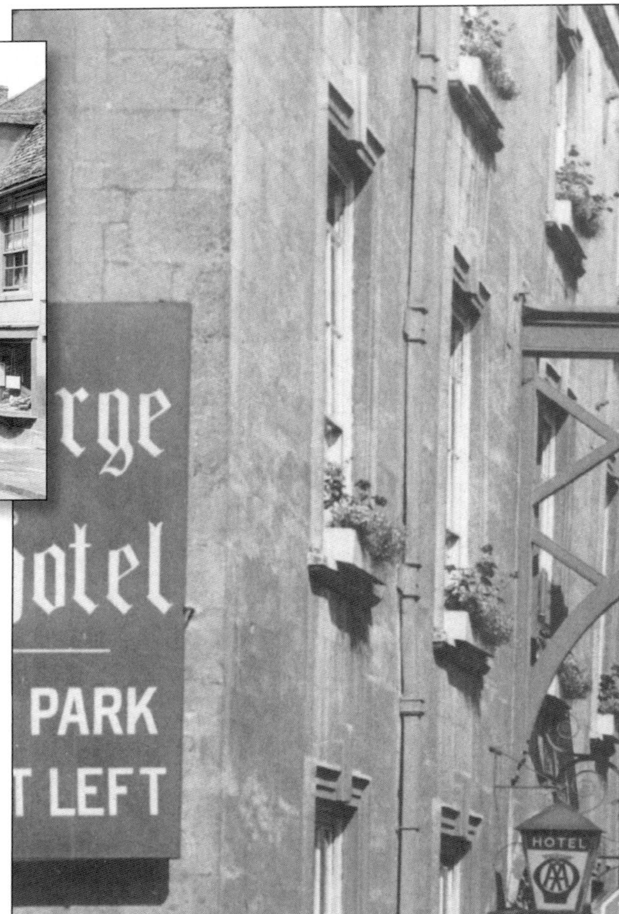

HIGH STREET, ST MARTIN'S c1955 S177051

The window boxes of the George Hotel are still a feature today, and the range of buildings on the right of the photograph continues to be used as shops, now antiques and furnishings, although previously they have included tailors, bakers and grocers. On the sky line, mid-way between the towers of St Mary's and St Michael's, is the statue of Justice on top of the prestigious Stamford Hotel. The only real change today is that the brick building just to the right of the two cars, which was home to a butcher's shop, was demolished in the early 1970s to widen the entrance to Water Street.

AND HIGH STREET, ST MARTINS

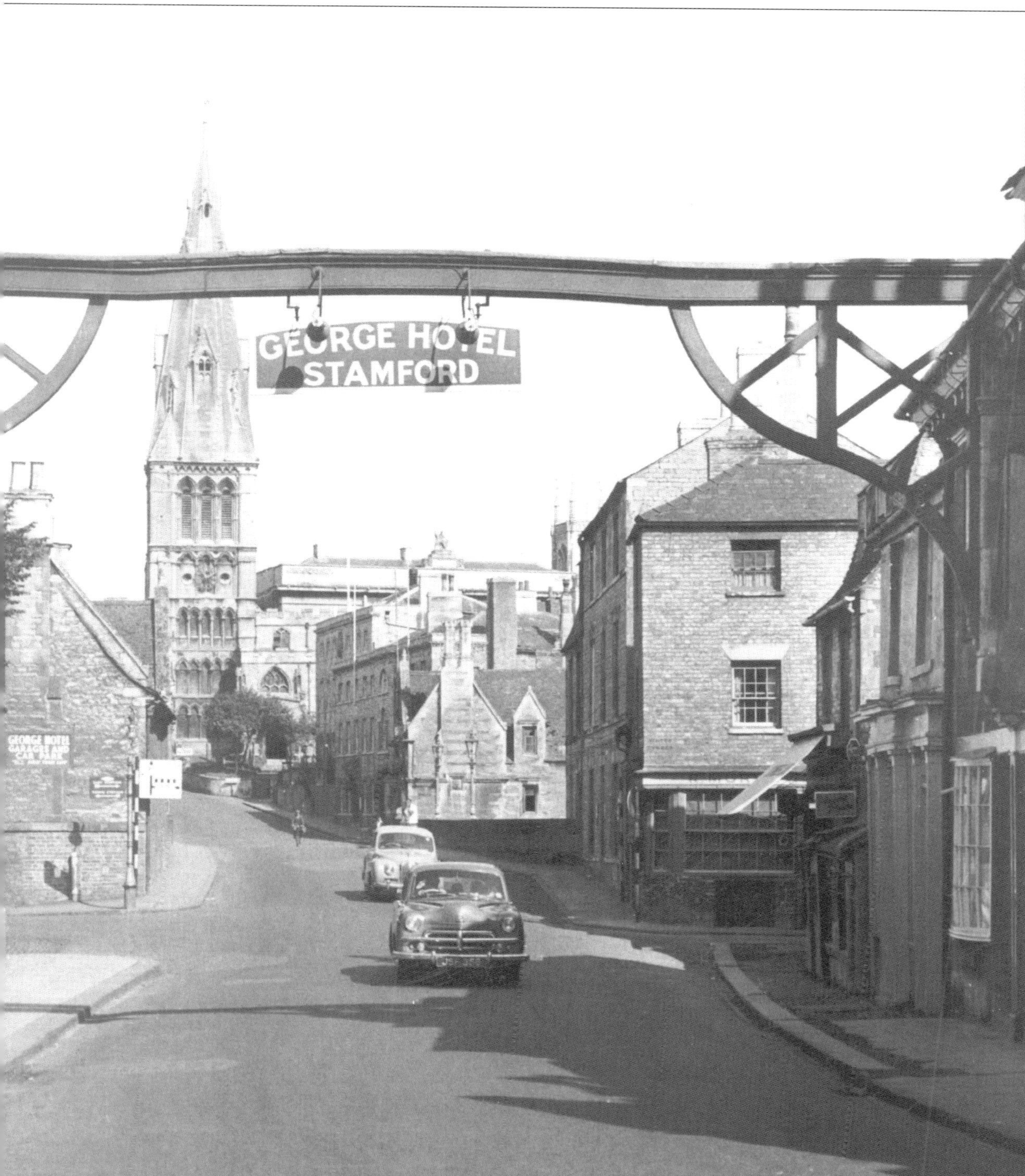

St Peter's Street, St Mary's Street

The impressive entrance into Stamford (72310, right) over Town Bridge and into the main part of the town, has not been arrived at by chance. The buildings in the foreground were part of a scheme by the Marquess of Exeter to improve the entrance to the town at the time that the bridge was replaced in the mid 19th century. The building on the right acted as a tollhouse for the bridge, much to the displeasure of the locals. The sign beyond the toll house reads 'Motors & Cycles', and appears to be associated with the Boat and Railway Inn, which occupied the site — its name can still be seen painted on the side of the building.

This approach to Stamford, through St Martin's, past the George Inn, over Town Bridge and finally up St Mary's Hill is still impressive today, and worthy of what has been described as 'the English country market town par excellence'.

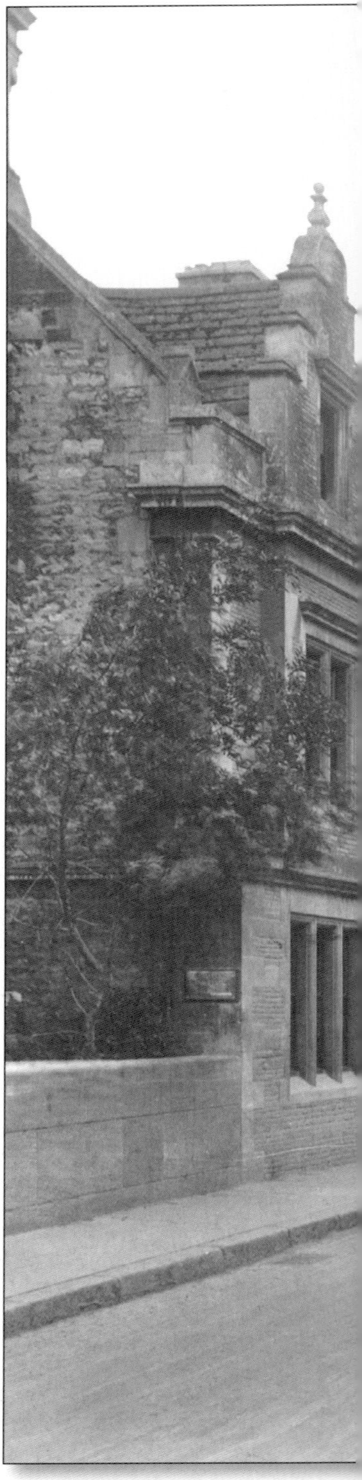

Below: St Mary's Church 1922 72329

The tower and spire of St Mary's church dominates the view. To the right is the Town Hall, which was originally situated over the north end of the bridge, with only a narrow arch for traffic. In 1776 it became a victim of early traffic congestion; it was demolished, and the new building constructed. In the foreground, left, the ironmongers stands beside the Norman Arch at the entrance to St Mary's Passage (72338, page 12). Above the lady's head is the sign to the Temperance Hotel, which was run around this time by John Bunning. Beyond this we have a glimpse of the sign for the Scotneys' Old Crypt Antiques, presumably taking its name from the vaulted 13th-century undercroft beneath No 13, now Fratelli's restaurant.

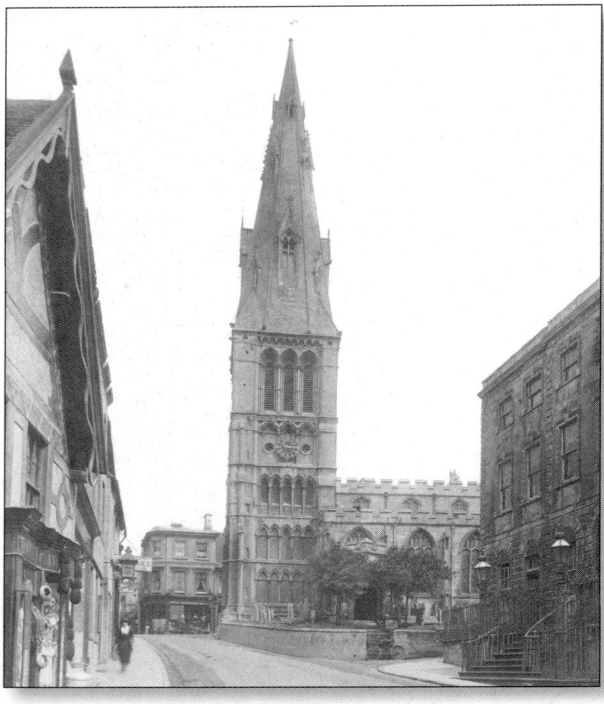

ST MARY'S HILL 1922 72310

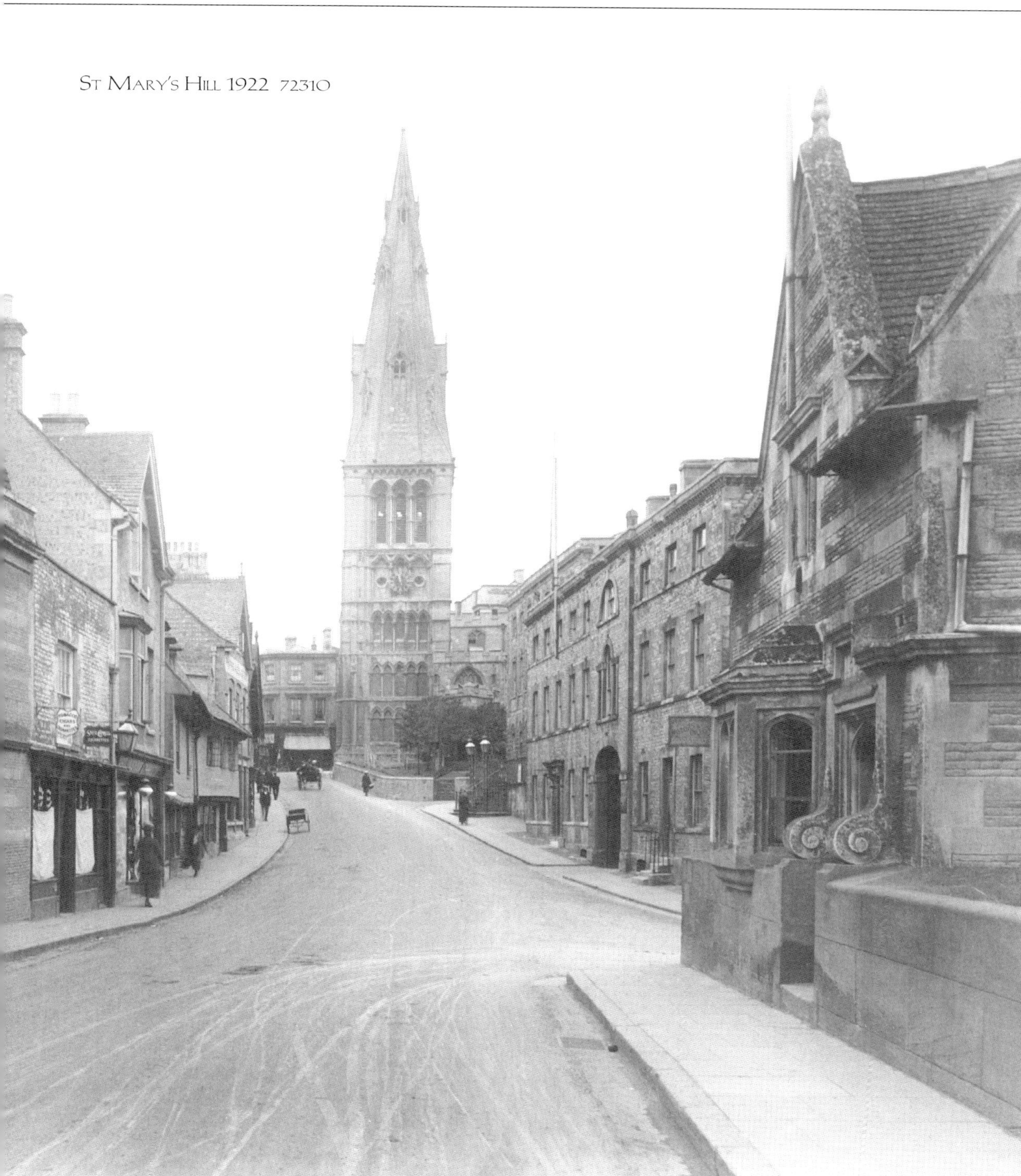

County Map

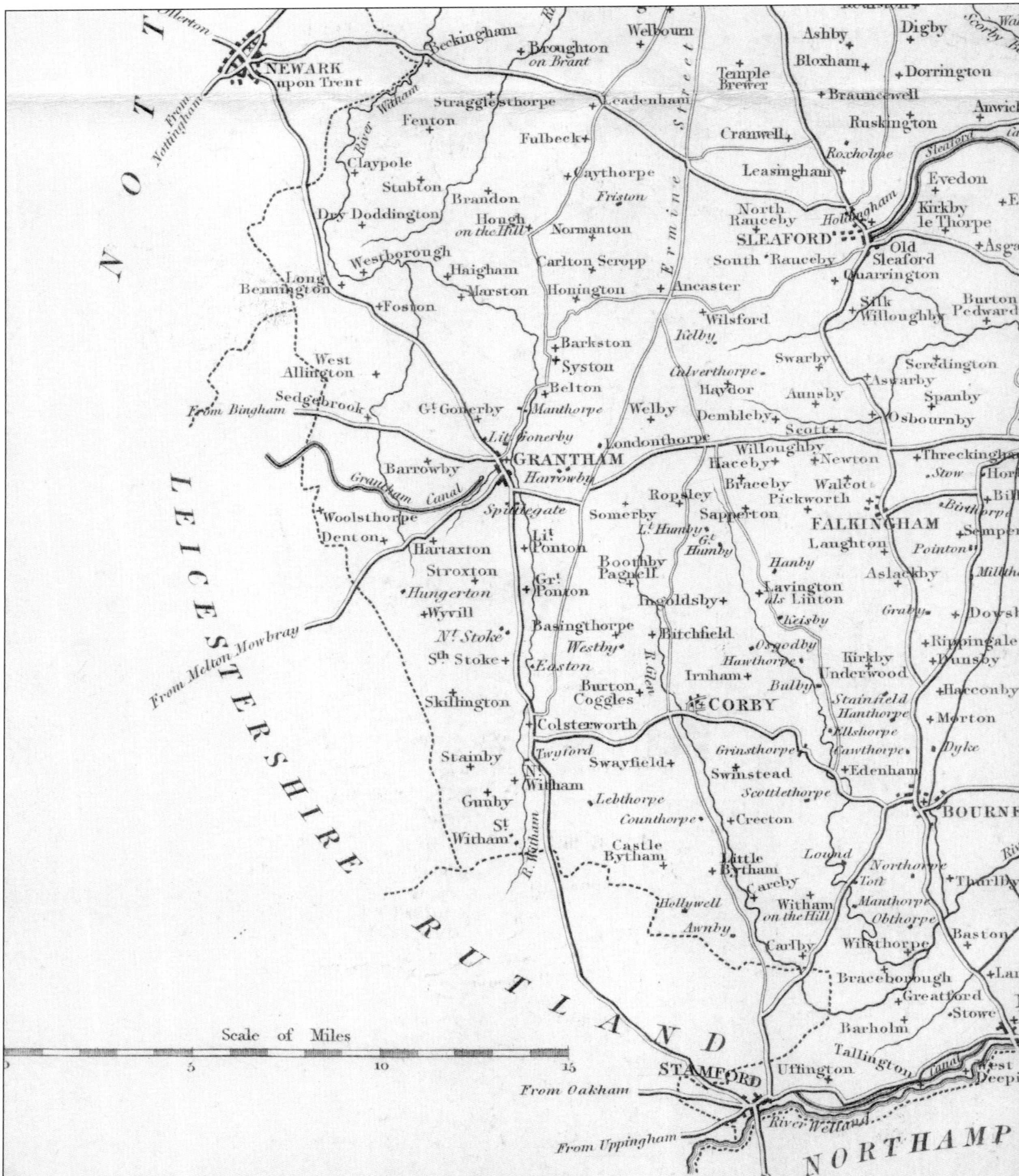

Ollerton
NEWARK
upon Trent
From Nottingham
Beckingham
Broughton
on Brant
Welbourn
Ashby
Digby
Bloxham
Dorrington
Temple
Brewer
Braunceweil
Anwick
River Witham
Stragglesthorpe
Leadenham
Fenton
Ruskington
Fulbeck
Cranwell
Roxholme
Claypole
Leasingham
Caythorpe
Evedon
Stubton
Friston
Brandon
North
Rauceby
Kirkby
le Thorpe
Dry Doddington
Hough
on the Hill
Normanton
SLEAFORD
Old
Sleaford
Westborough
Carlton Scropp
South Rauceby
Quarrington
Haigham
Long
Bennington
Marston
Honington
Ancaster
Foston
Silk
Willoughby
Burton
Wilsford
Kelby
Barkston
Swarby
Scredington
West
Allington
Syston
Calverthorpe
Asgarby
Belton
Haydor
Aunsby
Spanby
Sedgebrook
Gt Gonerby
Manthorpe
Welby
Dembleby
Osbournby
From Bingham
Lit Gonerby
Londonthorpe
Scott
Willoughby
GRANTHAM
Haceby
Newton
Threckingham
Barrowby
Harrowby
Stow
Braceby
Walcot
Grantham Canal
Ropsley
Pickworth
Spittlegate
Woolsthorpe
Somerby
Sapperton
FALKINGHAM
Denton
Lt Humby
Gt Humby
Laughton
Pointon
Hartaxton
Lit Ponton
Stroxton
Boothby
Pagnell
Hanby
Aslackby
Hungerton
Gr Ponton
Lavington
als Linton
Wyvill
Ingoldsby
Keisby
Graby
Basingthorpe
Osgodby
Nt Stoke
Westby
Bitchfield
Rippingale
From Melton Mowbray
Sth Stoke
Hawthorpe
Kirkby
Underwood
Dunsby
Easton
Irnham
Burton
Coggles
R. Glen
Bulby
Skillington
CORBY
Stainfield
Hanthorpe
Hacconby
Morton
Colsterworth
Elshorpe
Twyford
Grinsthorpe
Cawthorpe
Dyke
Stainby
Swayfield
Nt
Witham
Swinstead
Edenham
Scottlethorpe
Gunby
Lebthorpe
BOURNE
Counthorpe
Creeton
St
Witham
R. Witham
Castle
Bytham
Little
Bytham
Lound
Northorpe
Toft
Thurlby
Careby
Hollywell
Witham
on the Hill
Manthorpe
Obthorpe
Awnby
Carlby
Wilsthorpe
Baston
Braceborough
Greatford
Stowe
Barholm
Tallington
Canal
Uffington
West
Deeping
STAMFORD
From Oakham
River Welland
From Uppingham
LEICESTERSHIRE
RUTLAND
NORTHAMP
Ermine Street
Scale of Miles
5
10
15

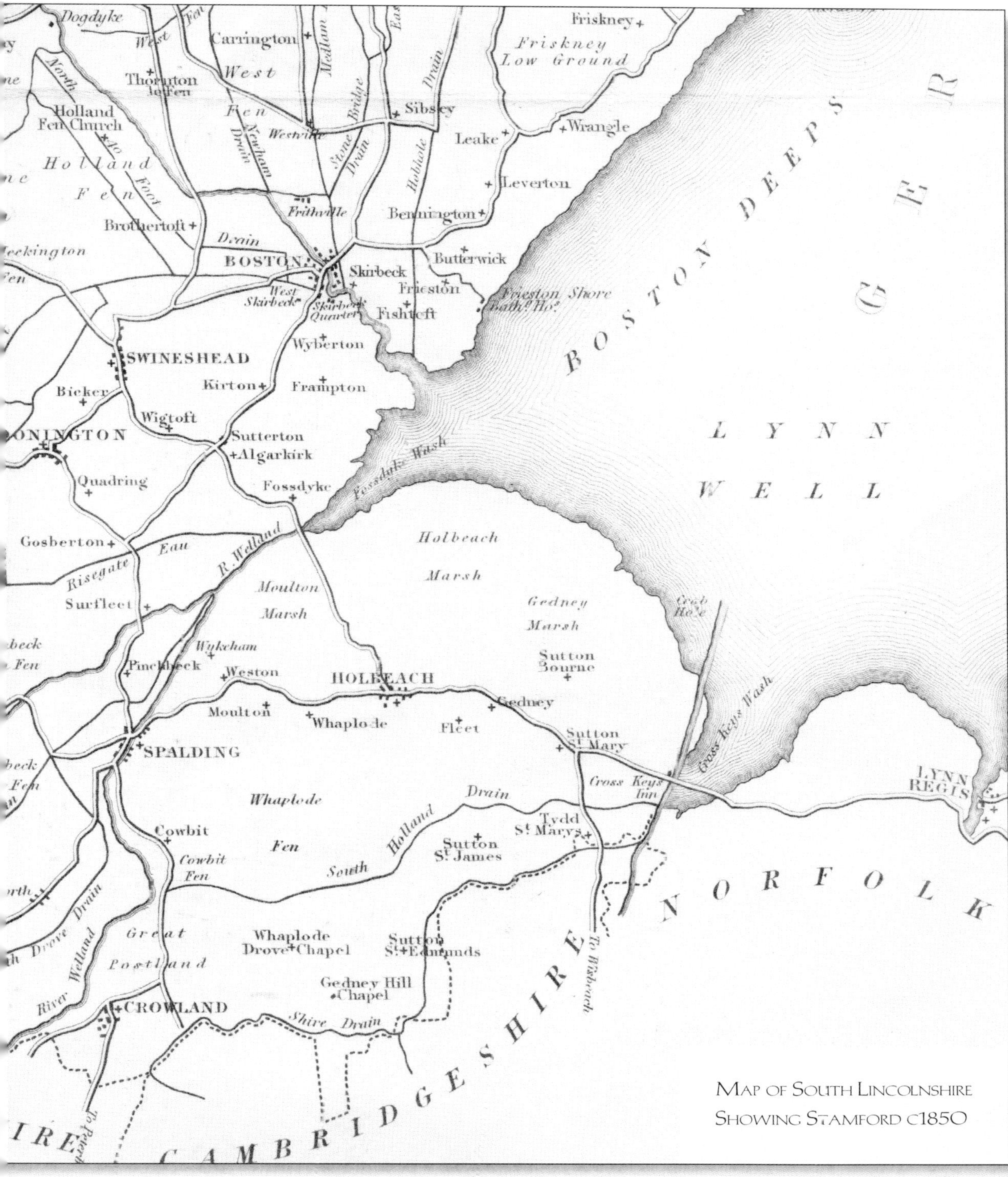

MAP OF SOUTH LINCOLNSHIRE
SHOWING STAMFORD C1850

Churches and Religious Buildings

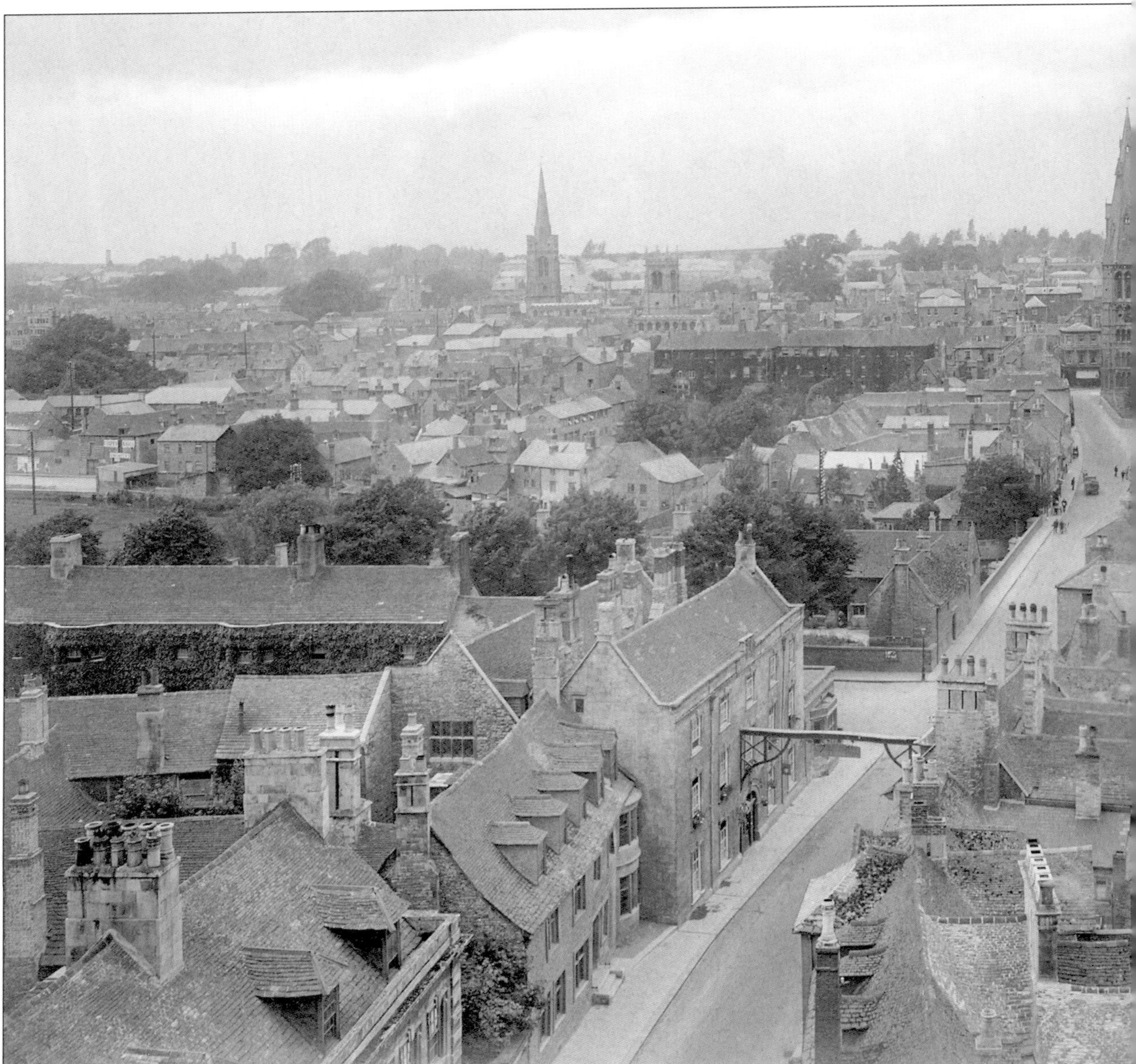

Even without its outstanding vernacular architecture, Stamford would deserve to be known on the strengths of its medieval churches alone. In its heyday, the town is believed to have had 14 churches; even today, five medieval churches survive, together with the gate of the Greyfriary and the outstanding Romanesque remains of St Leonard's Priory.

The tower of St Martin's church, standing south of the River Welland, was a familiar landmark on the Great North Road, as well as providing a viewpoint for the town's other churches. St Martin's itself was built wholly in the Perpendicular style by Bishop Russell of Lincoln towards the end of the 15th century; it contains the elaborate tombs of the Cecil family (72334 page 56). The windows of the church contain fine 15th-century glass, originally from Tattershall but installed here in 1757-60.

Churches and Religious Buildings

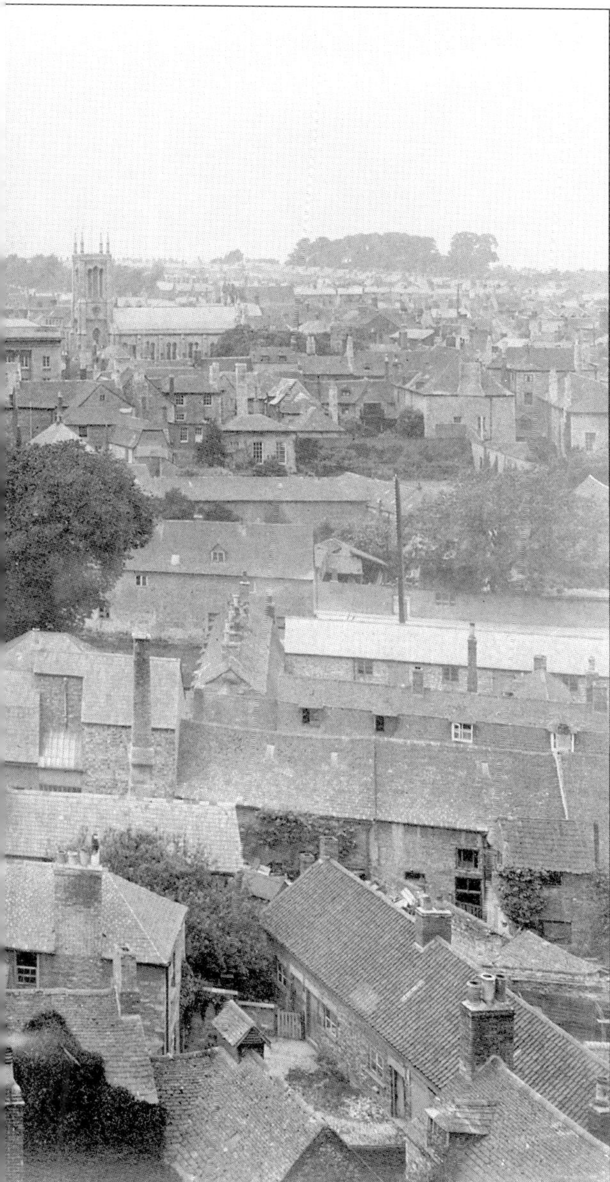

The View from St Martin's Church Tower 1922

72295

The layout of Stamford, climbing gently in terraces up from the Welland, is well shown in this photograph from St Martin's church tower. The churches of All Saints, St John, and St Mary stand out. To the right of the magnificent broach spire of St Mary's is the Victorian tower of St Michael's, now converted into shops. St George's church is just off the edge of the photograph to the right.

The church's new graveyard, off Barnack Road, is the final resting place of Daniel Lambert. At the time of his death aged 39 in 1809, he was the heaviest man in Britain. He weighed in at almost 53 stone, with a waist measurement of 9' 4" and leg circumference of 3' 11". He died in the Waggon & Horses Inn on a visit to Stamford races, and part of the inn had to be demolished to allow his coffin to be removed.

The rather damp view down the hill towards the George Hotel (72333, page 56) was taken from opposite St Martin's Antique Centre. The shop-fronts on the left-hand side have now gone, and so have the pinnacles on top of the Burghley Estate Offices, just beyond the old lamppost. The sign painted onto the house just beyond the church is advertising F L Gooch's veterinary surgery — it operated from No 19 High Street, St Martin's.

CHURCHES AND RELIGIOUS BUILDINGS

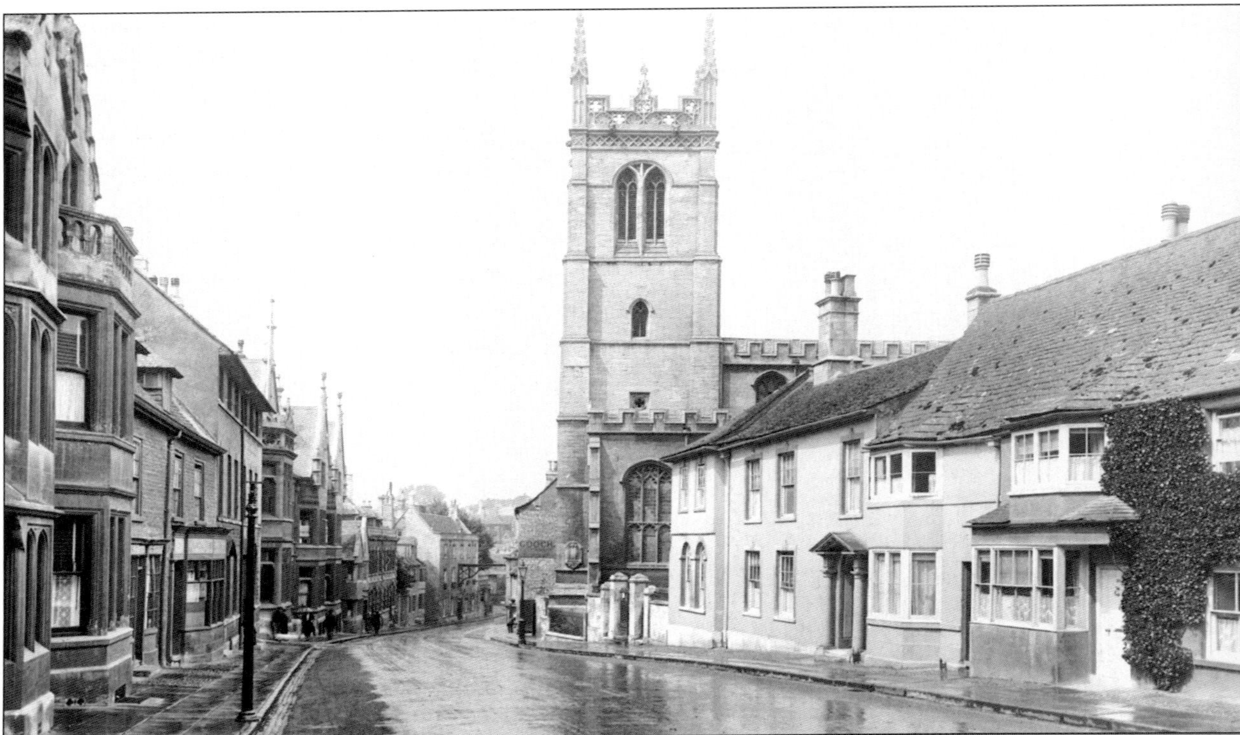

ABOVE: ST MARTIN'S CHURCH 1922 72333

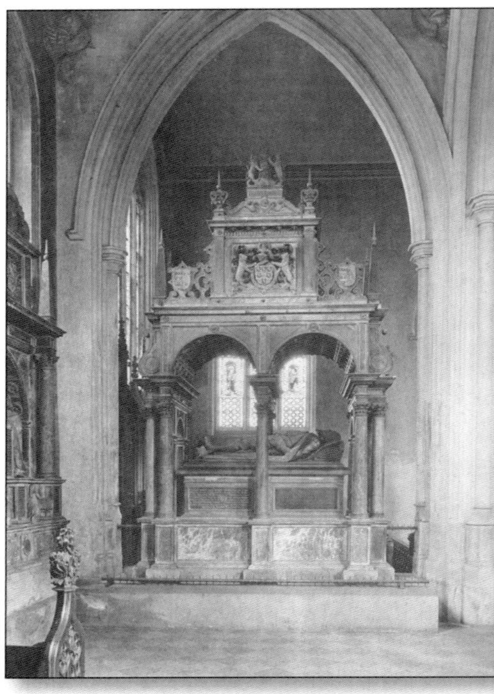

RIGHT: ST MARTIN'S CHURCH, THE BURGHLEY MONUMENT 1922 72334

This is the monument to William Cecil, Lord Burghley, builder of Burghley House and perhaps the most famous member of the Cecil family. He died in 1598 at the age of 78, and his elaborate tomb stands close to the altar. On the left is the monument to Richard and Jayne Cecil, his parents.

Churches and Religious Buildings

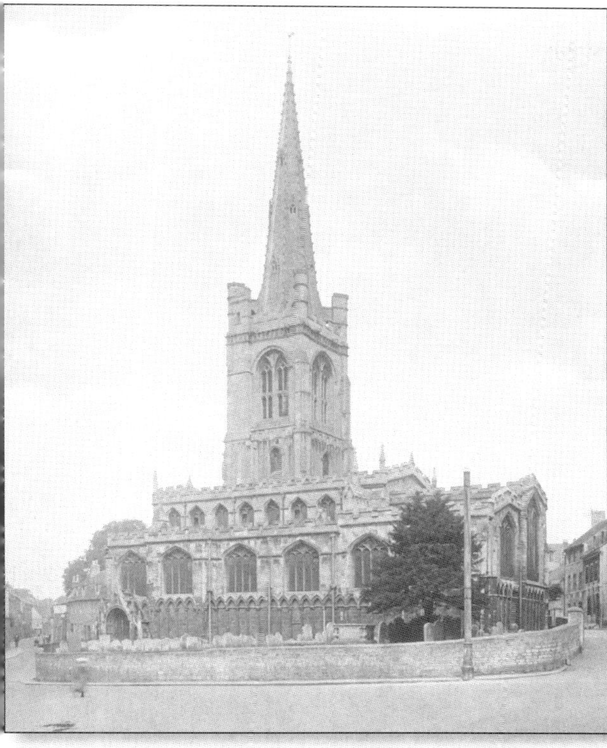

All Saints' church, adjacent to Red Lion Square, is one of Stamford's oldest churches. Although at first glance similar in style to St Martin's (it was rebuilt around 1461), it contains a good deal of 13th-century material, most evident from outside in the Early English blind arcading which can be seen in the south and east walls.

Inside the church, the south arcade of the nave has stiff leaf capitals (72327, below), characteristic of the Early English period, which contrast with the plainer ones of the north arcade (which may date from the time of the rebuilding). The alterations were the work of the wool merchants John and William Browne.

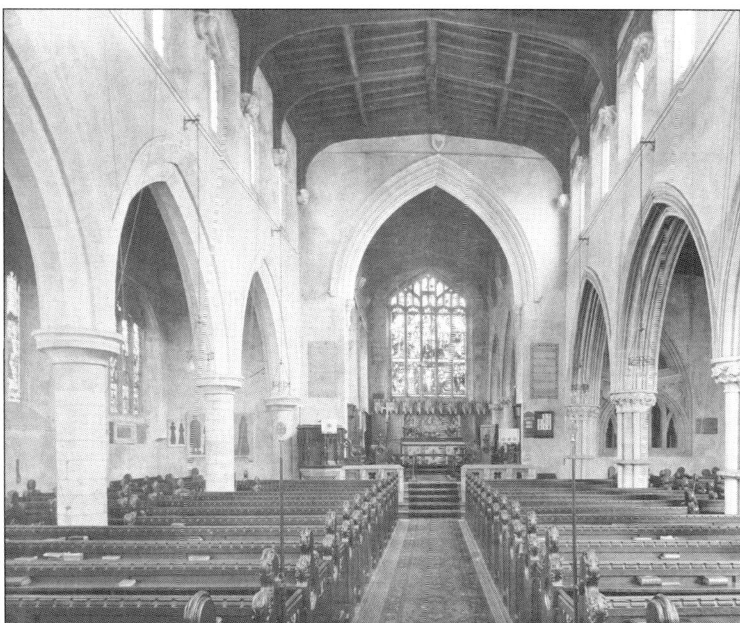

Above: All Saints' Church 1922 72324

In this view All Saints' appears to rise in tiers from an almost deserted Red Lion Square. The blind arcading is clearly visible. There is a strong similarity in the design of the towers of All Saints', St John's and St Martin's churches.

Left: All Saints' Church, the Interior 1922 72327

The rebuilding of All Saints' church in the 15th century was largely funded by the Brownes, a family of wealthy wool merchants. Some of the family memorial brasses can be seen attached to the wall on the left. The interior today is virtually unchanged, except that the boards listing the Ten Commandments have been removed from either side of the chancel arch and a new carpet has been fitted.

Churches and Religious Buildings

The church of St John the Baptist stands virtually on the other side of Red Lion Square from All Saints'. St John's is also in the Perpendicular style, and dates from c1450 when it was rebuilt by local merchants. Inside the nave carries an impressive angel roof. Despite the widening of the entrance into St John's Street in the 1930s, it is still a tight squeeze for pedestrians and vehicles alongside the church, as we can see from photograph (S177025, right). The lorry is parked at the entrance to Red Lion Square, giving an idea of what close neighbours St John's and All Saints' are.

St Mary's Church is the most eye-catching of Stamford's churches, with a broach spire rising to 163 feet. The spire dates from the early 14th century, one hundred years later than the tower on which it stands. Inside, the church gives the impression of being almost square, with the chancel hidden behind J D Sedding's 1890 rood screen (72332). The screen is topped by a cross designed by Harold Bailey, and was dedicated as a war memorial in 1920, shortly before the photograph was taken. Someone has taken a lot of trouble to arrange the hymn-books with regimental precision. The north chapel has a particularly fine blue and gold-embossed ceiling.

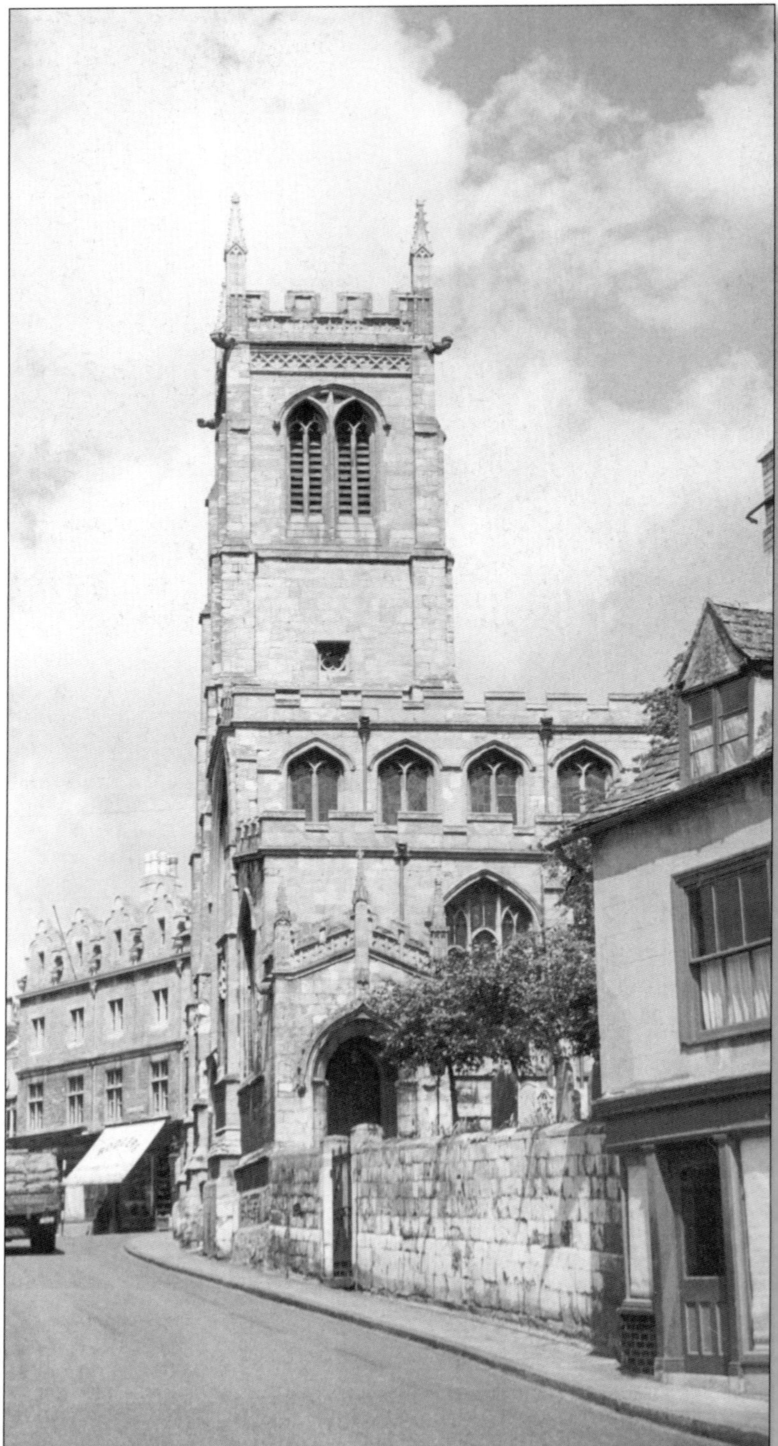

St John's Church c1955 S177025

Churches and Religious Buildings

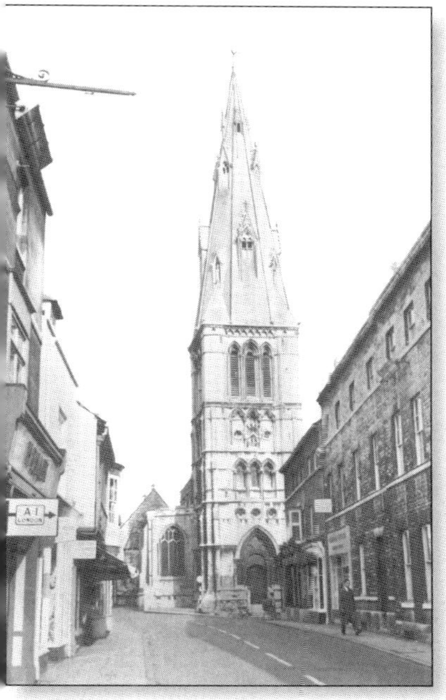

St Mary's Church c1955 S177060

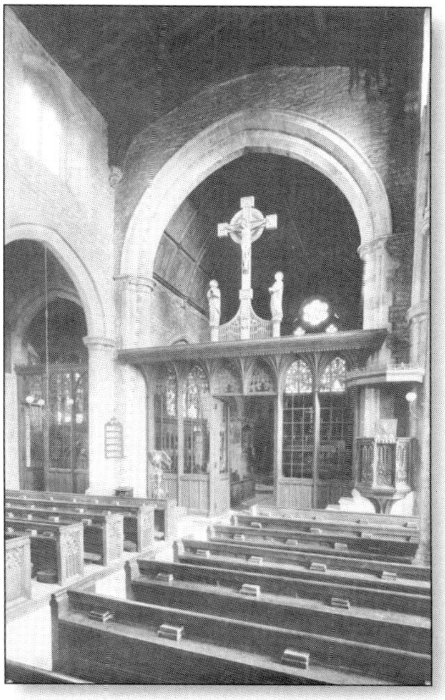

St Mary's Church, the Rood Screen 1922 72332

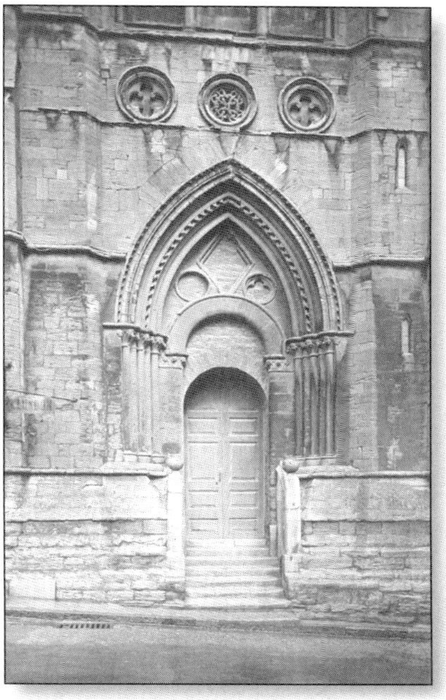

St Mary's Church, the West Door 1922 72330

The west door, tower and spire of St Mary's church hold a wealth of architectural detail, with blind arcading, niches holding statues of the four Evangelists, and elaborate openings in the spire. The 1922 wooden door is still in place today, but the decorative balls on the steps and the rather murky sign showing the way to London have gone.

St George's, situated further east in St George's Square, (S177009, page 60) is much more shy and retiring. The church is 13th-century, or possibly earlier, although parts were rebuilt in 1449, and further changes were made by a 19th-century restoration. St George's church achieved a measure of fame as the setting used for St Botolph's churchyard in the BBC's 1993 production of 'Middlemarch'. The square that surrounds the church is one of the best-preserved Georgian features of the town, or indeed in the country, and a number of the buildings may be familiar to watchers of 'Middlemarch'.

Other remains from the medieval period include a gateway dating from the middle of the 14th century, the last surviving part of Stamford's Greyfriary (72322 and S177001, page 60) which was the wealthiest of the four friaries in the town. An early 19th-century engraving shows the gate free standing without any building behind it, but in 1848 it was incorporated into the lodge of the Stamford and Rutland Infirmary which stands on a busy roundabout where the roads from Spalding and Bourne meet.

About half a mile to the east of the town centre are the remains of St Leonard's (72340, pages 62-63) a 12th-century Benedictine priory founded by Durham Abbey. The nave of the original church survives, and the layout of further elements of the priory has been found through excavation. The surviving arches would originally have led into a northern aisle, while the cloisters were on the other side. At the eastern end a central tower would have stood between the nave and the chancel, giving the church a cruciform pattern.

In addition to these churches, the centre of Stamford has a Roman Catholic church, which opened in 1865 and stands on Broad Street, a Methodist chapel of 1886 on Barn Hill, and a United Reformed church, dating from 1819, in Star Lane.

Churches and Religious Buildings

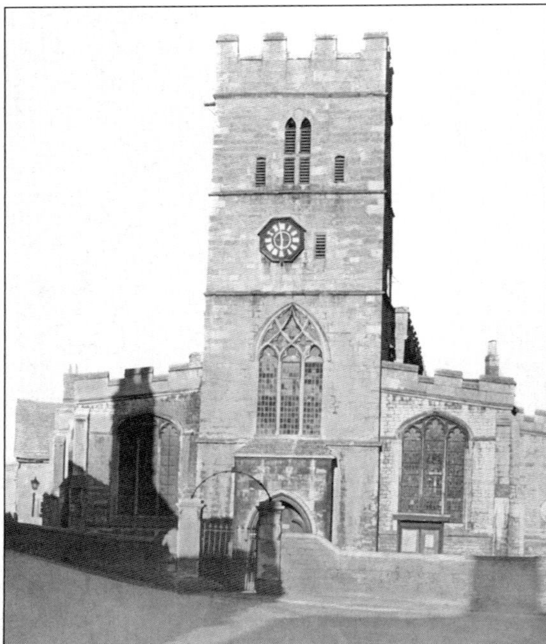

Above: St George's Church c1955 S177009

Below Left: The Infirmary Gateway 1922 72322

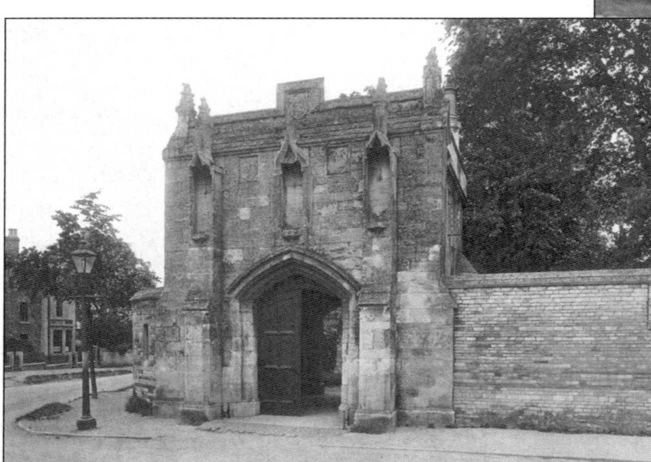

The Old Infirmary Gate c1955 S177001

The lamppost has disappeared and the tree has grown since 72322 was taken, but otherwise little has changed. A plaque has been fixed to the wall above the bench: it is still there today, and states incorrectly that this is the site of the house of the Whitefriars. The pinnacles above the gate have since been renewed.

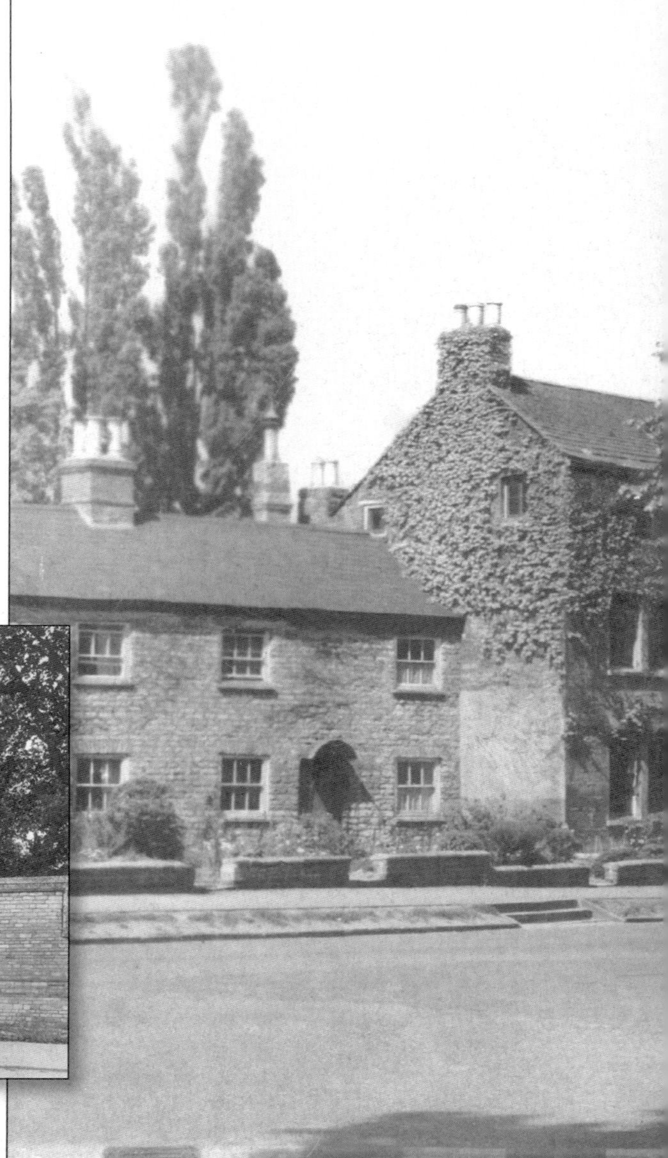

Churches and Religious Buildings

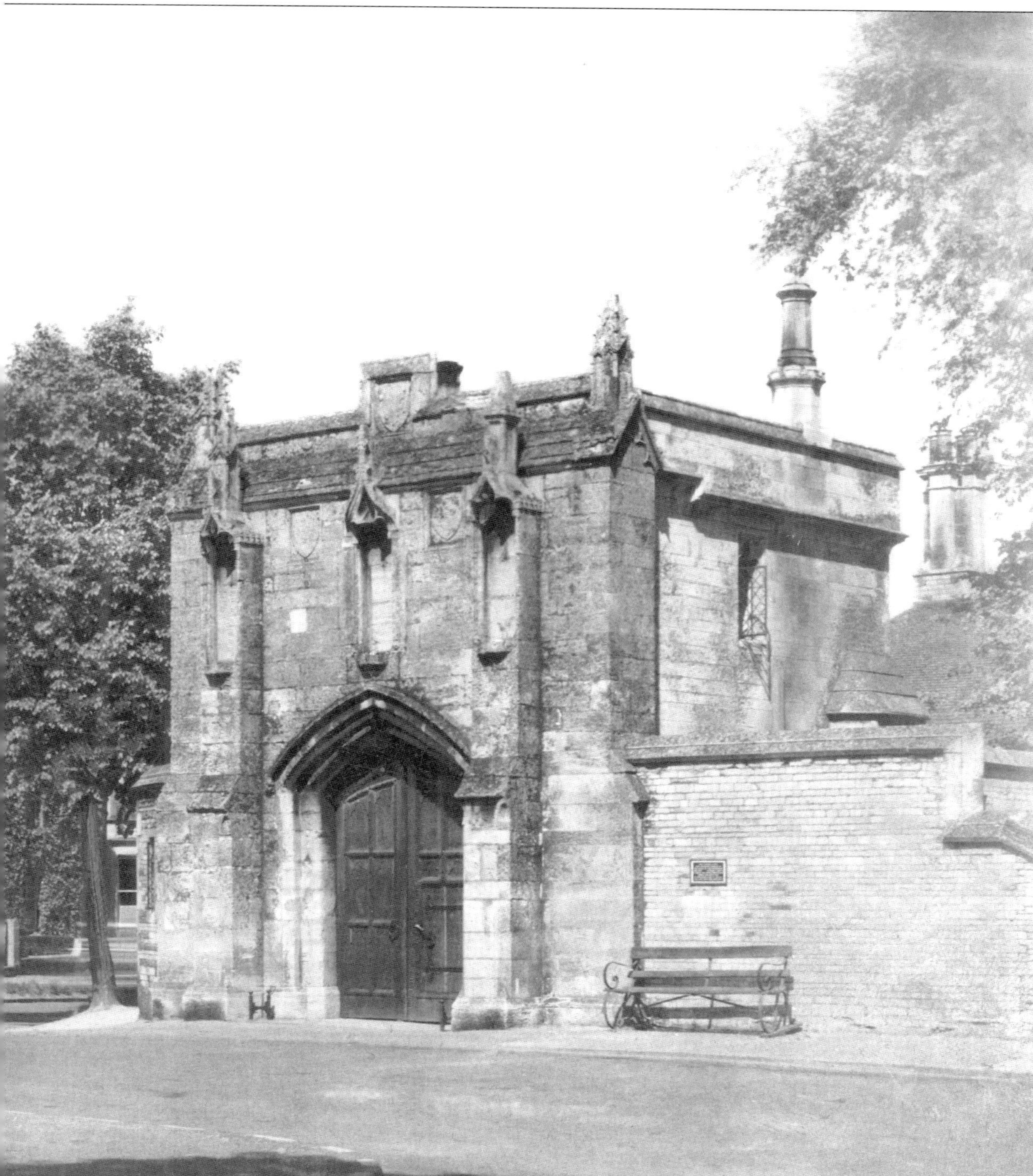

Churches and Religious Buildings

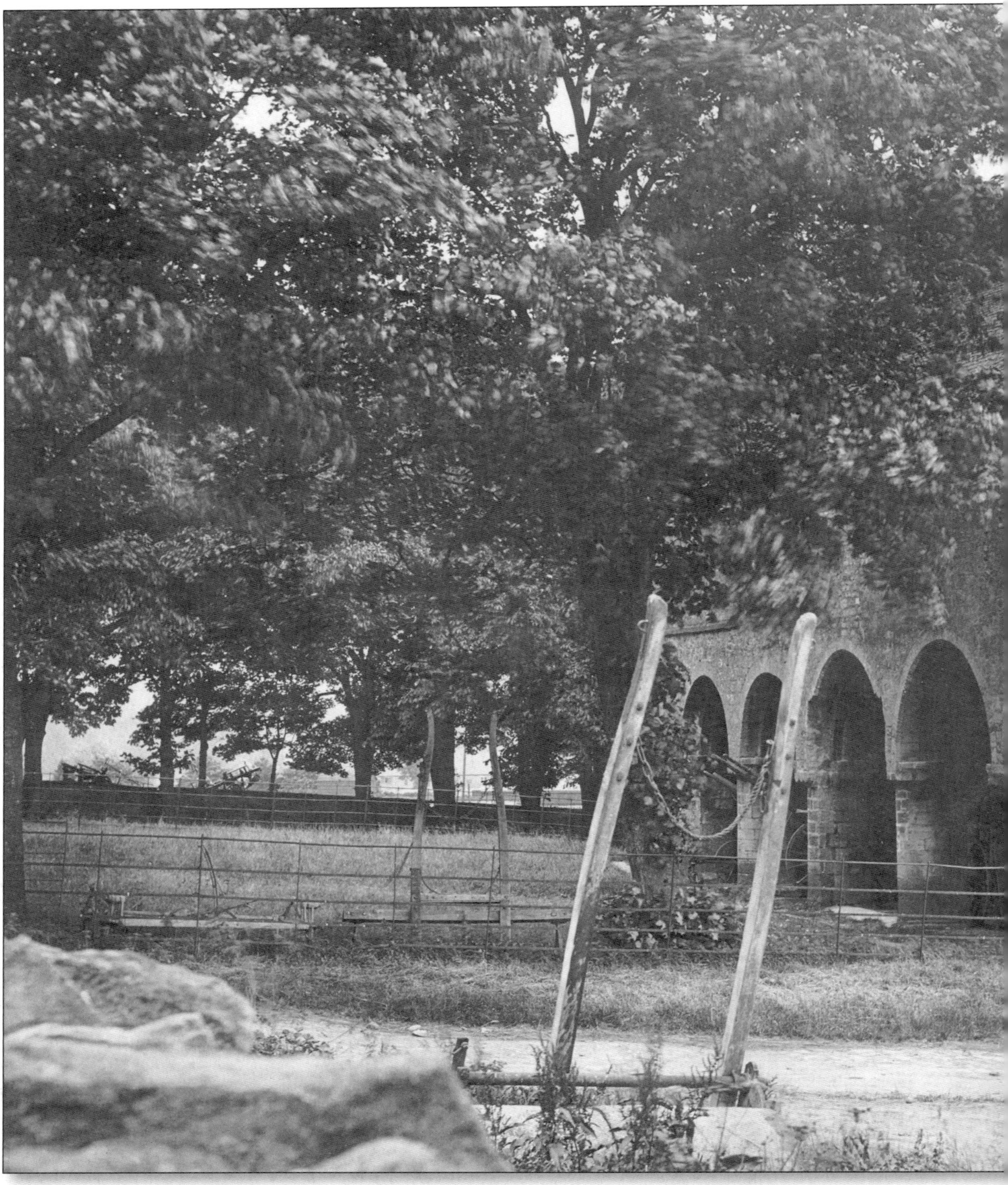

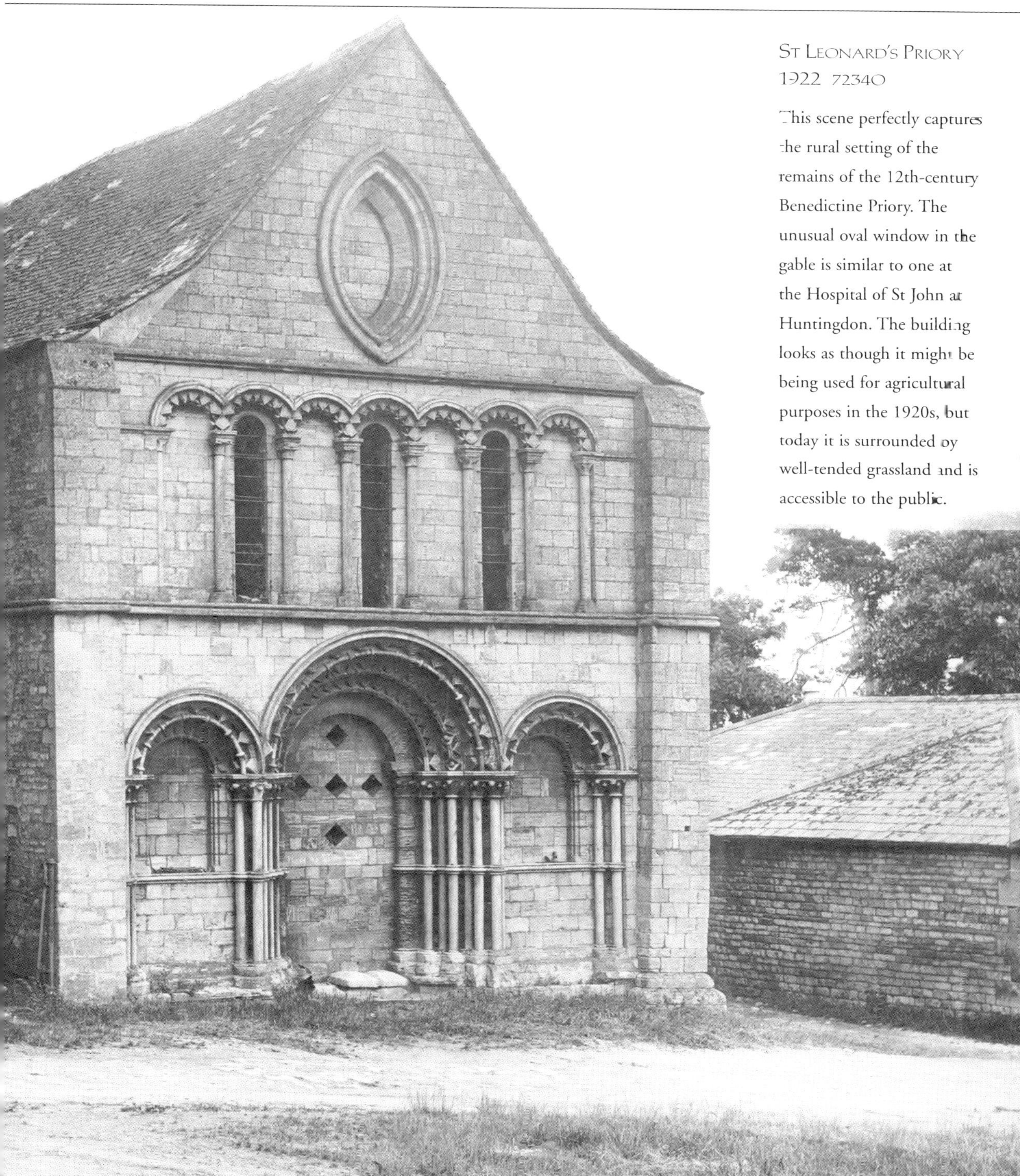

ST LEONARD'S PRIORY
1922 72340

This scene perfectly captures the rural setting of the remains of the 12th-century Benedictine Priory. The unusual oval window in the gable is similar to one at the Hospital of St John at Huntingdon. The building looks as though it might be being used for agricultural purposes in the 1920s, but today it is surrounded by well-tended grassland and is accessible to the public.

Hostelries

Although an important route in the early medieval period, the Great North Road did not have any great influence on the development of Stamford at that time. This was no doubt because the poor condition of the road, coupled with the primitive nature of early coaches, deterred all but the most hardy and wealthy of travellers. But by the 17th century, things were beginning to change. An advertisement of 1658 boasted that Stamford could be reached by coach in two days from London for the cost of one pound — while the whole journey to York was predicted to take four days. This marked the bumpy start to the coaching era, but improvement to the construction and maintenance of the road (by 1769 the journey time from London had been halved) heralded a period of prosperity for the town. Indeed, by 1830 the road was so busy with coaches that the first mutterings were heard that Stamford needed a bypass; in the event it had to wait a further 130 years before one was built.

As a town that owed much of its prosperity to coaching, it should come as no surprise that Stamford developed some most comfortable and prestigious hotels for long-distance travellers. Those approaching Stamford from the south, for example, would pass the doors of the George, the most famous of Stamford's hostelries. Although it is speculated that an inn may have stood on this site for a thousand years, the first mention of the George occurs in the 16th century. The present front of the building dates from 1724, when it was rebuilt to accommodate the increasing coaching trade. The 'gallows' sign that spans High Street St Martin's (72305) is thought to be an attempt at curing instability in the front wall arising from these changes, rather than an instrument of justice. It certainly provides a memorable entrance to Stamford from the south.

Much less long-lived than the George was the Stamford Hotel, with its imposing roofline and statue of Justice facing out over the valley to the south — it is still prominent today in views of the town. The hotel was conceived on a grand scale, in part to provide a base for political opposition to the Cecil family. Building work was started in 1809, but not completed until 1816. It is said that at the time of the hotel's construction an attempt was made to secure the demolition of St Mary's church to improve the prospect to the south. It is doubtful whether the town ever needed a hotel of this grandeur, and the timing of its creation was certainly unfortunate, as it coincided with the arrival of the railway and the rapid erosion of the coaching trade. The hotel was converted into a shopping centre in 1983.

The numerous fairs held during the year also ensured that there was no shortage of business for the town's lesser inns. November would no doubt have been a particularly profitable month, as it marked the town's ancient custom of bull running. This involved tormenting and chasing the unfortunate beast through the streets

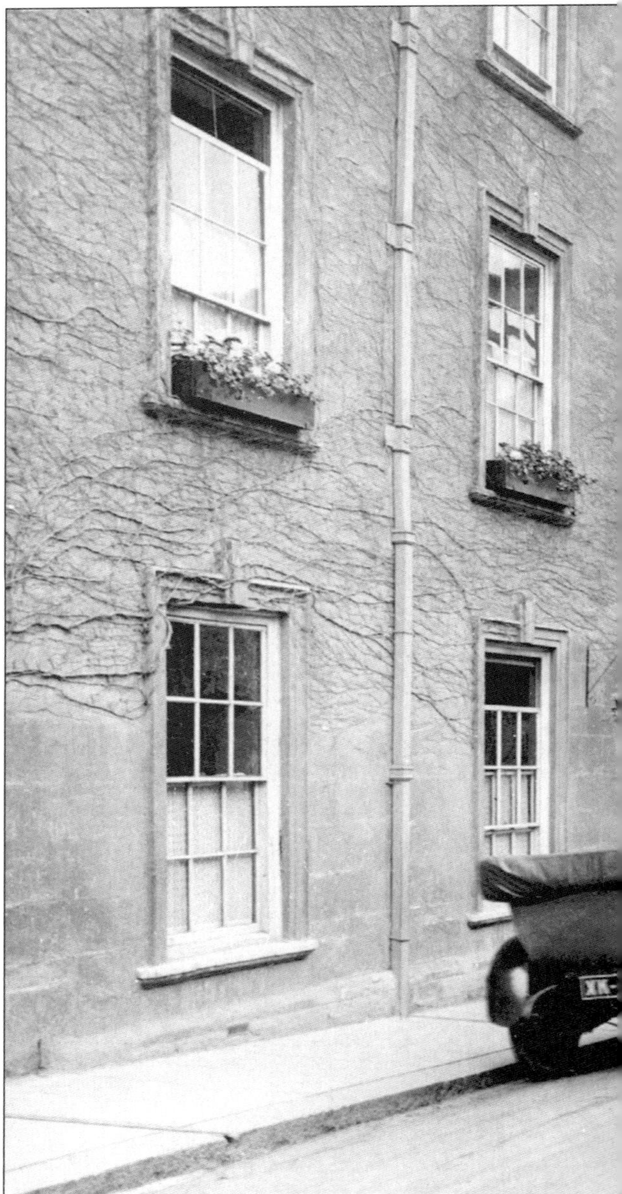

of the town, before it was driven off Town Bridge into the Welland. It was then slaughtered for the evening feast. The bull running, or 'rebel's riot feast', gave the common people an opportunity to enjoy themselves up to, and often well beyond, the point of anarchy; enterprising landlords cashed in by staging their own private, or 'stop' bull runnings at other times of the year. In 1776 the landlord of the Half Moon inn (72320, page 68) closed off Star Lane to hold a 'stop' bull running. The bull bolted into the kitchen of the Half Moon, with customers fleeing up the chimney and out through the windows. In the words of the 1896 guide to Stamford: 'there was good sport, many persons being tossed and gored and one man having an eye knocked out'. The custom was eventually banned in

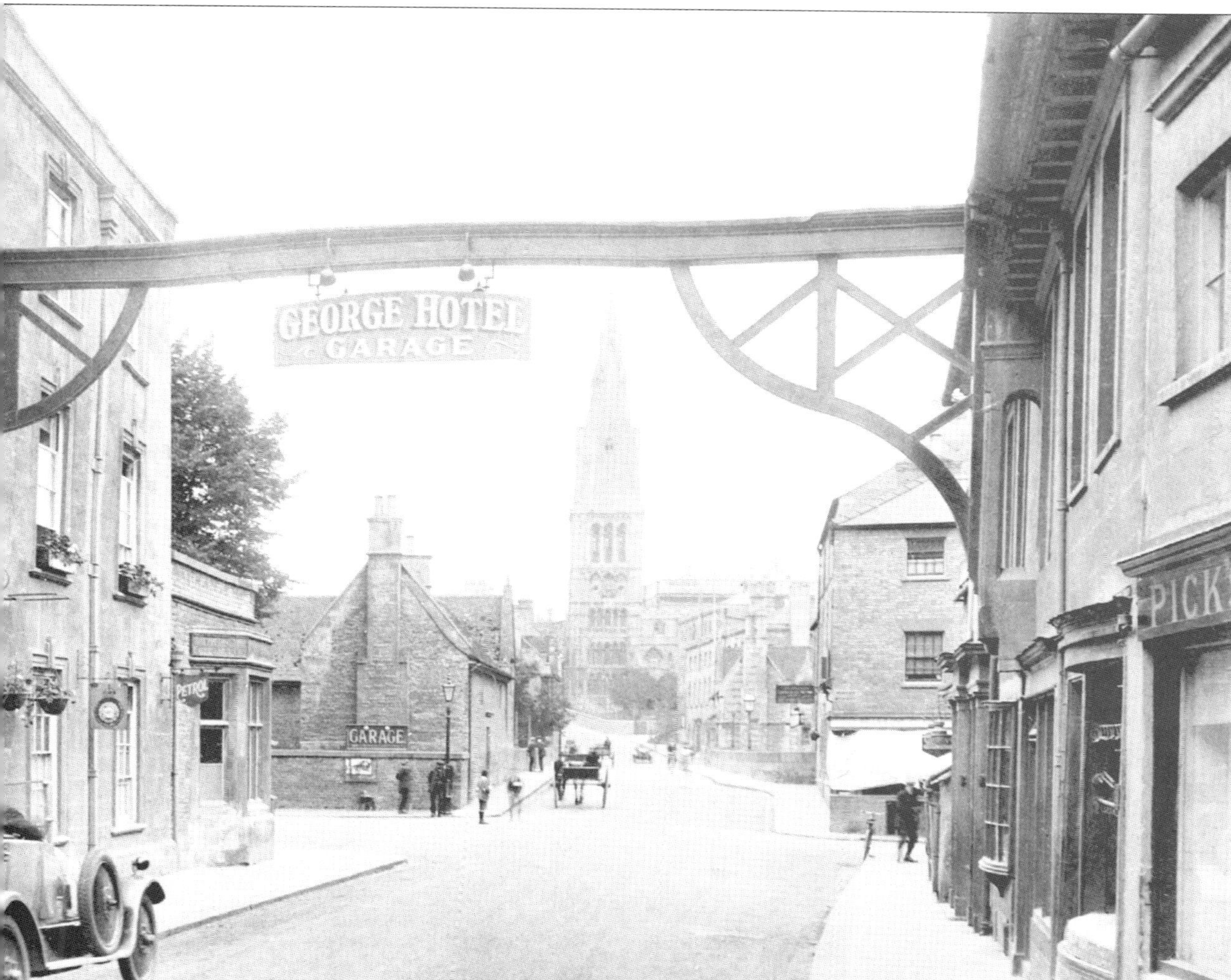

THE GEORGE HOTEL 1922 72305

The 1920s motorist appears well catered for, with both garaging and petrol to hand. The days of floodlighting have arrived too, although at this time the lights are illuminating the George's sign rather than the front of the building as they do today. Note the old fashioned AA sign on the wall of the hotel.

Hostelries

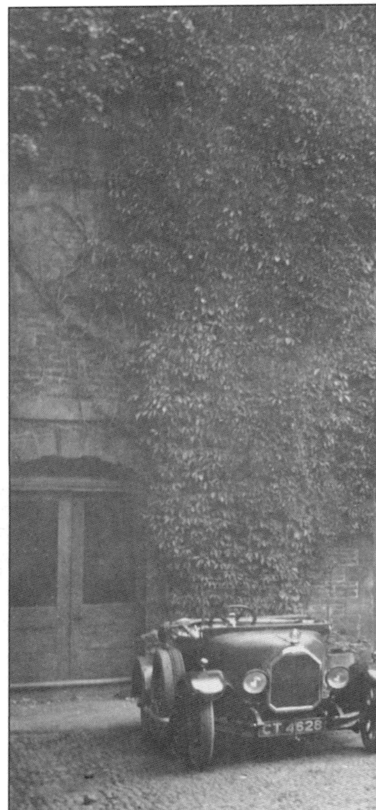

Right: The George Hotel Courtyard 1922 72321B

The courtyard is still walled with ivy, although it is not used for parking cars today.

Below Left: The George Hotel, a Bedroom 1922 72321D

Below Right: The George Hotel, the Dining Room 1922 72321C

These two photographs give a fascinating insight into what is must have been like to stay in a well-appointed hotel eighty years ago, before the word en-suite had entered the hotelier's language — the wash jugs are clearly intended for more than show. The fireplace, while impressive, looks rather draughty — it is perhaps just as well that a thick eiderdown is provided.

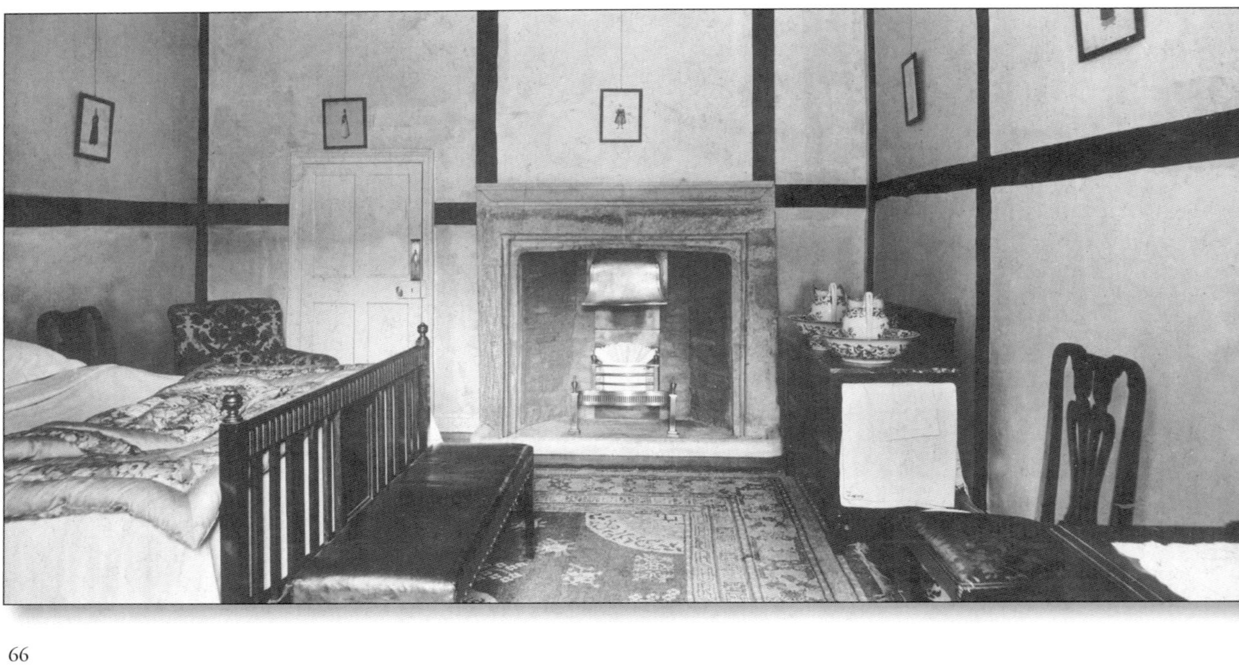

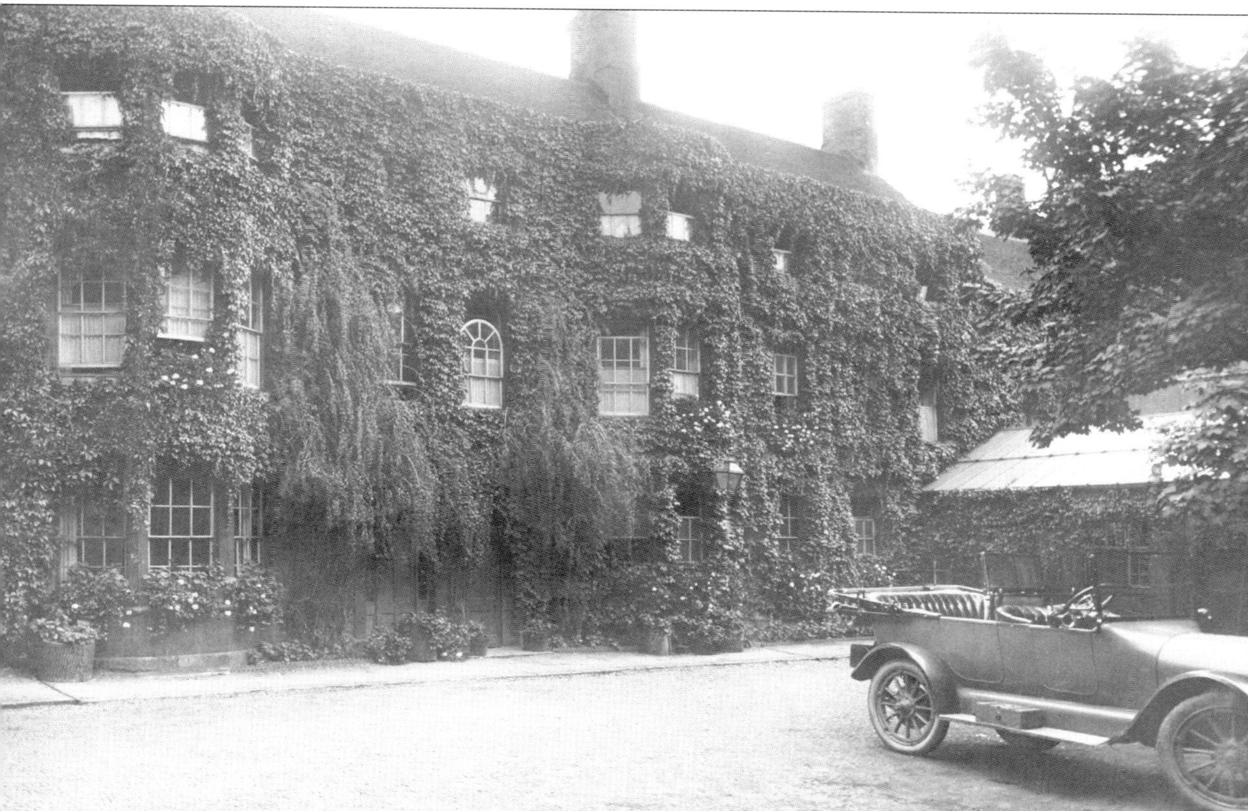

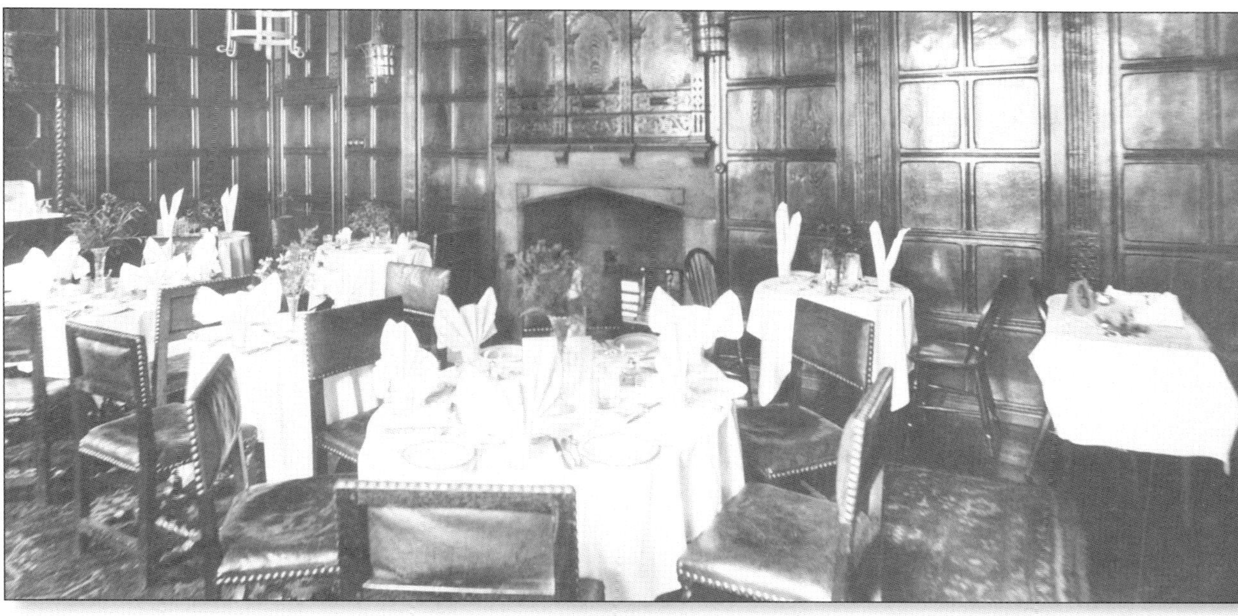

HOSTELRIES

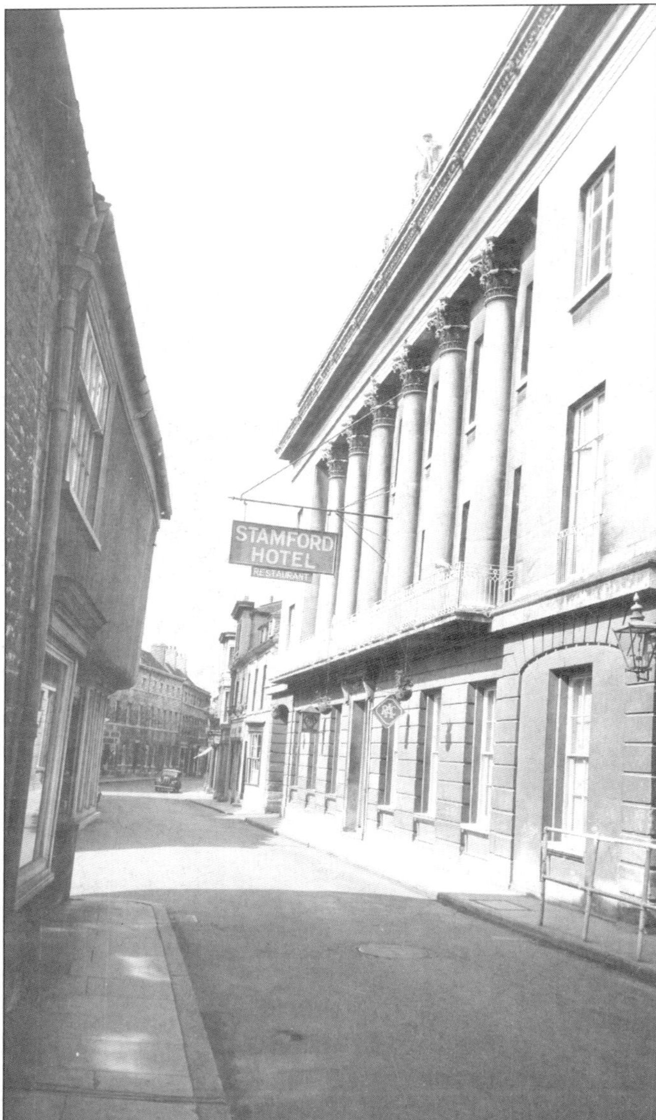

LEFT: THE STAMFORD HOTEL C1955 S177045

The grand Regency façade of the Stamford Hotel looks rather out of place squeezed in among the other buildings of St Mary's Street. On the right of the photograph, protected by railings as a concession to increasing traffic levels, is the exit from Cheyne Lane (S17706Z).

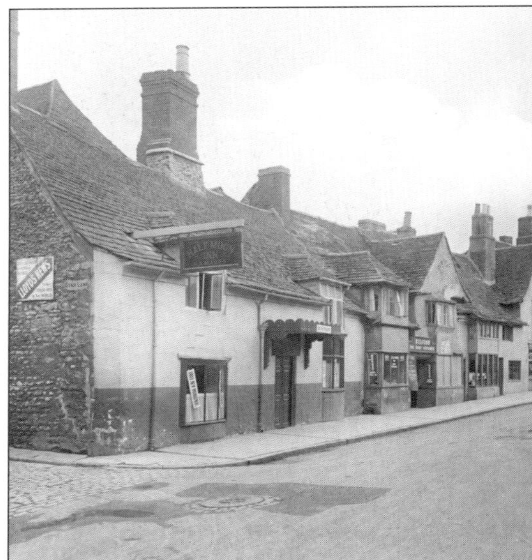

ABOVE: OLD HOUSES 1922 72320

This view of St Paul's Street shows the Half Moon Inn as it was before being rebuilt in 1938, and before the entrance to Star Lane (left) was widened in 1923. On demolition, some of the fabric of the old inn was found to date from the 13th century.

1839, due as much to the prohibitive cost of policing as to any more enlightened attitude towards animal rights.

The old London Inn, an early 19th-century building, fell victim to a traffic scheme that aimed to solve the problems caused by one of the right-angled bends of the medieval town. The scheme was intended to include a relief road across the meadows, although fortunately this element was never constructed. The new building, shown in S177047 (right), was built in 1939/40 by Phipp's brewery in Northampton. Note the 'A1 Grantham' signpost, a reminder that the main road continued to run through the town centre until the bypass was built to the west in 1960.

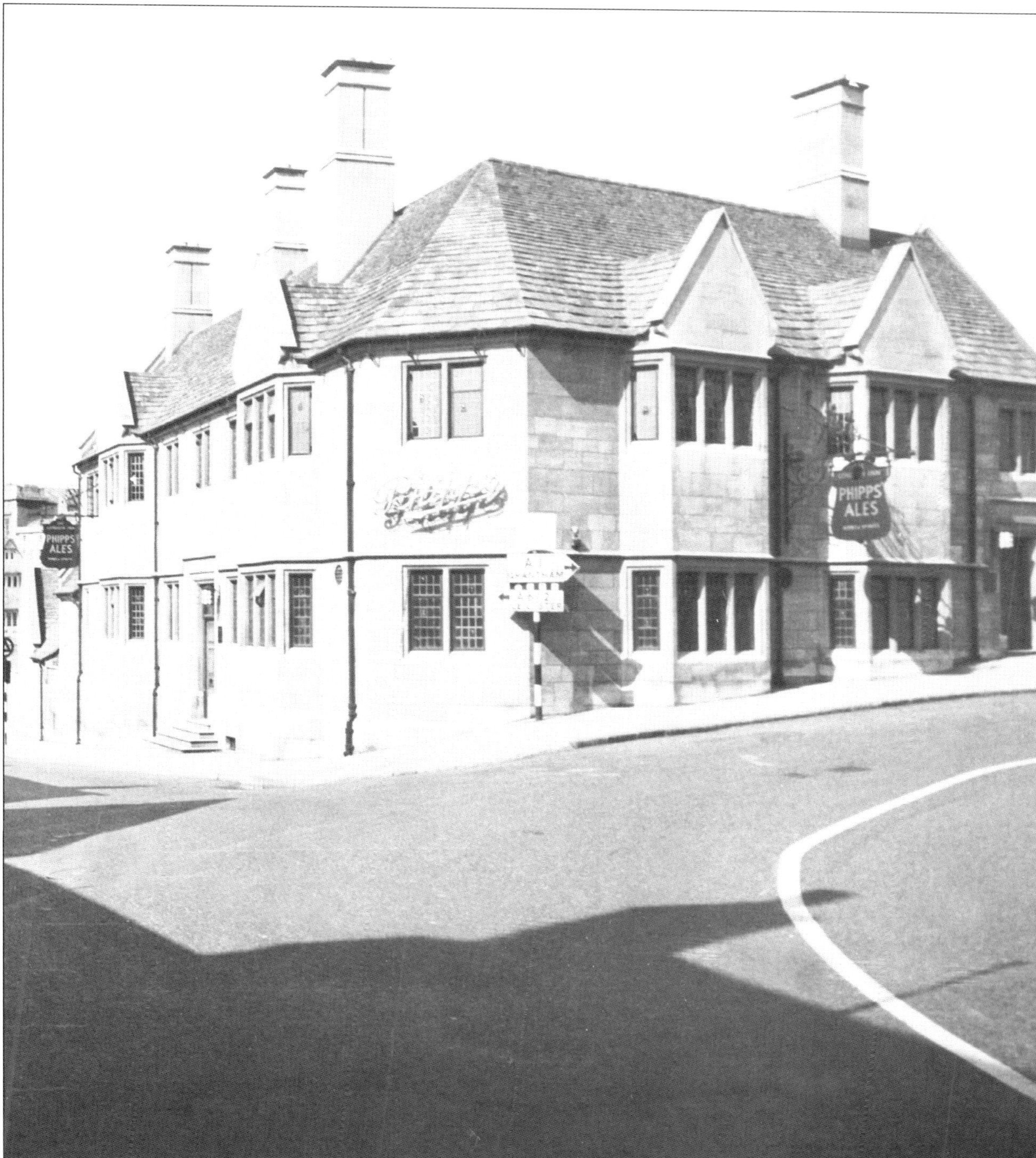

THE LONDON INN c1955 S177047

Around Stamford

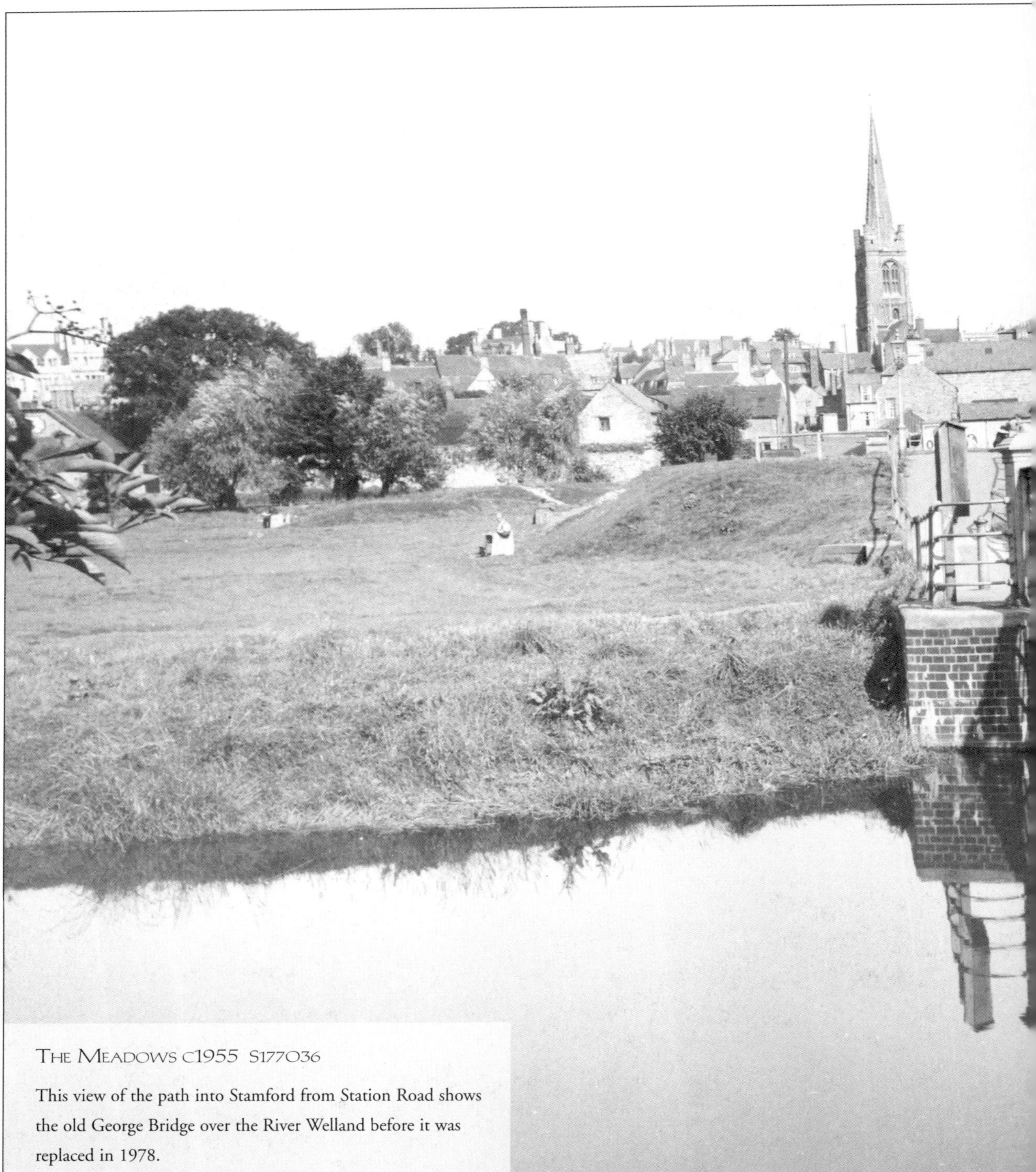

The Meadows c1955 S177036

This view of the path into Stamford from Station Road shows the old George Bridge over the River Welland before it was replaced in 1978.

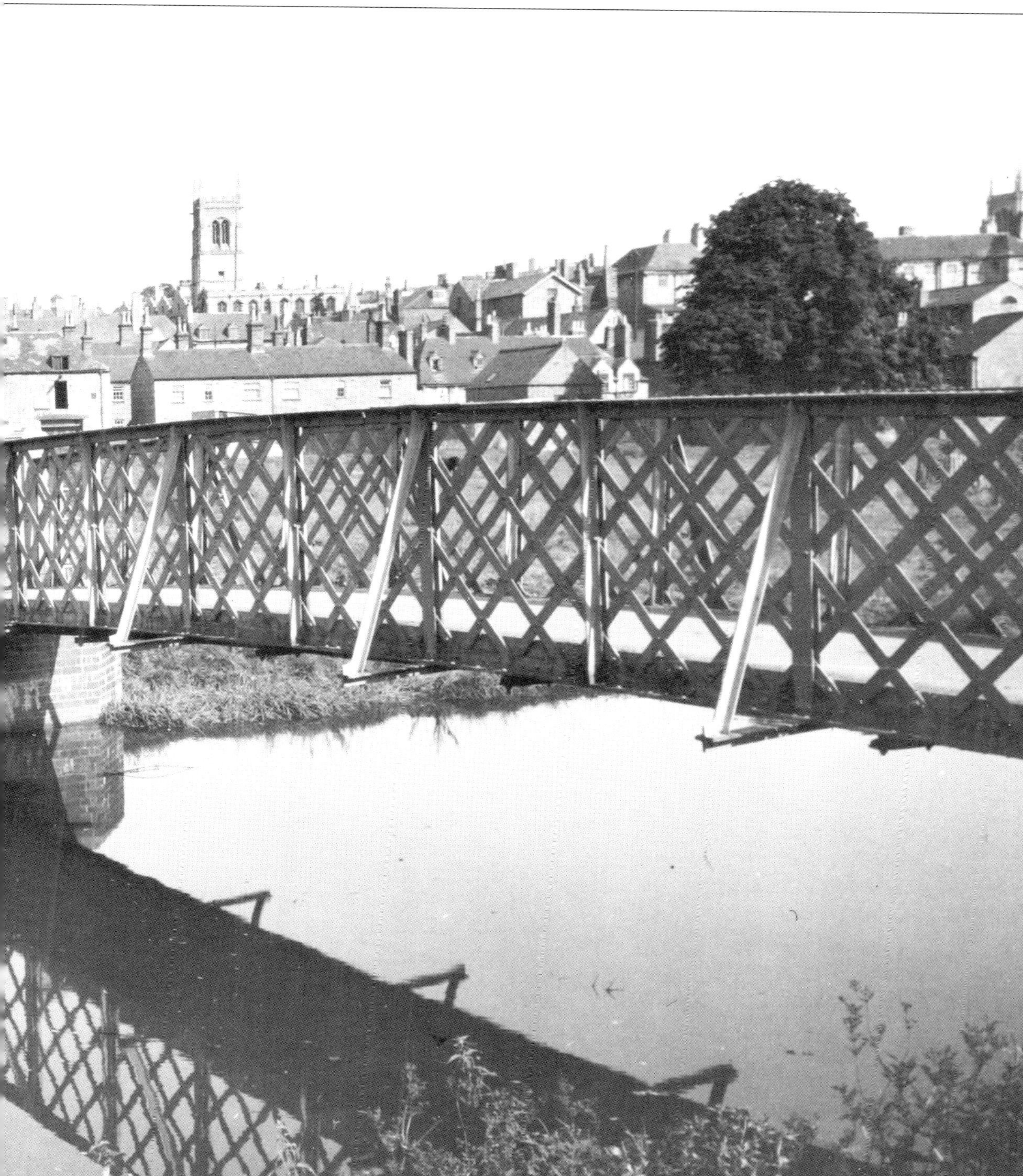

Around Stamford

The landscape to the west of Stamford is one of interfolding limestone hills and valleys and the remnants of the great forests of Rockingham and Kesteven. It is attractive countryside, studded with villages drawing on fine locally-available building stone and slates. East of the town, the land falls away towards the Fens, through which in the past the Welland provided, albeit intermittently, a navigable corridor to the sea. The river and its meadows form the centrepiece of the town. The enclosure movement was late in affecting Stamford, and at the time that the remaining open fields around the town were enclosed in the second half of the 19th century, the value of the meadows was recognised; they survived as common land.

Although there has been a bridge over the Welland at Stamford since medieval times, the present Town Bridge was built in 1849. It was constructed from Bramley Fall stone (a type of millstone grit) which was brought in by the railway. The cost of the bridge was £8,500, £5,000 of which was paid by the Midland Railway as part of the deal giving them access to the town. The Marquess of Exeter immediately reinstated the tolls on the bridge when it opened, which led to a confrontation with indignant locals. However, the tolls remained in place until 1868.

Photograph 72314 (page 74-75) of the Town Bridge was taken from the most easterly tip of the meadows between the Welland and the Mill Stream, a location now dominated by a large willow. Although the Welland looks tame and slow-flowing in this picture, a marker set on the parapets of the bridge shows the point reached by the notorious flood of 1880. Beyond the bridge we can see a smoking chimney, possibly belonging to the town's power station, in the industrial area which lay alongside Wharf Road.

The tranquil scene taken looking downstream from the bridge (72315, page 77) has in fact seen more changes than most in Stamford. The entrance down to the river on the right of the photograph still survives today as a flight of steps leading from the patio of Pizza Express, but the old buildings beyond have now all gone, making way for the new warehouse-style apartments of Saxon Court. Over the river is the chimney of J C Grant's brass and iron foundry, built in 1845 — it has had a variety of industrial uses since. The sign on the gable end to the left of the chimney advertises 'Corn & Offals by Cumberlands'.

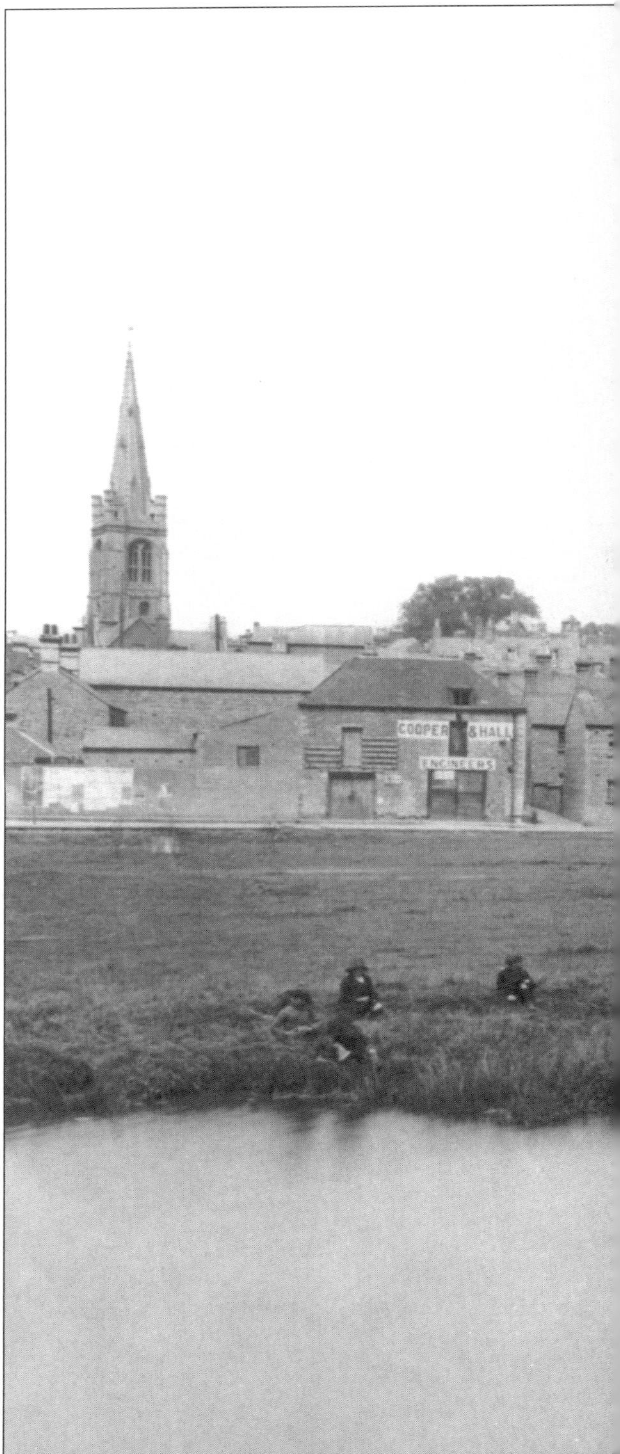

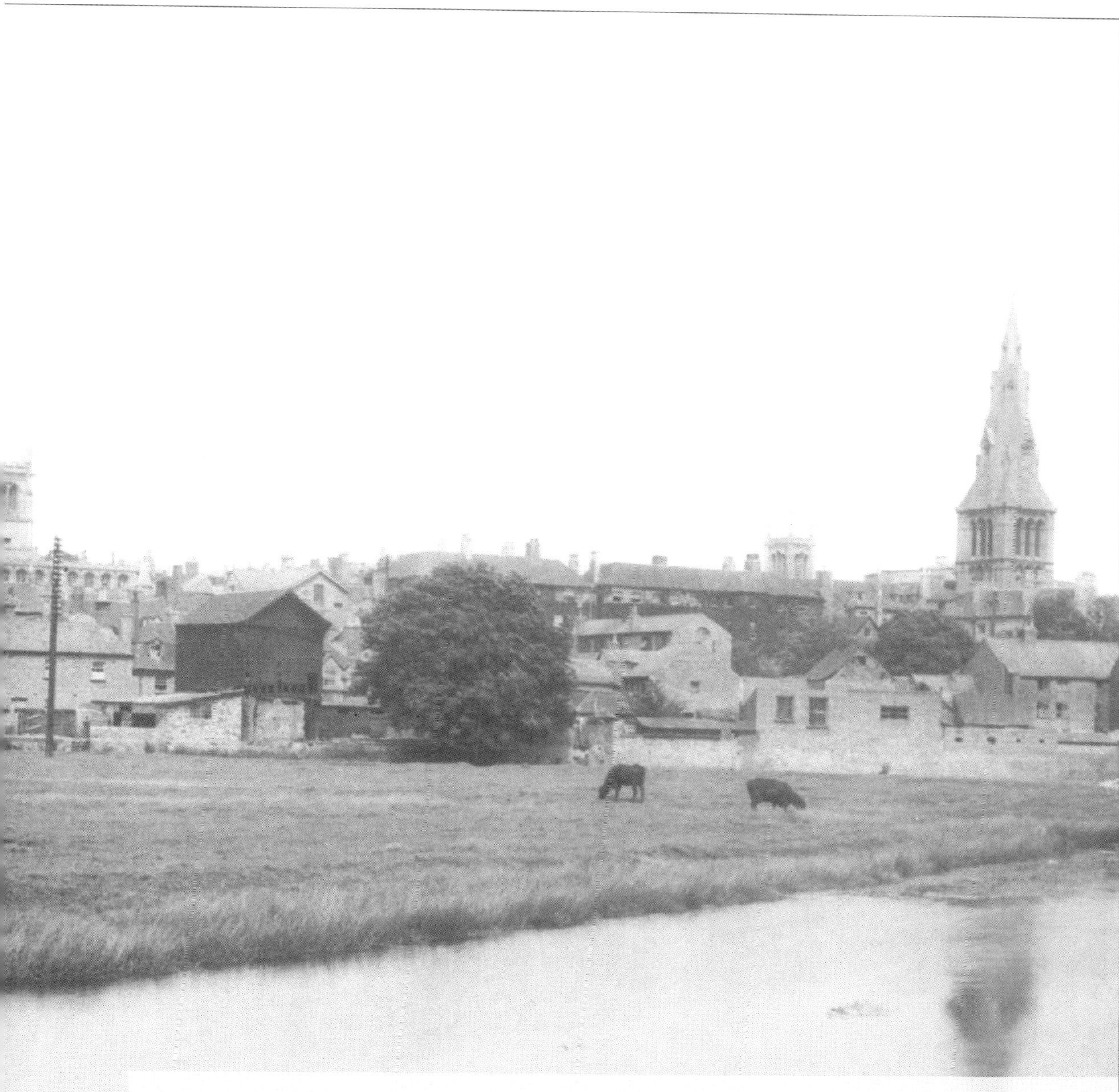

THE VIEW FROM THE MEADOWS 1922 72297

Just above the left-hand end of the bridge in S177036 (page 70) and here in 72297 we can see buildings which in the 1920s housed Cooper & Hall, the engineers. By the time the later photograph was taken, the roof appears to have fallen into disrepair, and it was only a few more years before the building, along with the cramped terraced housing alongside, was demolished to make way for a car park.

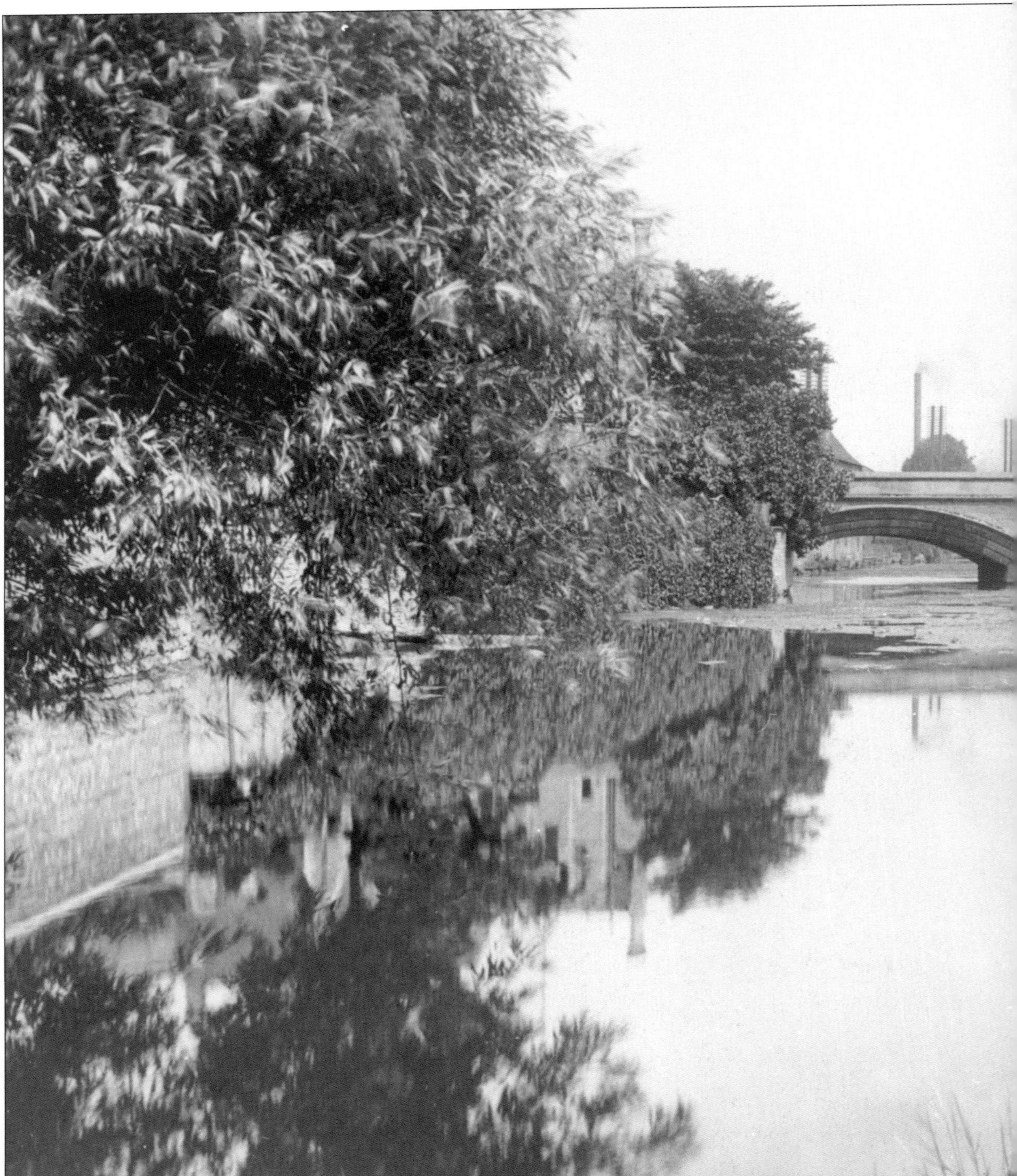

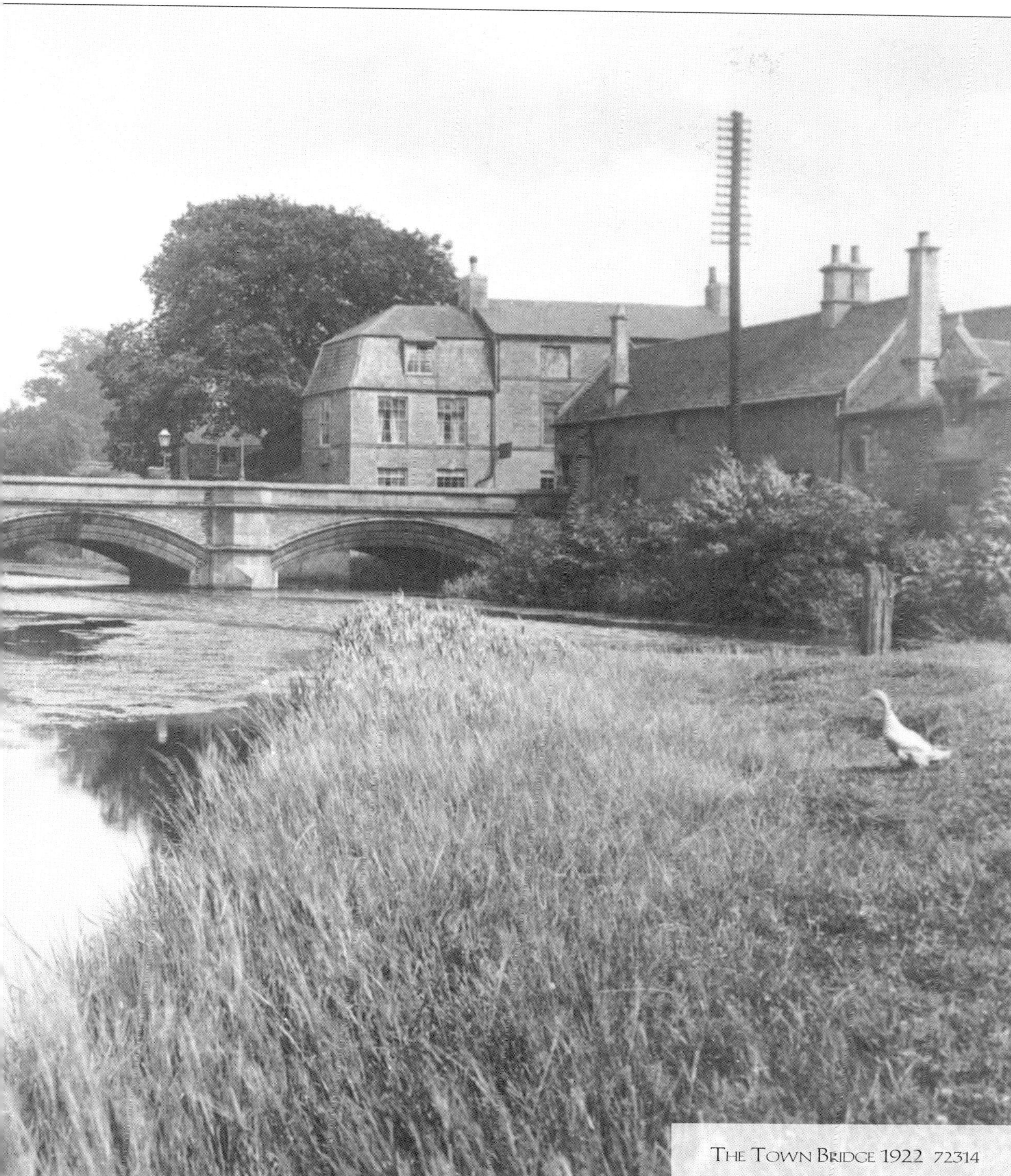

THE TOWN BRIDGE 1922 72314

Around Stamford

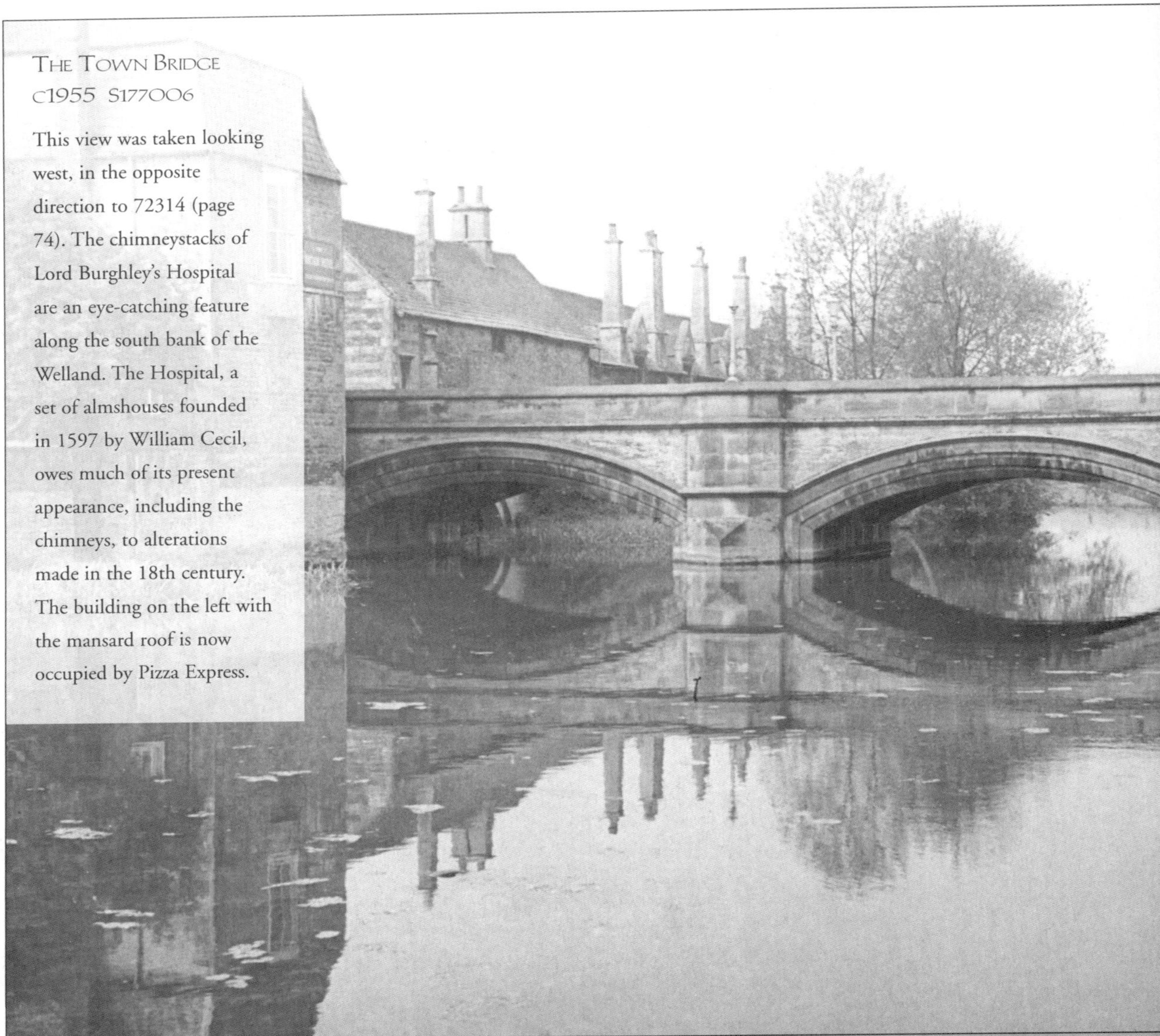

The Town Bridge
c1955 S177006

This view was taken looking west, in the opposite direction to 72314 (page 74). The chimneystacks of Lord Burghley's Hospital are an eye-catching feature along the south bank of the Welland. The Hospital, a set of almshouses founded in 1597 by William Cecil, owes much of its present appearance, including the chimneys, to alterations made in the 18th century. The building on the left with the mansard roof is now occupied by Pizza Express.

Given the presence of the Great North Road, and the patronage of the Cecils, it is understandable that from Tudor times onwards the area around Stamford became popular for the location of the country houses of the aristocracy. South of the river, on rising ground, are the grand houses of Burghley and, now in ruins, Wothorpe. Burghley was built between 1565 and 1587 by William Cecil, Lord Treasurer to Queen Elizabeth I, as his country estate. It stands within a magnificent park and gardens, which owe their current form to the genius of Capability Brown in the early 18th century.

Burghley House (72323A, pages 78-79) remains virtually unchanged since its completion, despite being placed under siege, if only for one day, by Parliamentary forces in July 1643. Certainly nothing has changed on the outside of the house since the view from the south-west was taken in 1922.

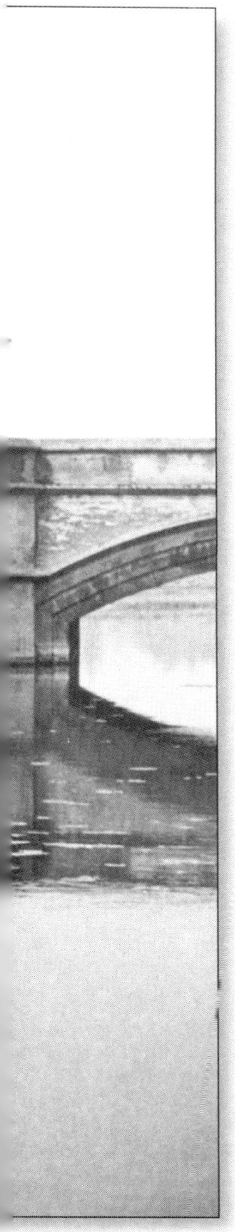

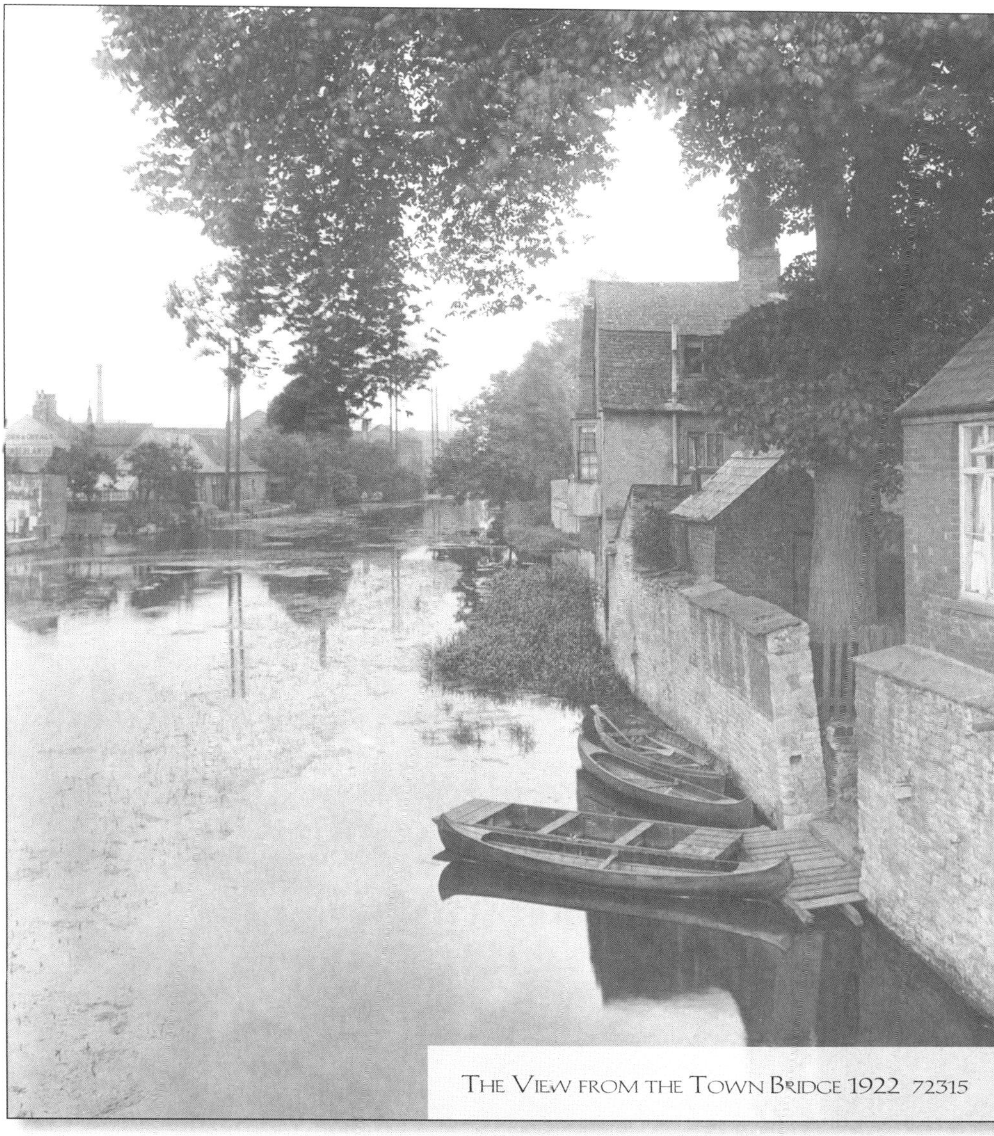

THE VIEW FROM THE TOWN BRIDGE 1922 72315

Wothorpe House was built in the early 17th century by Thomas, the son of William Cecil, who went on to be made first Earl of Exeter by James I. It is believed that the house was constructed for the widows of the family; in its heyday it would have been an impressive dwelling. The house was briefly defended during the Civil War by Royalist troops, immediately before the siege of Burghley House.

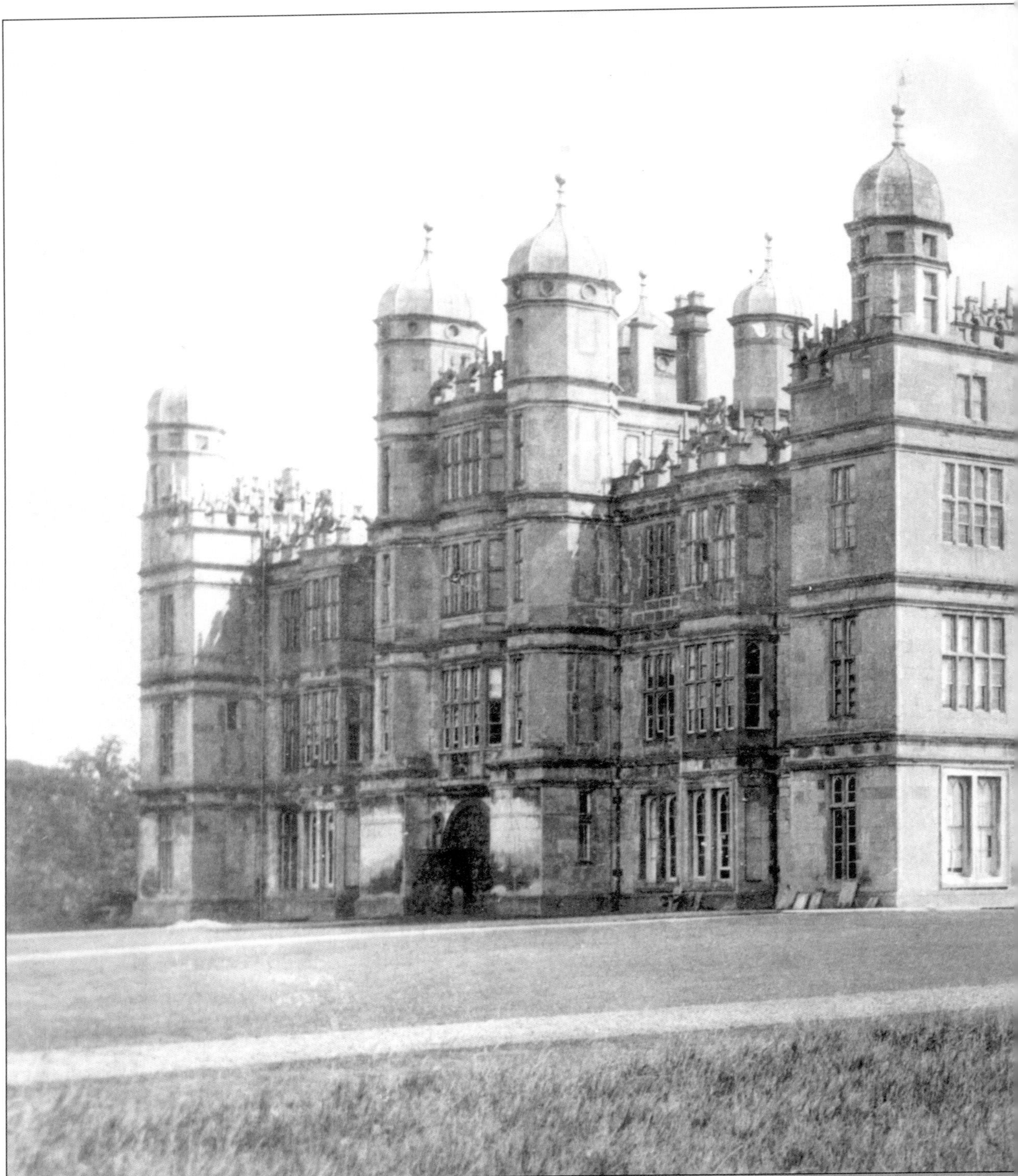

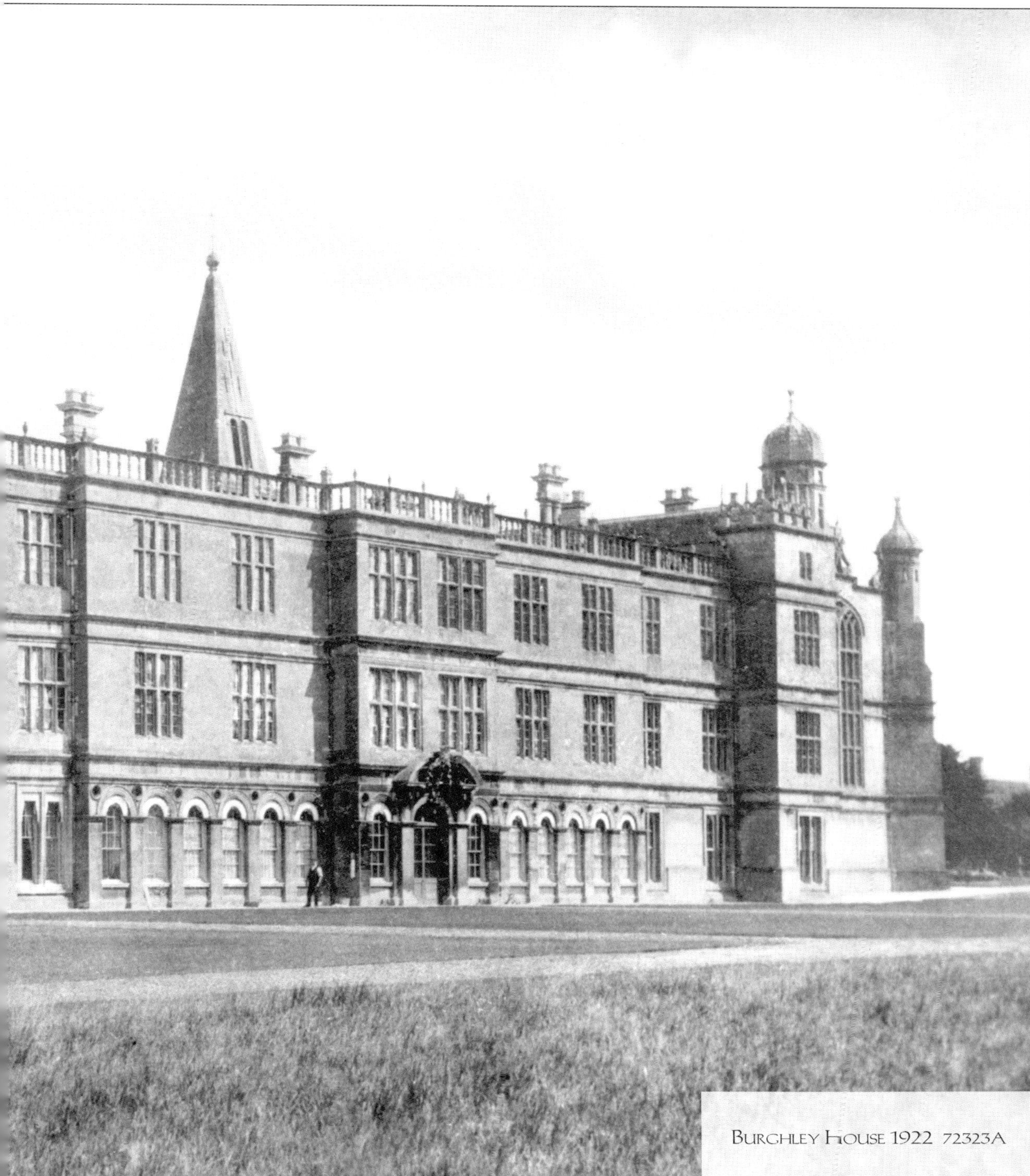

BURGHLEY HOUSE 1922 72323A

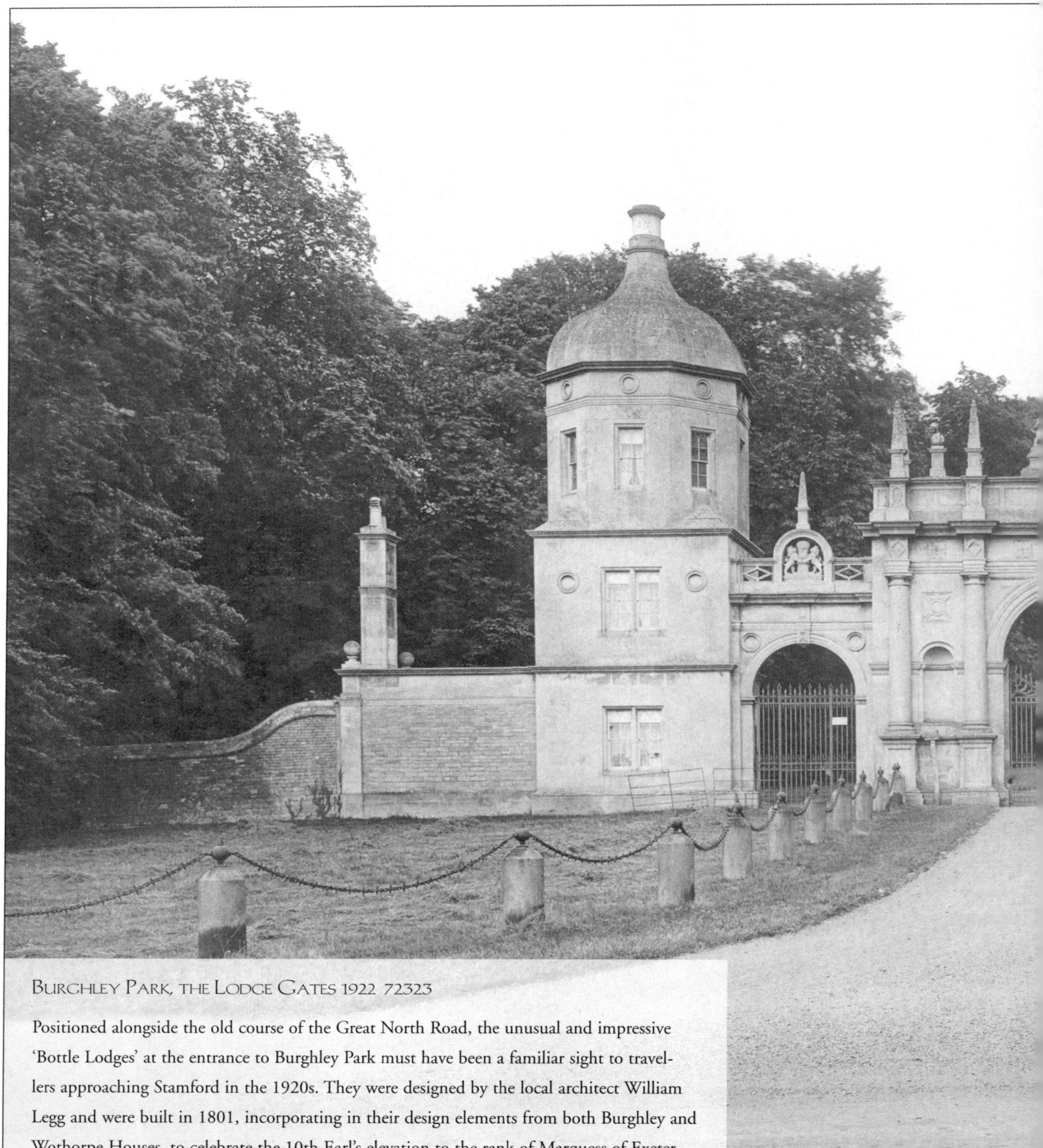

BURGHLEY PARK, THE LODGE GATES 1922 72323

Positioned alongside the old course of the Great North Road, the unusual and impressive 'Bottle Lodges' at the entrance to Burghley Park must have been a familiar sight to travellers approaching Stamford in the 1920s. They were designed by the local architect William Legg and were built in 1801, incorporating in their design elements from both Burghley and Wothorpe Houses, to celebrate the 10th Earl's elevation to the rank of Marquess of Exeter.

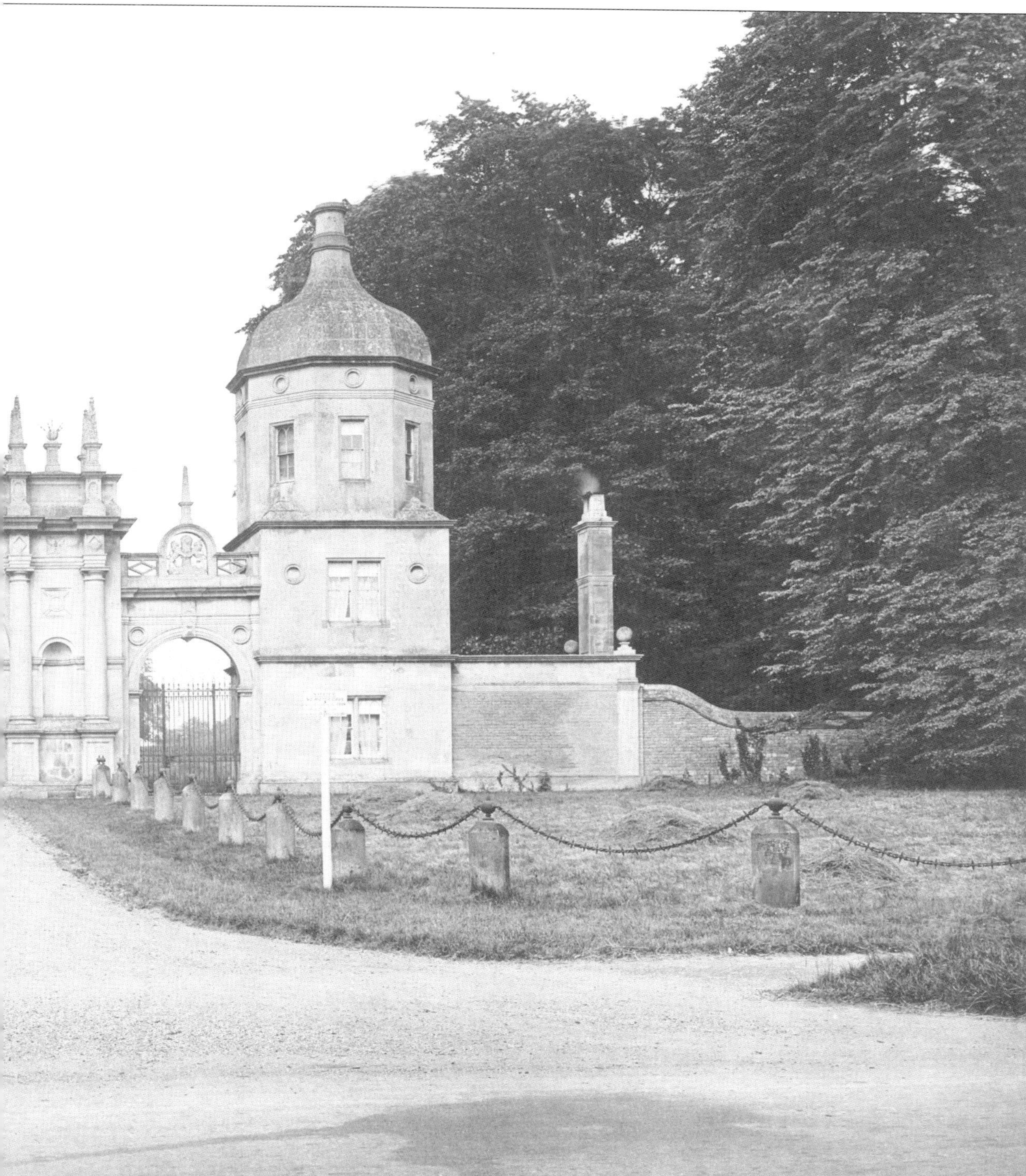

THE RUINS OF WOTHORPE HOUSE 1922 72342

The ivy-clad ruins of Wothorpe House have been an attraction for tourists for over a hundred years, and it is of no surprise that they were included by the Frith photographer in his collection of Stamford photographs. The site today may be approached by public footpath, about a mile south-west of Stamford.

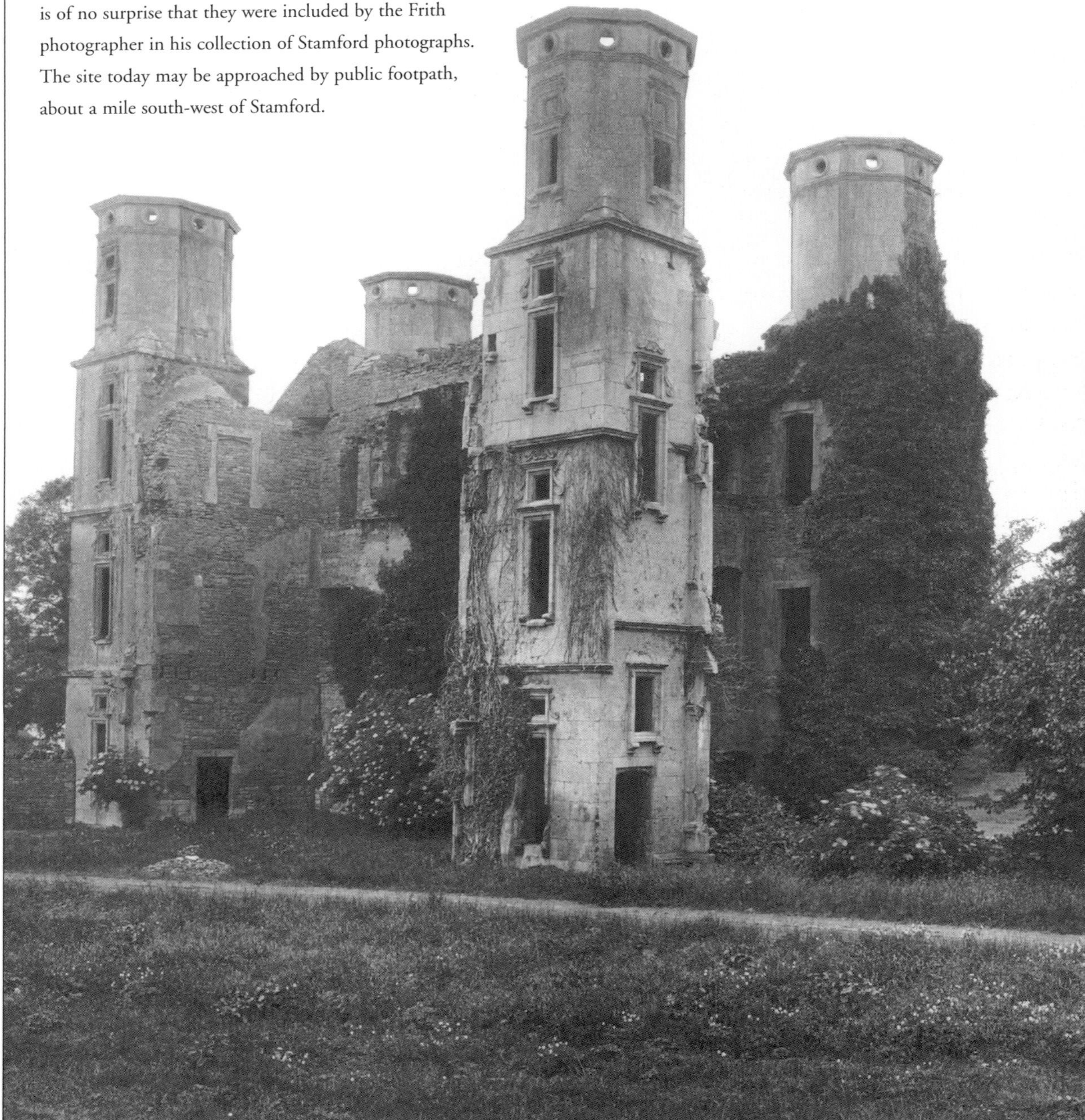

Bibliography

All Saints' Church, a short history & guide — *P Sharp (1987)*

Anglo-Saxon Lincolnshire — *P Sawyer (SLHA 1998)*

Brabner's Gazetteer of Britain *(1895)*

English Medieval Monasteries — *R Midmer (Heinemann 1979)*

Guide to Stamford & Neighbourhood — *G Burton (1896)*

Jarrold Guide to Stamford *(Jarrold Publishing 2000)*

Lincolnshire Churches Revisited — *H Thorold (Michael Russell 1989)*

Lincolnshire Curiosities — *H Peach (Dovecote Press 1994)*

Lincolnshire Railways — *S Squires (Lincolnshire Books 1998)*

Maypoles Martyrs & Mayhem — *Q Cooper & P Sullivan (1994)*

Roads & Tracks of Britain — *C Taylor (J M Dent 1979)*

Stamford as Middlemarch — *Stamford Museum Heritage Information Sheet (Lincolnshire County Council 1997)*

Stamford Mercury website — *www.stamfordtoday.co.uk*

Stamford Museum Town Trails *(Lincolnshire County Council 2001)*

Stamford Then & Now — *M Smith (Paul Watkins 1992)*

The Ancient Roads of England — *J Oliver (1936)*

The Book of Stamford — *A Rogers (Barracuda Books 1983)*

The Cyclists Route Book of Great Britain — *W J Spurrier (Iliffe & Son)*

The English Medieval House — *M Wood (Bracken Books 1983)*

The Making of the English Landscape — *W G Hoskins (Hodder & Stoughton 1977)*

The Market Town of Stamford 1900 — *K Ford (MAD Publishers 2000)*

The Official Handbook of Stamford *(1947)*

The Story of Stamford — *M Smith (1994)*

Ordnance Survey Map

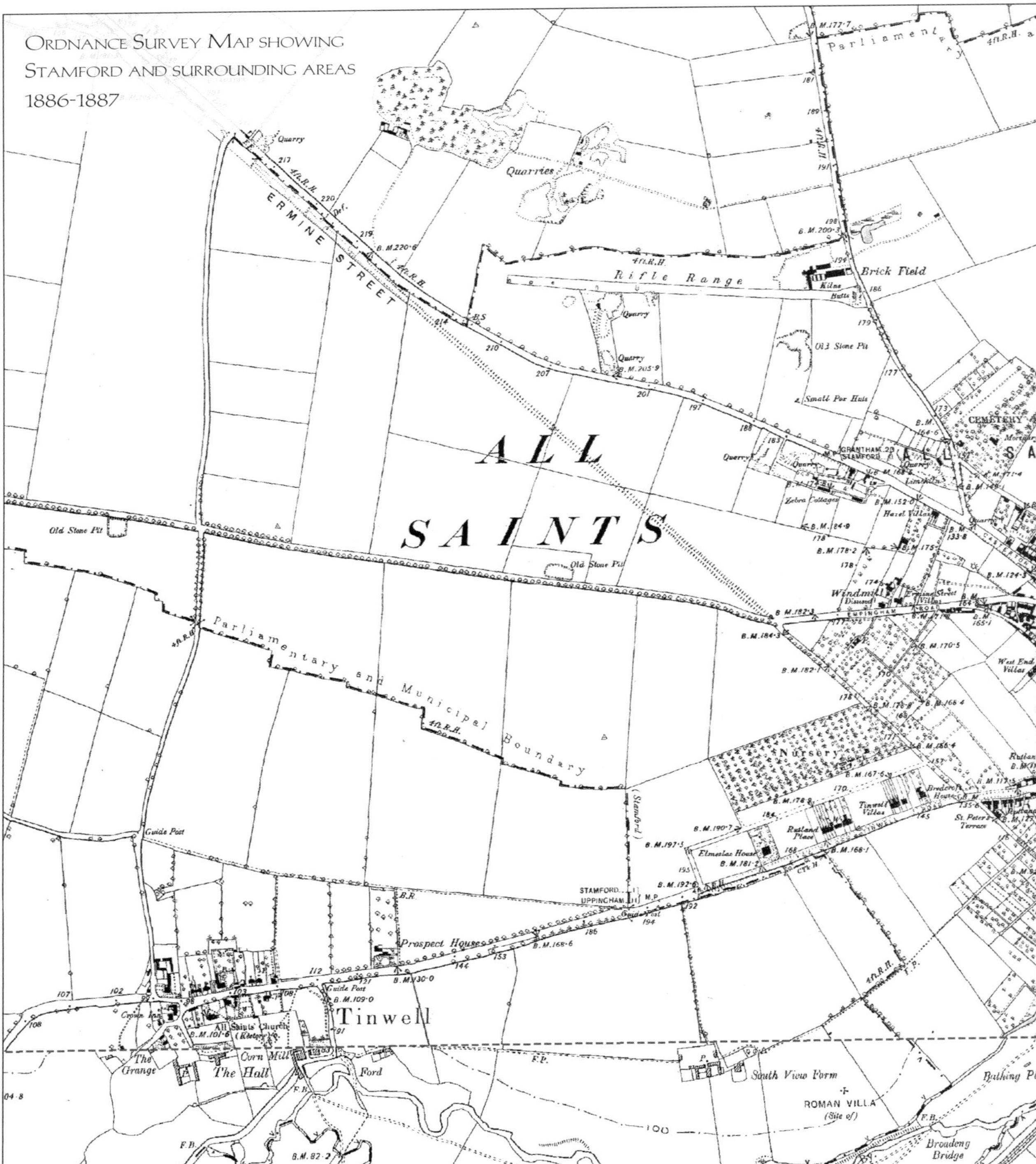

Ordnance Survey Map showing Stamford and surrounding areas 1886-1887

ORDNANCE SURVEY MAP

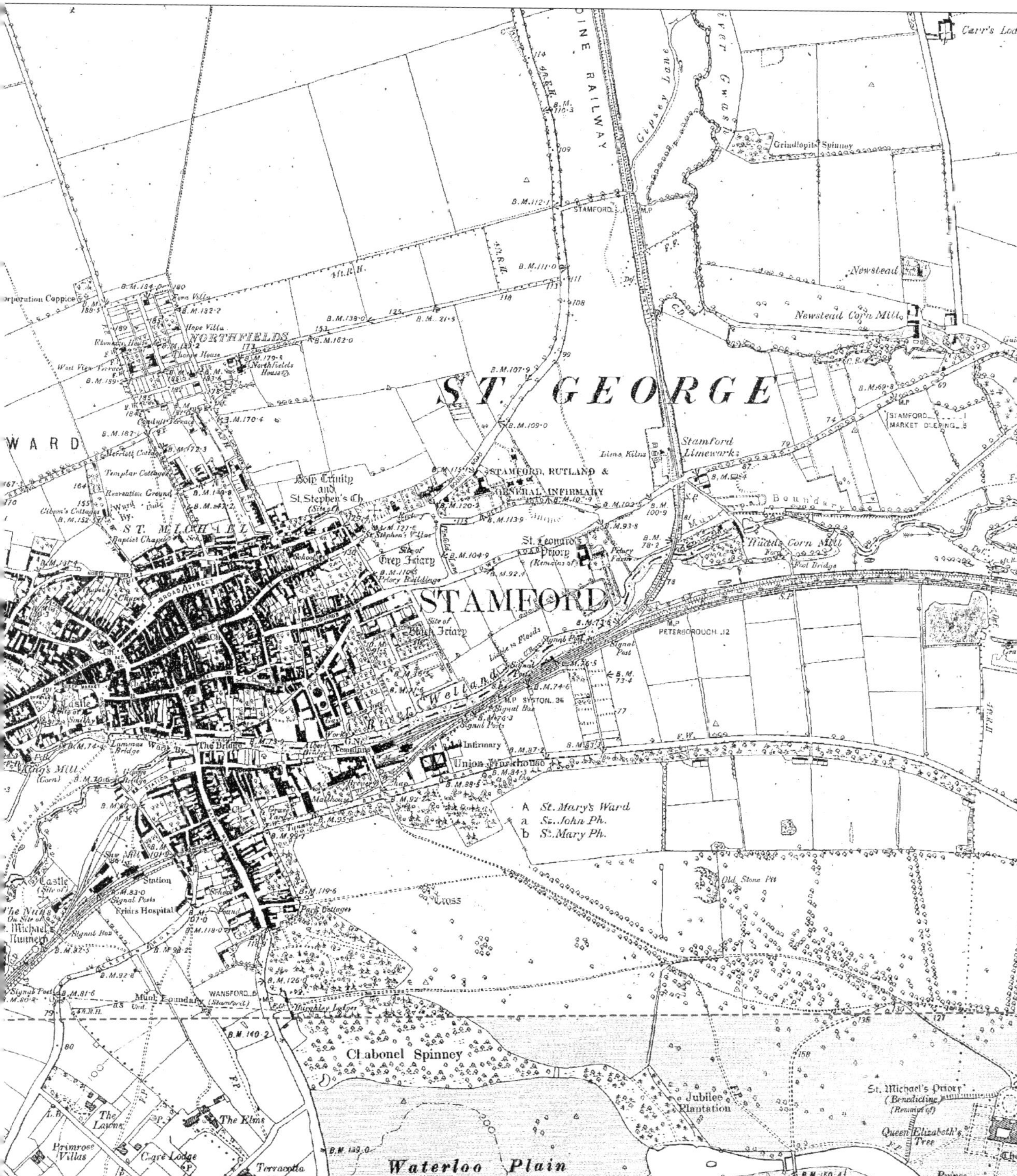

Names of Pre-Publication Buyers

The following people have kindly supported this book by purchasing limited edition copies prior to publication.

Roger Adams & Family of Stamford

John D Alcock, Stamford

Mr J W Alderman & Mrs R E Alderman

The Allan & Smith Families of Stamford

B Appleyard, Stamford

Patricia Ann Arling

Jean & John Atkinson for their Ruby Wedding 27/03/05

A V Baker, Stamford

Mr T & Mrs C Baker, Stamford

P Barlow

To Mary & Roy Barnes, Happy memories of Stamford from Doreen & Len

Violet Baxter

BBC Radio Lincolnshire

In memory of Alice & Ron Beach and Joan & Ken Batley

Neil & Mary Beaver

For Almuth & Jurgen Becker, Germany

The Bell Family, Stamford

Thelma & Larry Bell, Stamford

The Bennett Family, Stamford

Mr Maurice & Mrs Frances Bloodworth

Louise, Sam, & Millie Bowers, Stamford

Mr S A & Mrs S R Bowers, Stamford

G & C M Bradbury, Ryhall

Dianne C Bradford, Stamford

In memory of Joan & Stan Bradshaw

Pam & Dave Bradshaw, Felixstowe, Suffolk

The Bramley Family, Stamford

Miss T K Brazier & Mr S G Hammock

Maureen & Wally Brooks, Stamford

Stuart James Brooks

J E Broughton, Stamford

Doreen Brown, Stamford

The Brown Family, Stamford

The Brown Family, Vine Street, Stamford

Elizabeth Burnside

John Burrows, Stamford

Alec & Renée Burt

Beryl Butcher, Stamford

Kathleen Cadby

Wembley & Doris Camping, Ryhall, Stamford

Mr & Mrs D R & S R Chappell, Stamford

Maureen Chong

Brian Christie, Stamford

Frances O Clark, Colin V Clark

Terence Martin Clarke

Bob & Barbara Cleveland, Stamford

Ian & Carmen Collis

Mr M T & Mrs J Conneely, Stamford

Phyllis Grace Cook

Gordon & Pat Copson, Stamford

Terry Corby

Kate, Patrick & Michael Coulsey, Stamford

B Couzens, Stamford

Martin Cragg, Skegness

Trevor & Jean Cunnington, Stamford

Mr Simon Curtis

Marjorie & Malcolm Darke

The Dartnell Family

James & Deanna Davies, Stamford

Allan & Anne Dawson, Stamford

In memory of L F Dobbs, Stamford

Remembering John Dolby, shopowner & printer

For Paul Downs, in memory of Nanny & Grandad

Michael Duffy, Stamford

In memory of Len Earey, Stamford

George T Earl

Tony & Joan Emery, Stamford

The Foster Family, Australia

Gladys M Foster, Stamford

The Fowler Family, Stamford

Colin C Francis

Derek & Jane Freeman, Stamford

Tina Garratt, Stamford

Jane & Rick Gentle

In memory of Michael Gill, Stamford

To my son Howard Gladman, from your father

To my son Martyn Gladman, from your father

To my son Steven Gladman, from your father

Mrs I Goodes, Collyweston

Mr & Mrs Michael Gordon, Stamford

Our first home, Stamford 2005, J & S Grimm

Ian Andrew Hall

Bob, Carol, Ben & Alice Harkness, Stamford

Mr Darryl Harrison & Family, Stamford

Sam Harrison, Stamford

John & Daphne Hawkins

The Hawksworth Family, Stamford

Joan Hayes, Stamford

Jill Haynes, Stamford

Dedicated to the Haynes Family, Stamford

Tony Hayre for Fathers Day 2005

To Harold Henson, Peterborough, from Susan

Mr G W Hill, Stamford

Francis W G Howard, Stamford

In memory of Alex Hoyles

T J Hoyles, Anne, Julian & John

David Stephen Hudson, Stamford

Mrs S & Mr M Hyder

Arthur W Ingram

Mark W Ingram

Reverend Albert & Miss Polly Irwin

To Nanny Jane from A & P Jackson & Family

Betty & Harold Jackson, Casterton, Stamford 2005

Mr Milos Jarabak, Michalovce - Stamford

Glenys Johnston, Stamford 2005

Mr C R & Mrs D M Jones, Stamford

The Kendrew Family, Stamford

Chris & Jane Kew and Family

The Kippen Family, Stamford

Josh Kirby

Geoffrey Lea

David K Lee, Stamford

David & Sarah Lee

Hazel Lee

Michael S Lee, Stamford

Michael Sidney Lee of Stamford

David H Lenton, Stamford

For Jenson Dominic Lewis with love, Mum & Dad

Sarah Lindsey, Stamford

R S Long & M V Long, Stamford

Michael Longstaff, Stamford

Margaret Lowe

M Lynas, Stamford

In memory of Harry Mallard, Stamford

Stuart & Natasha Mann, Stamford (2003)

The Marshall Family, Stamford

Andrew P Matthews, Stamford

Dr & Mrs I Mowat, Stamford

Alan, Jacqueline & Simon Munford 2005

In memory of Gervais Musgrove & Tom Bell

T D Musgrove; Timothy D Musgrove, Stamford

The Needham Family, Tallington, Stamford

Mr D V & Mrs J E Newman

In memory of Joan & Jack Nicholls

Ann Norris

Mr & Mrs N Norris & Family

To Pam & Paul Oswald, Scotland

Brian Palmer, Barnack

Frederick C Palmer

Park Farm Bed & Breakfast, Careby

For Matthew A Parkinson, love Dad & Rose 1/6/05

Paul, Jane & Miles, Rutland Terrace

The Peck Family, Ryhall

The Peng Family, Stamford

Mr & Mrs R A Proctor, Stamford

Angela & Richard Ransom, Tallington

Frank & Joy Rawlings

Mr Ron Richardson, Stamford

Stanley & Joan Rickett and Family

Brian John Riley, Stamford

Suzie Robinson, Market Rasen

Mr & Mrs David Roe & daughter Alice

Trevor Rudkin

I P & P A Russon & Family of Stamford

Rutland Radio

St Gilbert's Primary School, Stamford

Mrs F E Sawyer, Stamford

Paul Sentance, Stamford

H E Sharpe & Sons, Great Casterton

The Sharpe Family, Stamford

David T Simpson

John & Barbara Smith, Tallington, Stamford

Michael James Rodwell Smith

Mick Smith, Lincoln

Sidney James Smith & Josephine Stella Smith, Stamford

Margaret Smyth, Gainsborough

To Nigel Stafford on his birthday

Stamford Day Centre

Stamford Mercury

Mary Steele

Jenny & David Stimson, Stamford

The Straker Family, Stamford

Mick & Sue Stretton, Stamford

Mr B C & B A Sumner

For Mrs Frances Talbot of Poynton

To Carmen & Keith Taylor, 'Forever friends', from Betty & Bob

Geoff Taylor, Boston

Pete, Jacqui, Chris & Claire Thompson

Mr J & Mrs P Tibbert, Senrad, 'The Tibbs', Stamford

Mr M J & Mrs D L Towell, Stamford

Ann Turner & Peter Turner

David 'Chutny' Turner & Paul Turner

Gavin J Tutcher, Stamford

To my loving father J E W Tyers

Janet J Upex

Robert & Margaret Vipan, Stamford

L P Voller, Peterborough

Stella & Barrie Westbury

Mr M J & Mrs L S Wilson, Stamford

The Woodin Family

The Woods Family at Newstead Mill Dairy

Gordon Earle Wright & Edith Lilian Wright

The Yarr Family

INDEX

FRITH PRODUCTS & SERVICES

Francis Frith would doubtless be pleased to know that the pioneering publishing venture he started in 1860 still continues today. Over a hundred and forty years later, The Francis Frith Collection continues in the same innovative tradition and is now one of the foremost publishers of vintage photographs in the world. Some of the current activities include:

Interior Decoration

Today Frith's photographs can be seen framed and as giant wall murals in thousands of pubs, restaurants, hotels, banks, retail stores and other public buildings throughout the country. In every case they enhance the unique local atmosphere of the places they depict and provide reminders of gentler days in an increasingly busy and frenetic world.

Product Promotions

Frith products are used by many major companies to promote the sales of their own products or to reinforce their own history and heritage. Frith promotions have been used by Hovis bread, Courage beers, Scots Porage Oats, Colman's mustard, Cadbury's foods, Mellow Birds coffee, Dunhill pipe tobacco, Guinness, and Bulmer's Cider.

Genealogy and Family History

As the interest in family history and roots grows world-wide, more and more people are turning to Frith's photographs of Great Britain for images of the towns, villages and streets where their ancestors lived; and, of course, photographs of the churches and chapels where their ancestors were christened, married and buried are an essential part of every genealogy tree and family album.

Frith Products

All Frith photographs are available Framed or just as Mounted Prints and Posters (size 23 x 16 inches). These may be ordered from the address below. From time to time other products - Address Books, Calendars, Table Mats, etc - are available.

The Internet

Already ninety thousand Frith photographs can be viewed and purchased on the internet through the Frith websites and a myriad of partner sites.

For more detailed information on Frith companies and products, look at these sites:

www.francisfrith.co.uk
www.francisfrith.com
(for North American visitors)

See the complete list of Frith Books at:
www.francisfrith.co.uk

This web site is regularly updated with the latest list of publications from The Francis Frith Collection. If you wish to buy books relating to another part of the country that your local bookshop does not stock, you may purchase on-line.

For further information, trade, or author enquiries please contact us at the address below:
The Francis Frith Collection, Frith's Barn, Teffont, Salisbury, Wiltshire, England SP3 5QP.
Tel: +44 (0)1722 716 376 Fax: +44 (0)1722 716 881 Email: sales@francisfrith.co.uk

See Frith books on the internet at www.francisfrith.co.uk

Dear Adianto, [illegible] Christmas!

Love, Grandpa and Grandma Hamilton

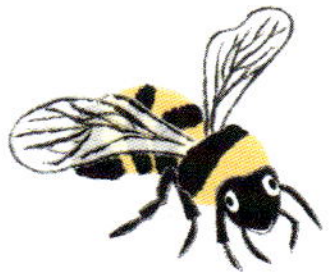

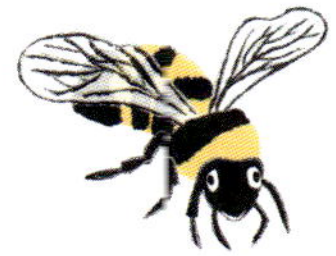

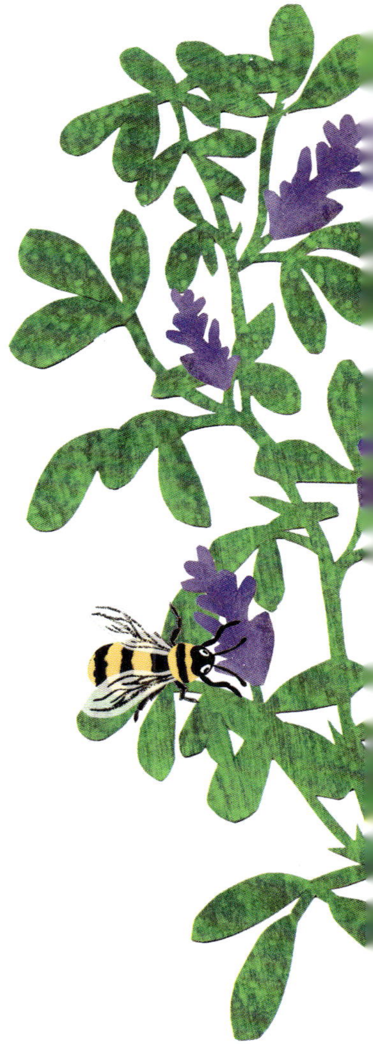

Alfalfabet
A to Z

The Wonderful Words from Agriculture

written by Carol Watterson
illustrated by Michela Sorrentino

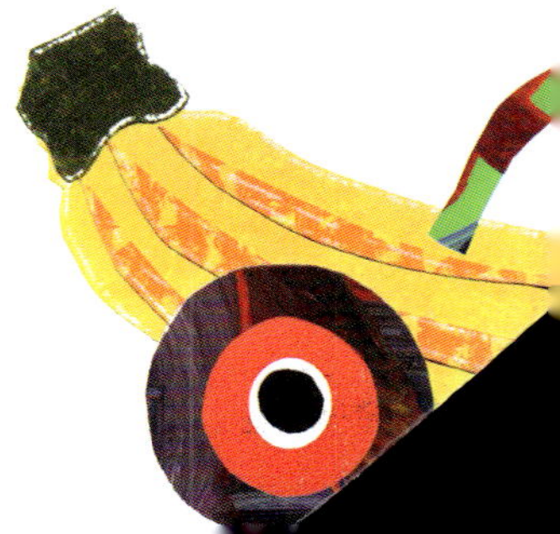

British Columbia Agriculture in the Classroom Foundation

What is Agriculture?

Agriculture (ag-ri-kuhl-cher) is a big word that means working together on many things. Think of all of the things we do to make the food we eat — that's agriculture. It's people working together to grow plants and raise animals to make things we need. It's also growing crops to feed the animals. We work on agriculture in many places — on the farm, at the ranch, in the forest and the sea.

Agriculture grows alfalfa for the Angus, hay for the horse, canola for our cooking oil and wheat for our bread. It gives us milk from cows, honey from bees, eggs from hens and wool from sheep.

Agriculture is all around you. Look around and you will see so many things we make from the plants and animals we raise — paper, crayons, pencils, soccer balls, your sweater and even the shoes on your feet.

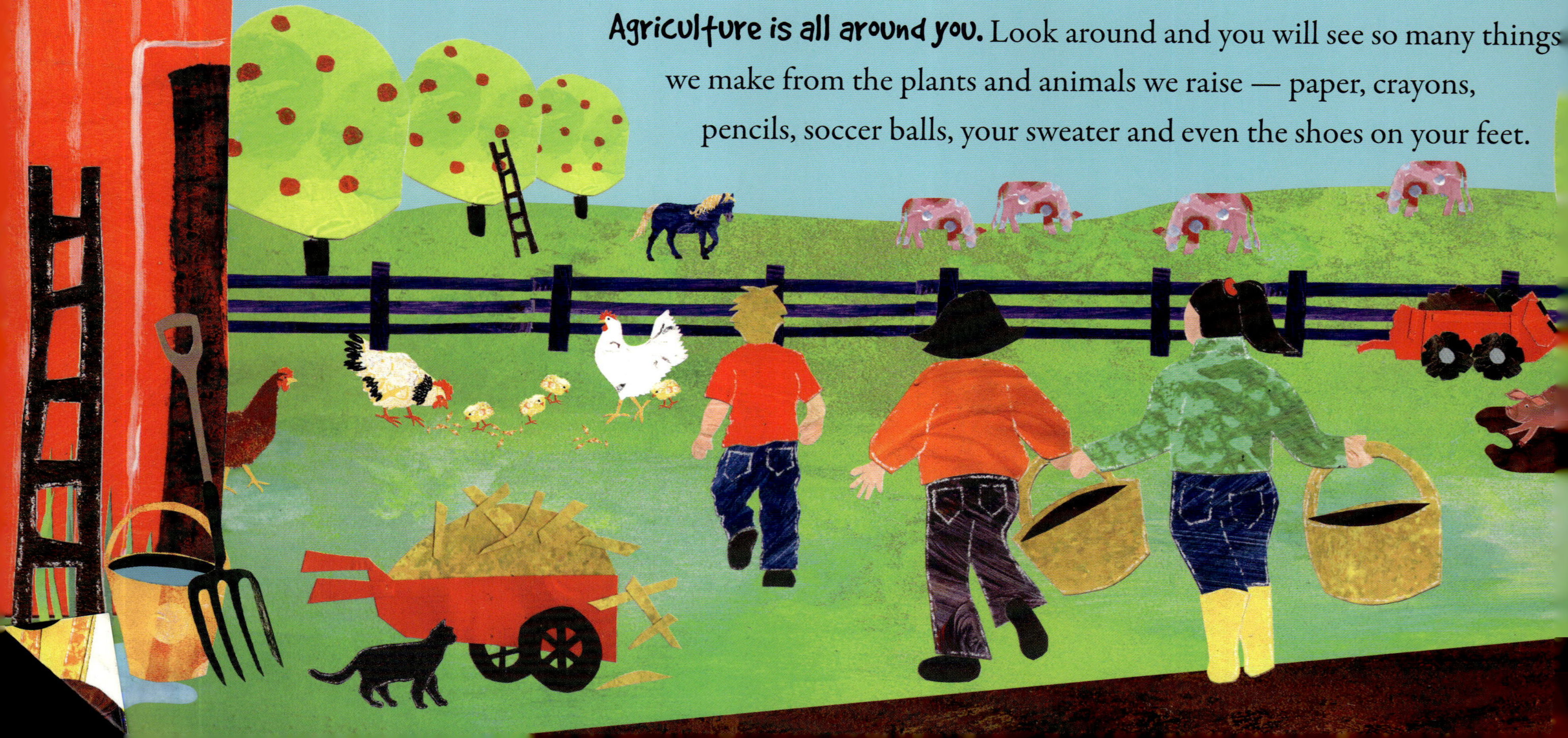

Let's turn the page and meet some of the wonderful words from agriculture.

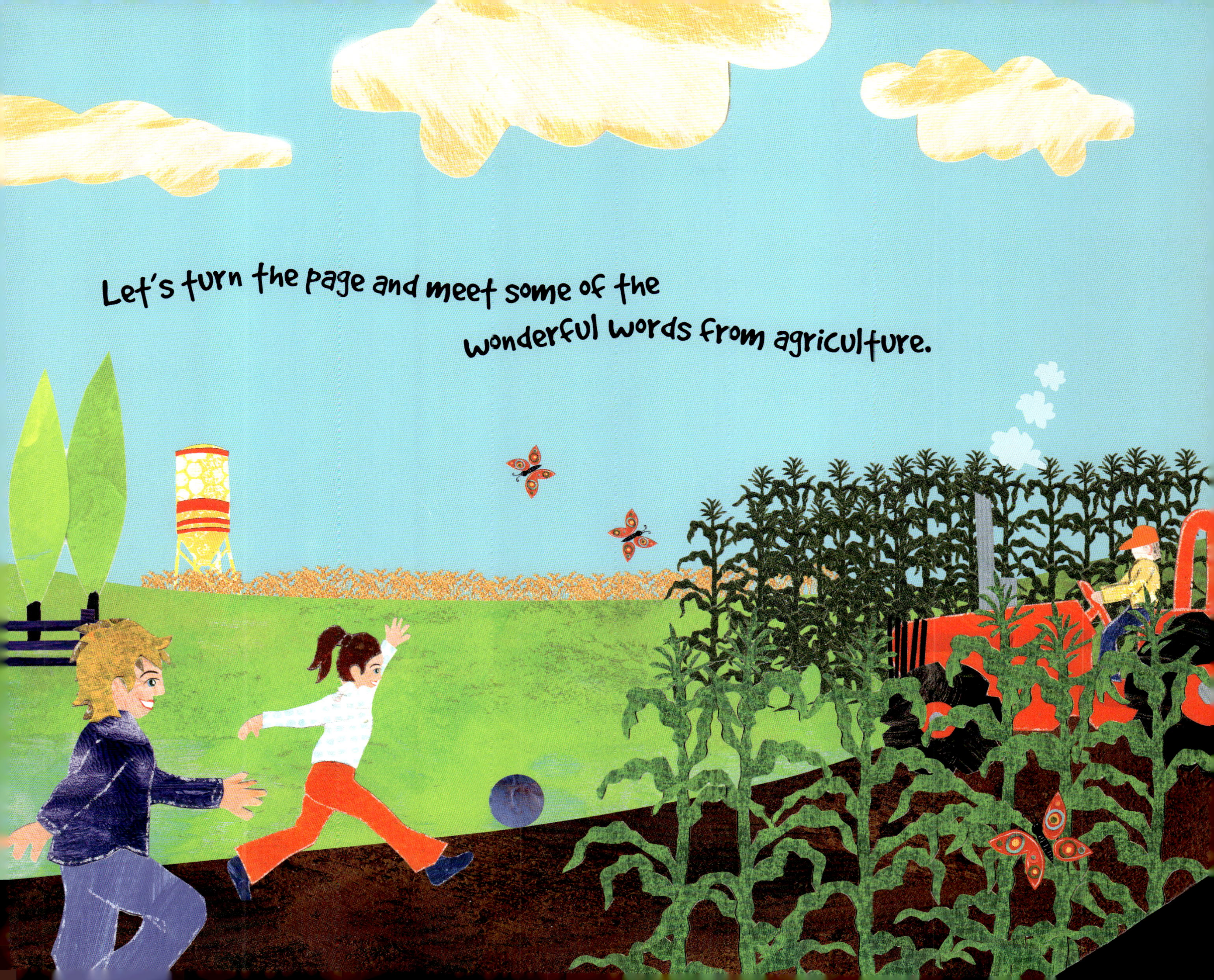

Aa Ants on Asparagus

Spring is here!

Who are those green soldiers poking their heads through the dark earth?

Asparagus! They are the first to arrive.
One, two, three – more green spears shoot up.
Knobby crowns reach for the sun while ants tickle their tender stalks.

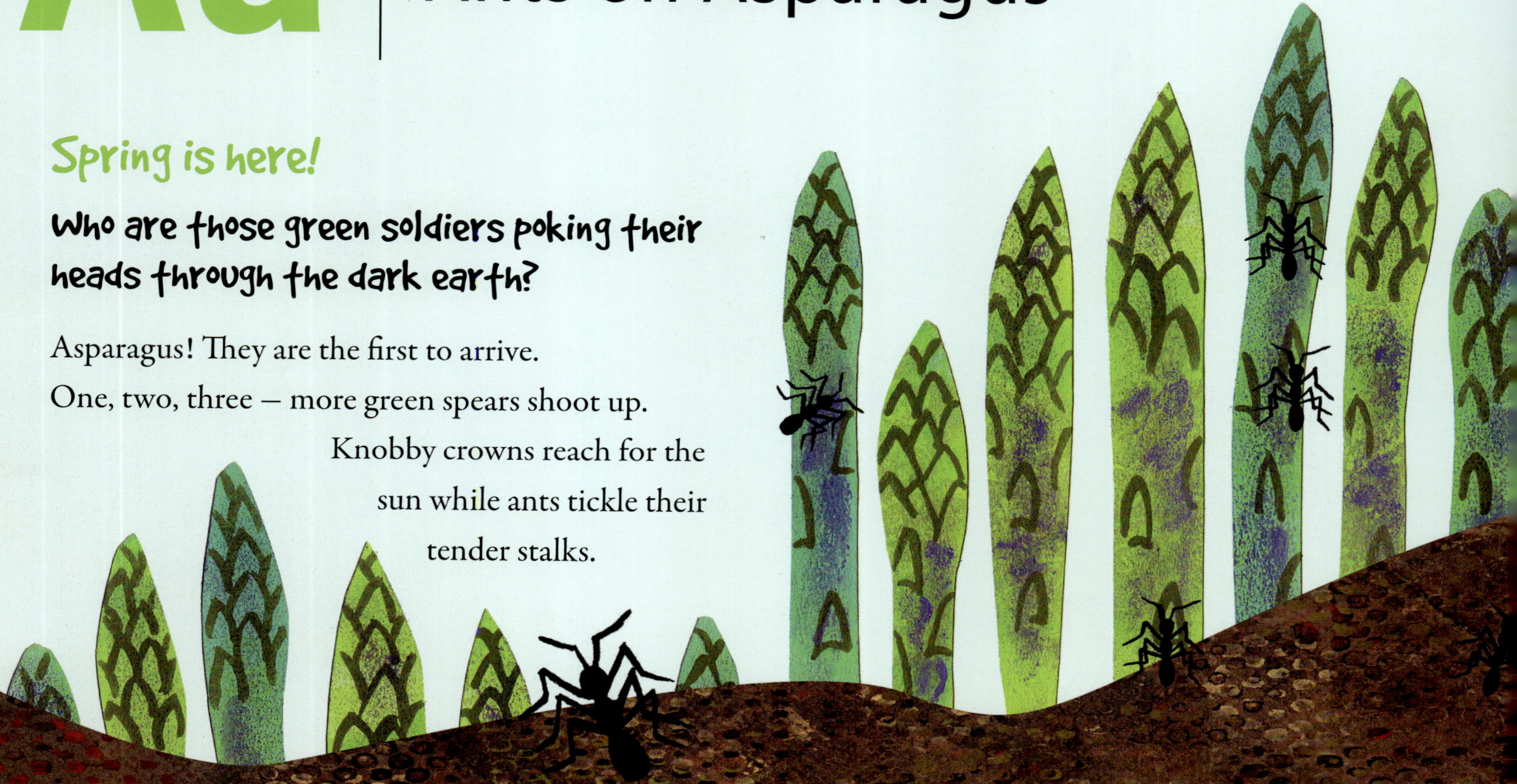

Warm spring weather softens the earth. It's time for the farmer to get the soil ready for planting. Many crops, like wheat and corn, grow from seeds that the farmer plants each spring.

Asparagus doesn't need to be planted every spring. The farmer harvests only the stalks and leaves the ts in the soil. Next spring, the plant will grow new shoots from its roots.

Can you name some fruits that grow on trees?

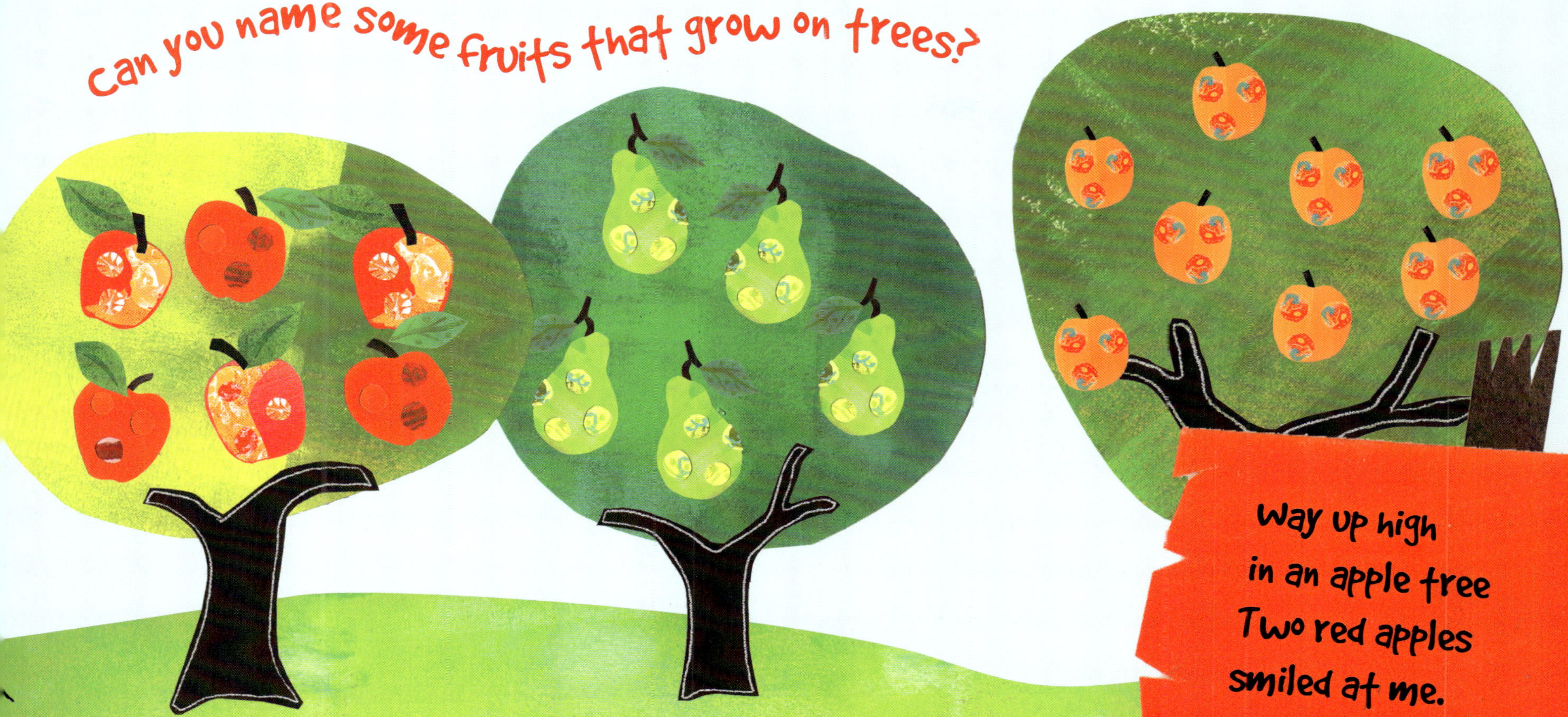

Way up high
in an apple tree
Two red apples
smiled at me.
I shook that tree
as hard as I could.
Down came the apples
and m-m-m
they were good.

The apple tree is full of fruit. These crispy, sweet **Ambrosia** apples are ripe and ready to pick.

Apricot trees are the first to blossom each spring. April blossoms fall and make room for bright orange summer fruit.

Did you know that not all pears are yellow? **Anjou** pears can be green or red.

Let's turn the page and find a yellow pear.

Bb | Blueberries, Beetles and Beans

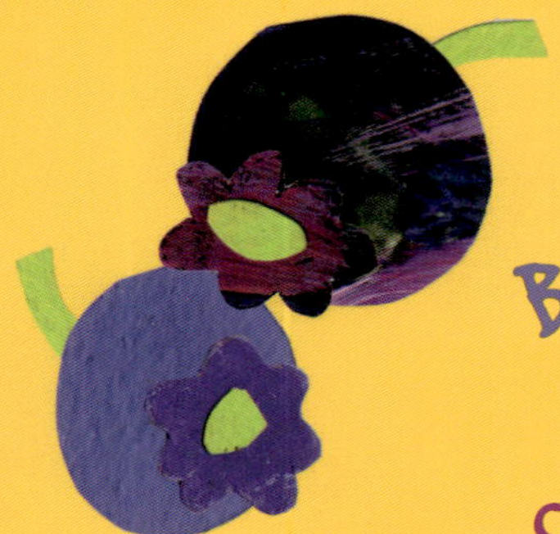

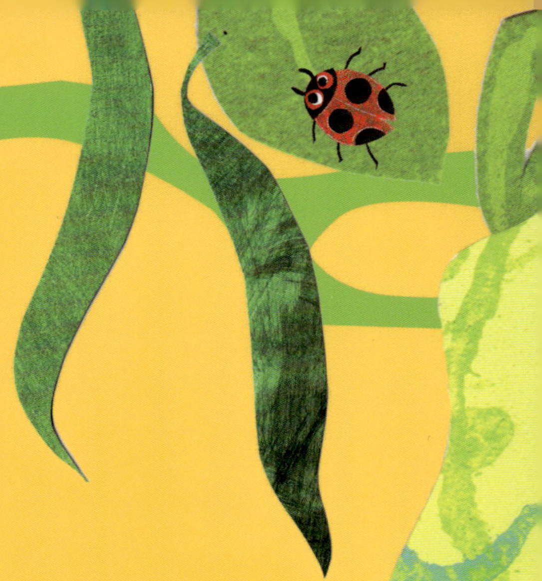

Brown beans jump, blueberries bounce and red beetles hide.

Curly, long, smooth and bumpy – fruits and vegetables come in all sorts of shapes and sizes. Some of them are named for their colour. Did you know that blueberries were once called star berries because of the star shaped pattern left by the flower on the end of the fruit?

Most berries grow on bushes that produce new berries every summer. One blueberry bush may produce more than 3,000 berries in one season! Blueberries aren't blue at first. As they ripen, the berries turn from green, to red, to purple and then blue – that's when they are ripe and ready to pick.

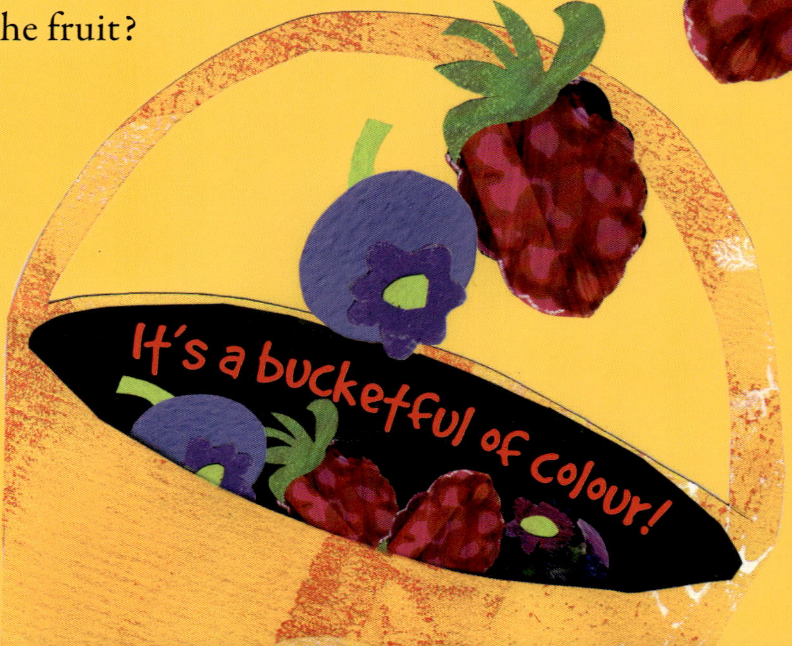

Clip, Clop, Crunch

Cc

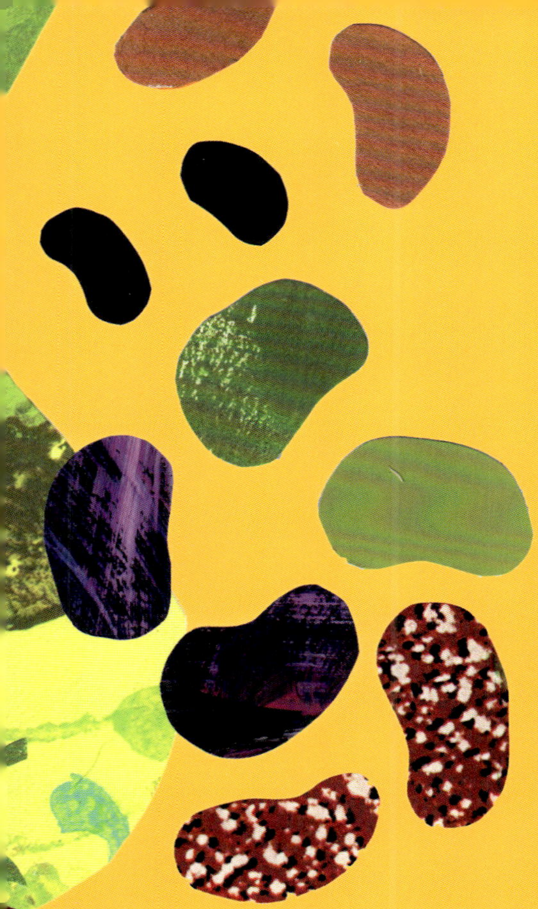

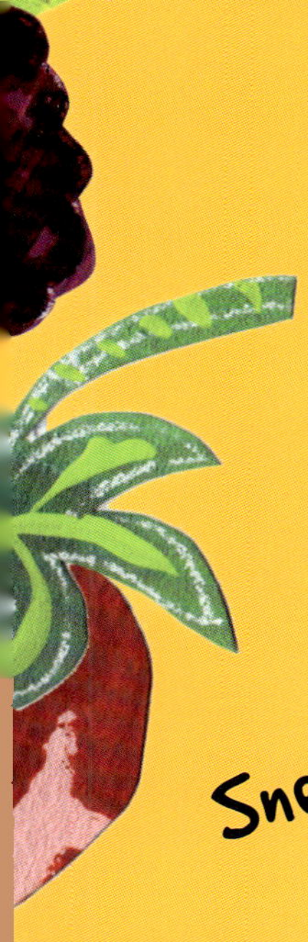

Carrots are a crunchy treat.

Horses also munch on alfalfa hay, grass and oats. Apples too!

Did you know that not all carrots are orange? Some types of carrots are red, yellow, purple and even white.

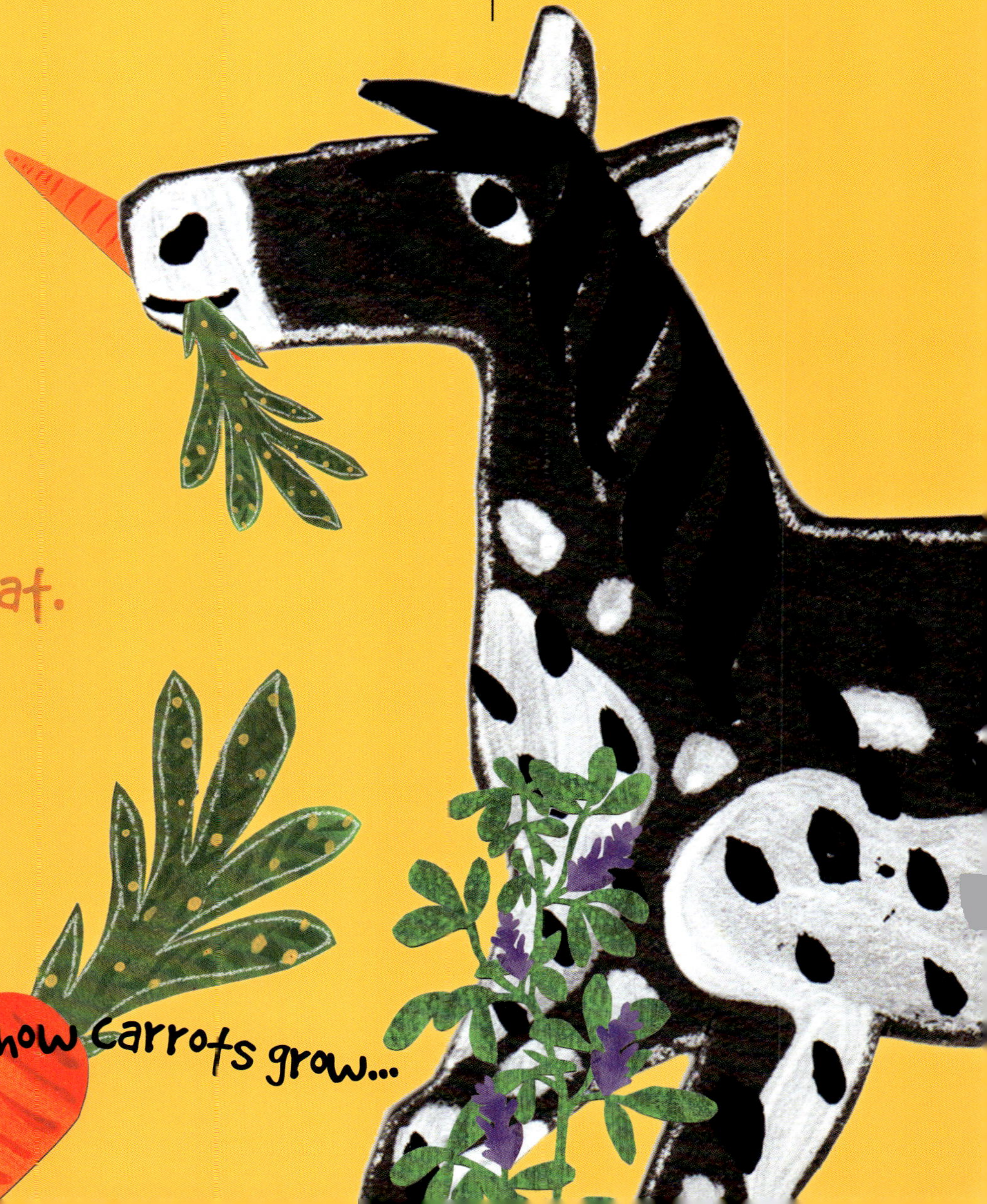

Sneak a peek on the next page to see how carrots grow...

Dd

Dig in for Dinner

Look down. Vegetables are hiding in the deep dark soil.

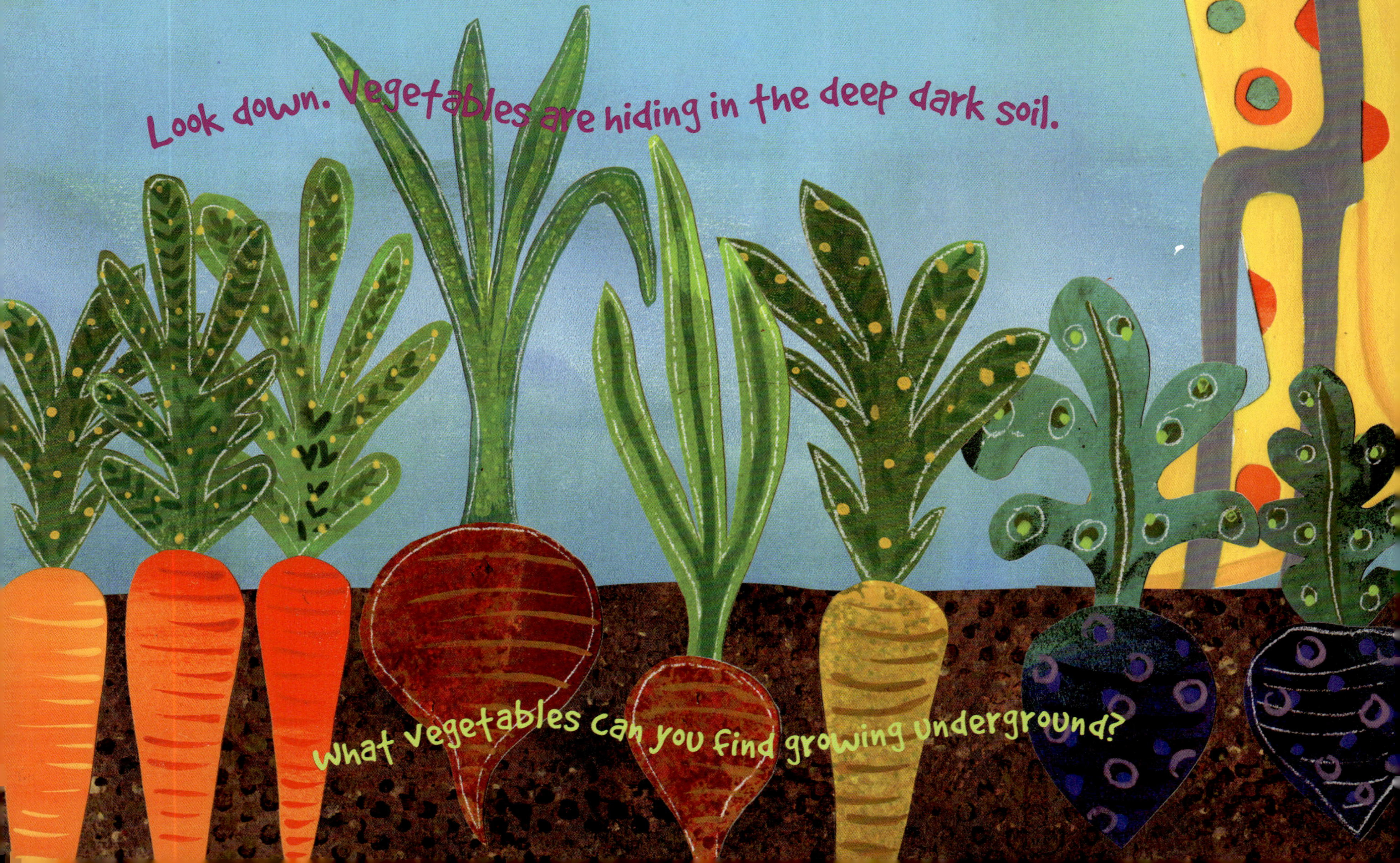

What vegetables can you find growing underground?

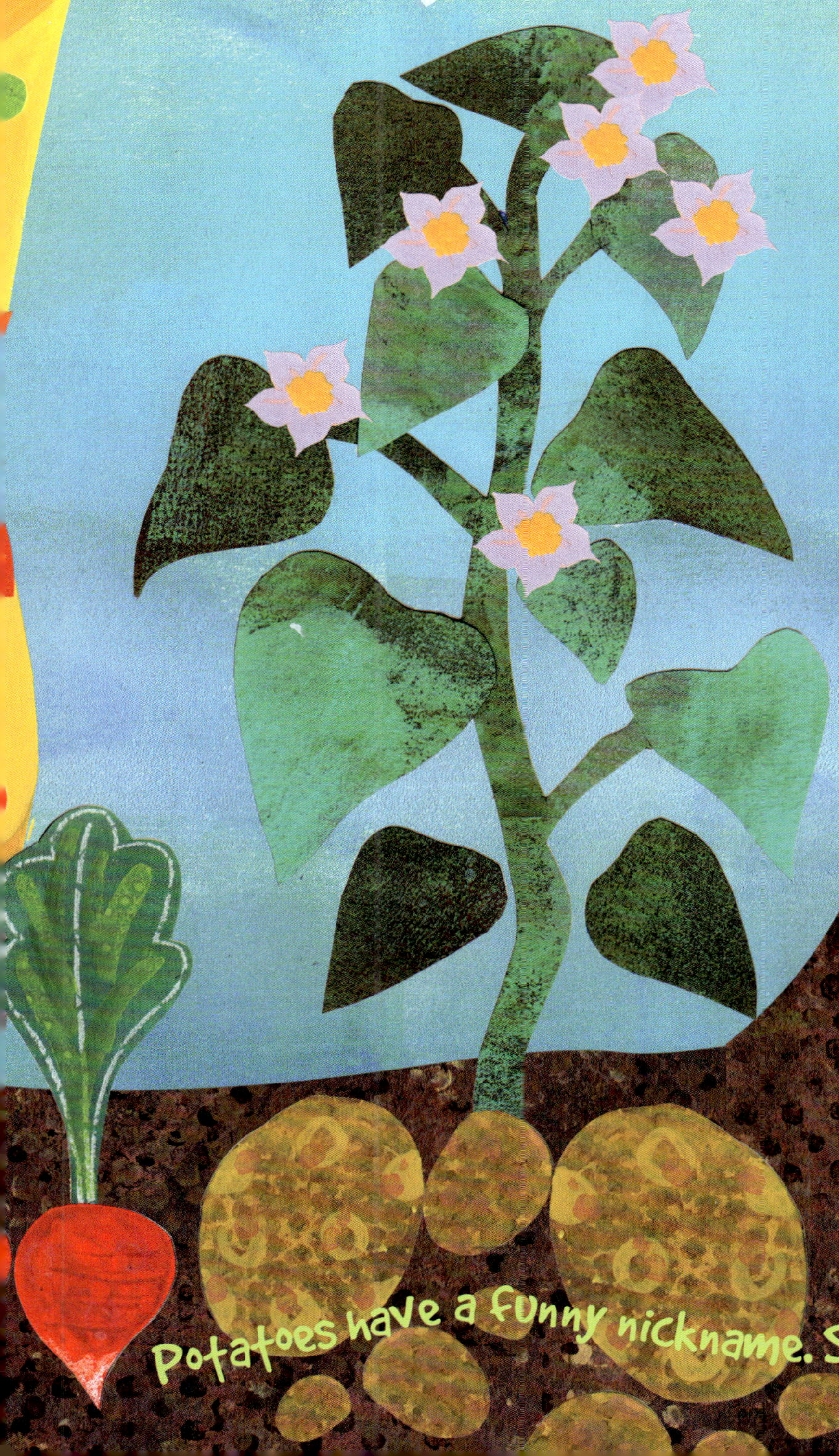

Something magical is happening underground.

Root vegetables are drawing in nutrients from the rich soil and slowly developing from tiny seeds into bumpy globes and cone-shape wonders. Dig down, grab onto a leafy top and give it a good yank. **POP! out comes dinner.**

Did you know that there's a plant hiding inside every potato?

To grow a potato you plant a potato.

A plant sprouts from the seed potato's eyes. Leafy tops reach for the sky while roots dig down deeper into the earth. There, in the dark, something else happens. More potatoes grow from the plant's underground stems. These underground tubers are the part of the plant we eat. **Get digging!**

Potatoes have a funny nickname. Spuds. How do you like to eat your spuds?

Ee | Eager Ewes

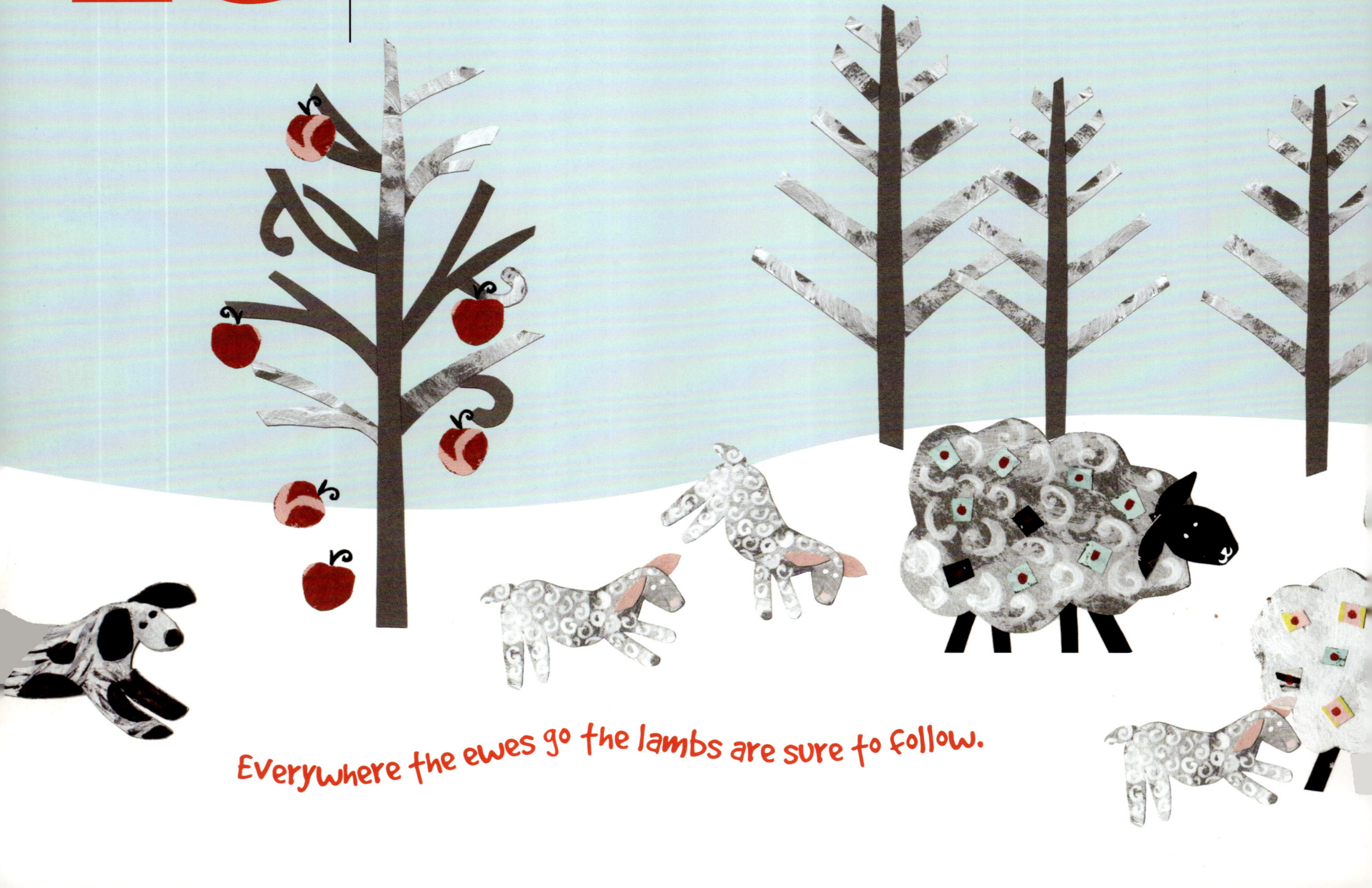

Everywhere the ewes go the lambs are sure to follow.

Five Fleecy Facts

1 **Female sheep are called ewes** and male sheep rams.

2 **Sheep do not like to be alone.** They flock together in groups and have a strong instinct to follow their leader. If the lead ram jumps over a stick and the stick is taken away, the other sheep will still jump over the spot where the stick was!

3 **Sheep eat grass and grain** and are called ruminants. This means they have four parts to their stomach.

4 **Sheep provide us with many useful things** like wool, meat, sheepskin, milk and cheese. Fat from sheep, called tallow, is used to make candles and soap.

5 **Sheep have an excellent sense of smell.** That's because they have scent glands in front of their eyes as well as on their feet. They sure don't like to get their feet wet!

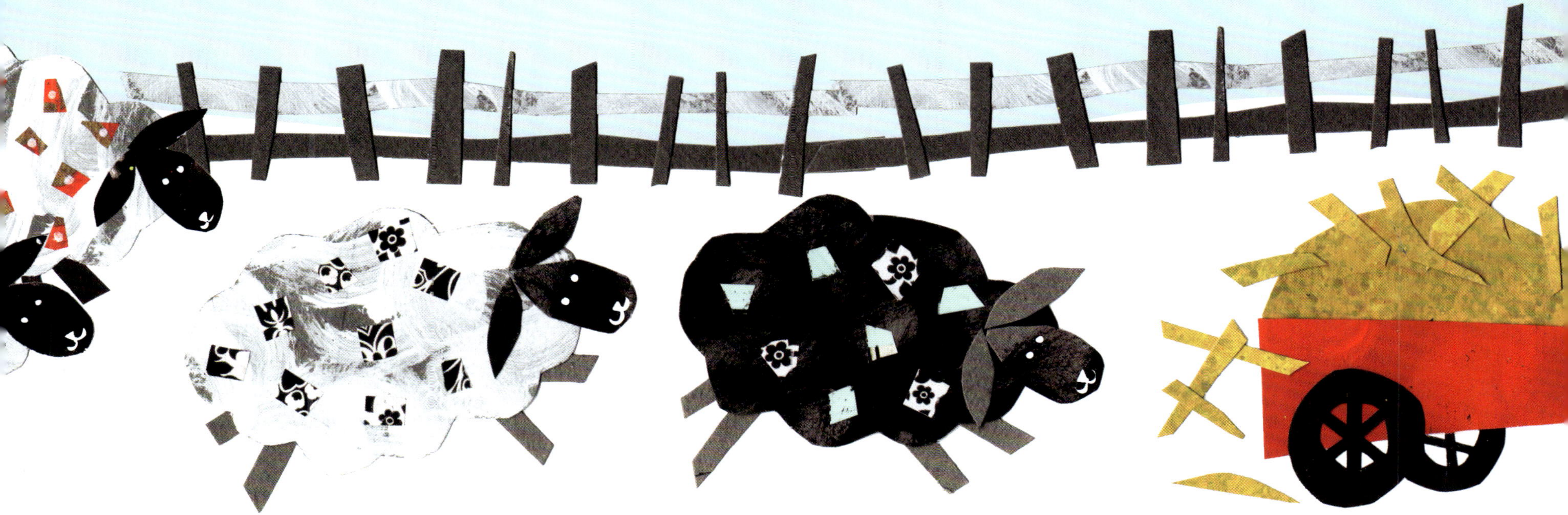

Ff

Flip Flop Fry

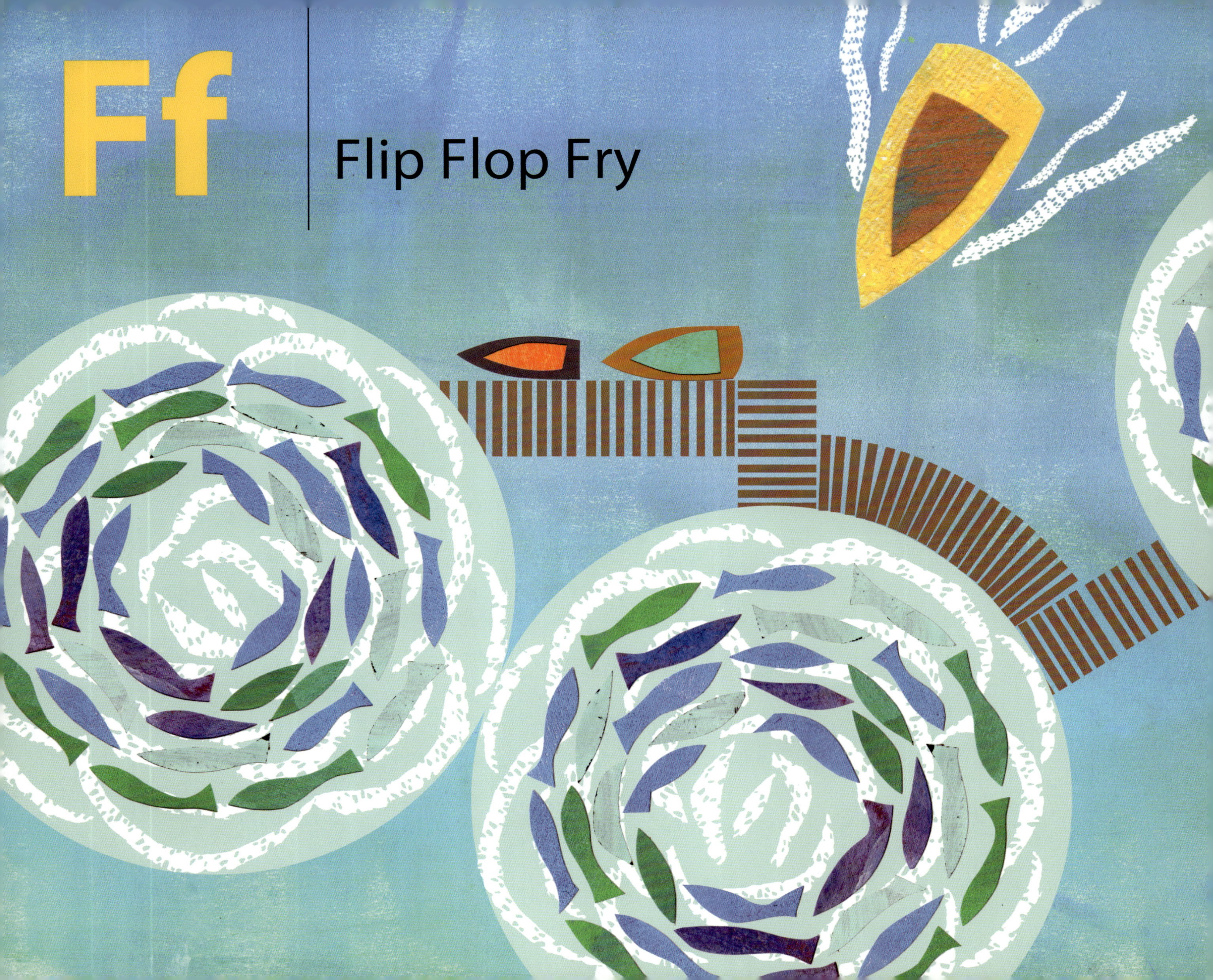

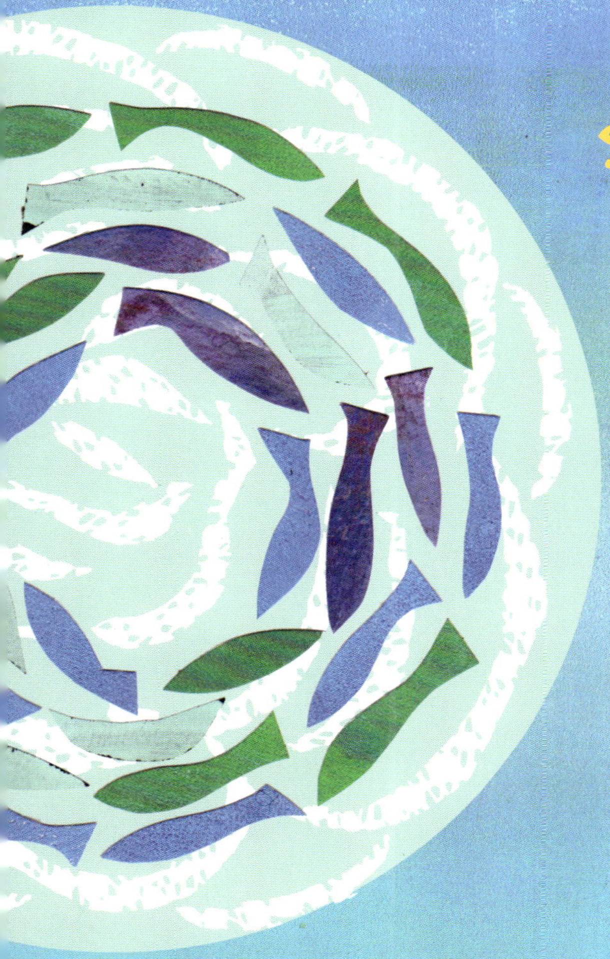

See the flashes of silver fins on the water? It's young salmon fry on a fish farm.

Did you know that some farms are on water? Aquaculture (ah-kwuh-kul-cher) is the name for the farming of plants and animals that live in water.

Young salmon, called fry, are raised in the ocean in floating cages where they are fed and have plenty of room to swim. These fry started their lives as eggs in a hatchery. When they were large enough the fry were moved here by boat to their saltwater farm. They will be reared here in tanks until they are fully-grown salmon.

Fish farms also raise shellfish. These are sea animals whose skeletons are on the outside of their bodies. Oysters, clams, scallops and mussels are raised in the ocean on floating farms until they are big enough to be harvested.

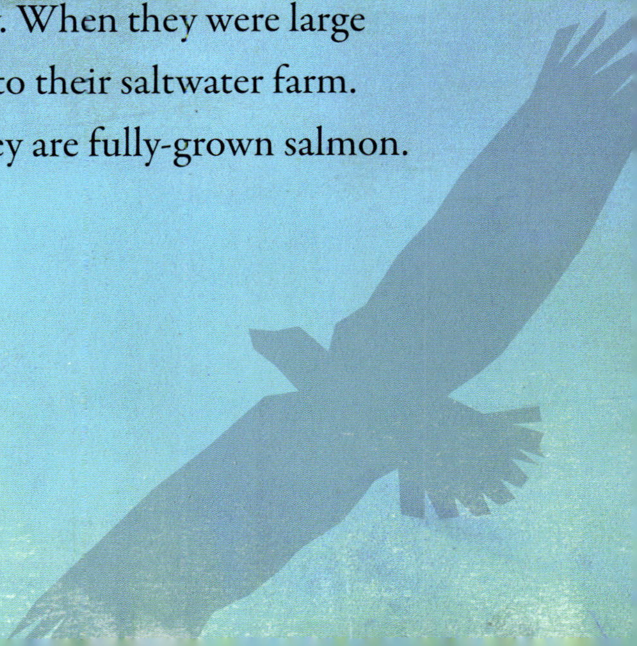

Gg

Gaggle of Giggling Geese

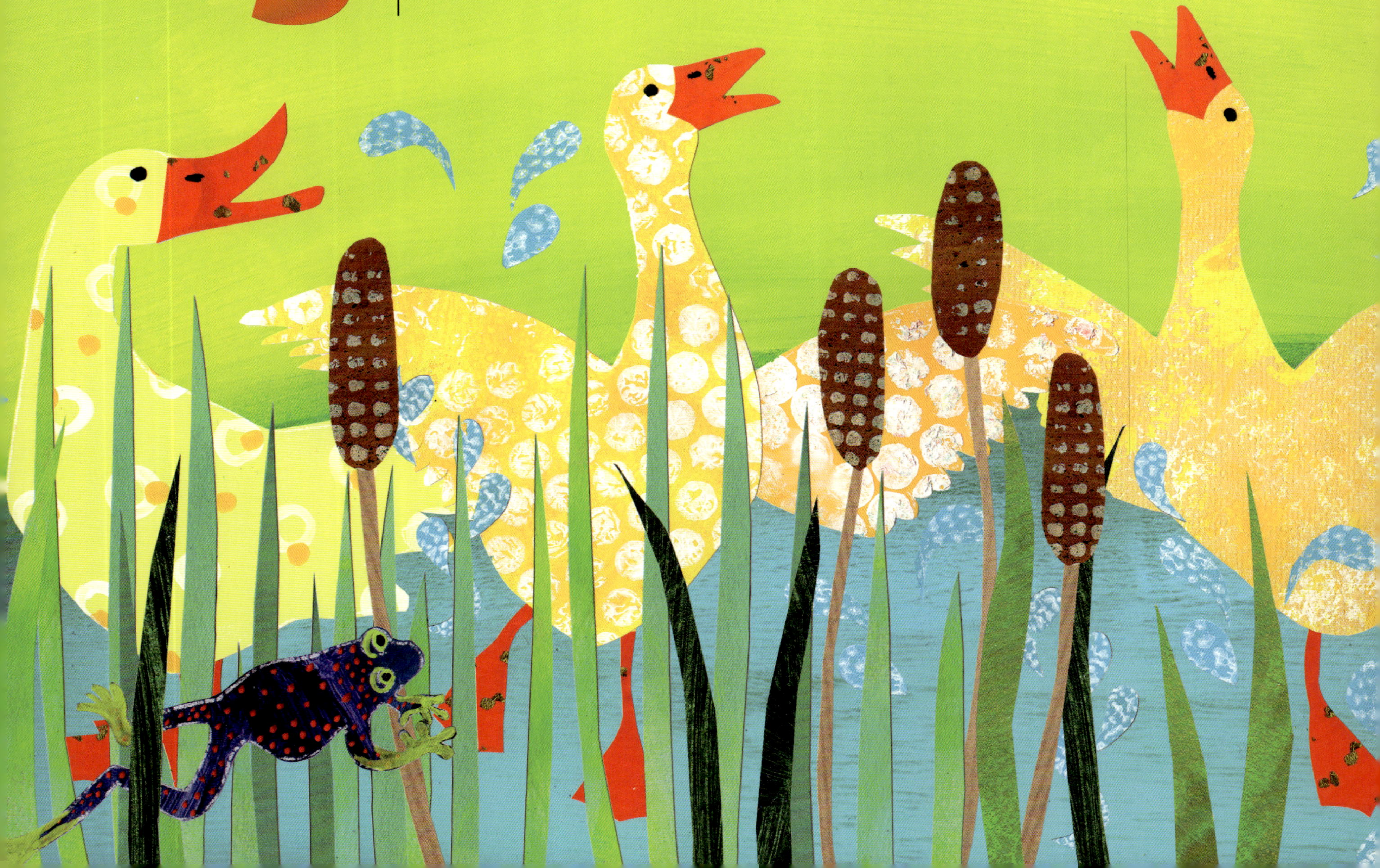

Geese don't really giggle. They honk. When they are mad they hiss.

Geese are good lawn mowers.

A goose's bill is shaped like a triangle, with sharp notches along the edges. The notches help a goose cut through dry grass and short plants which they love to eat. The geese eat the weeds but not the crops. This makes the farmer happy.

Geese honk for different reasons.

One honk means *"Hello"*. More than one honk usually means trouble. That's why geese make good guards on the farm. Loud honking is useful when predators such as raccoons or foxes sneak into the barnyard.

A group of geese is called a gaggle.

Although geese on a farm don't fly or swim like wild geese they love to frolic together in the water. It makes them giggle. **Can you giggle like a goose?**

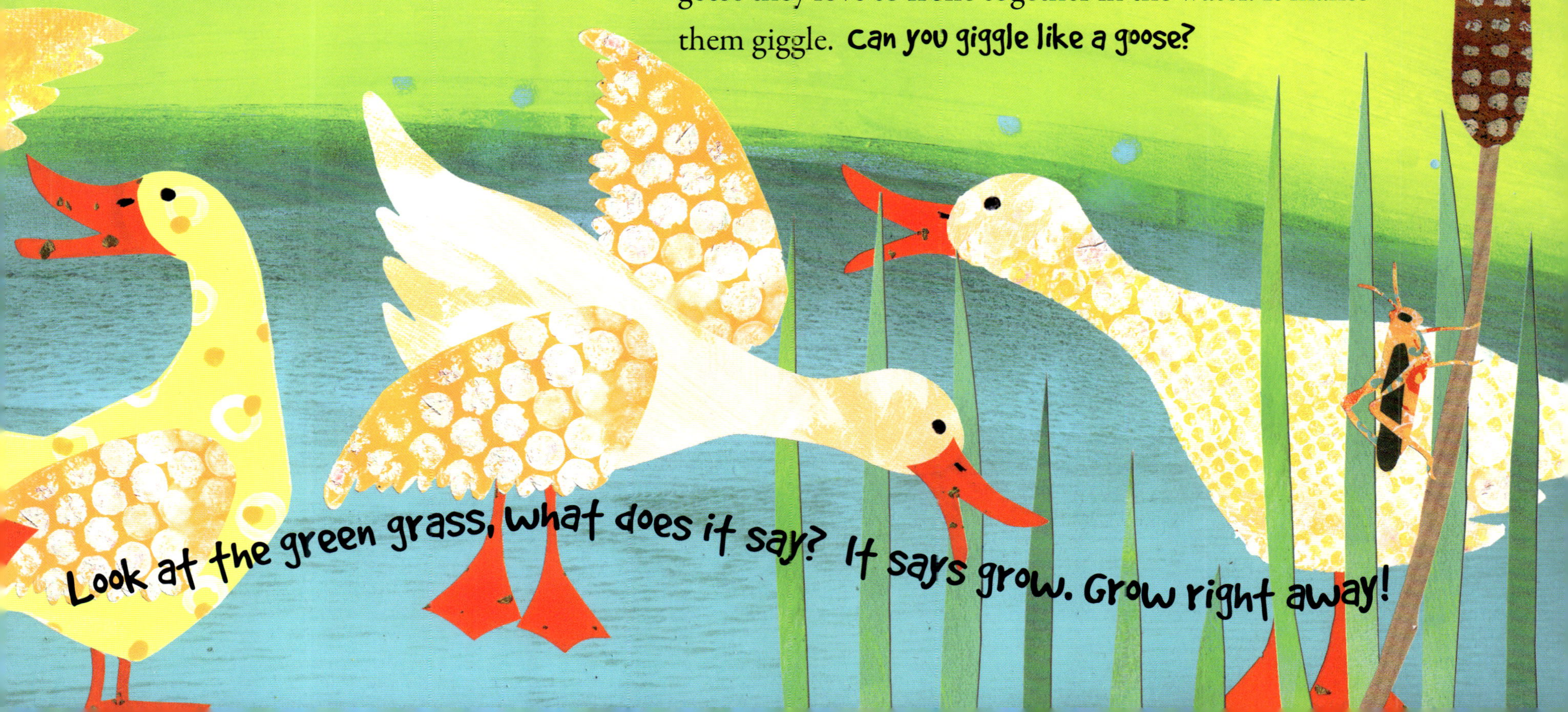

Look at the green grass, what does it say? It says grow. Grow right away!

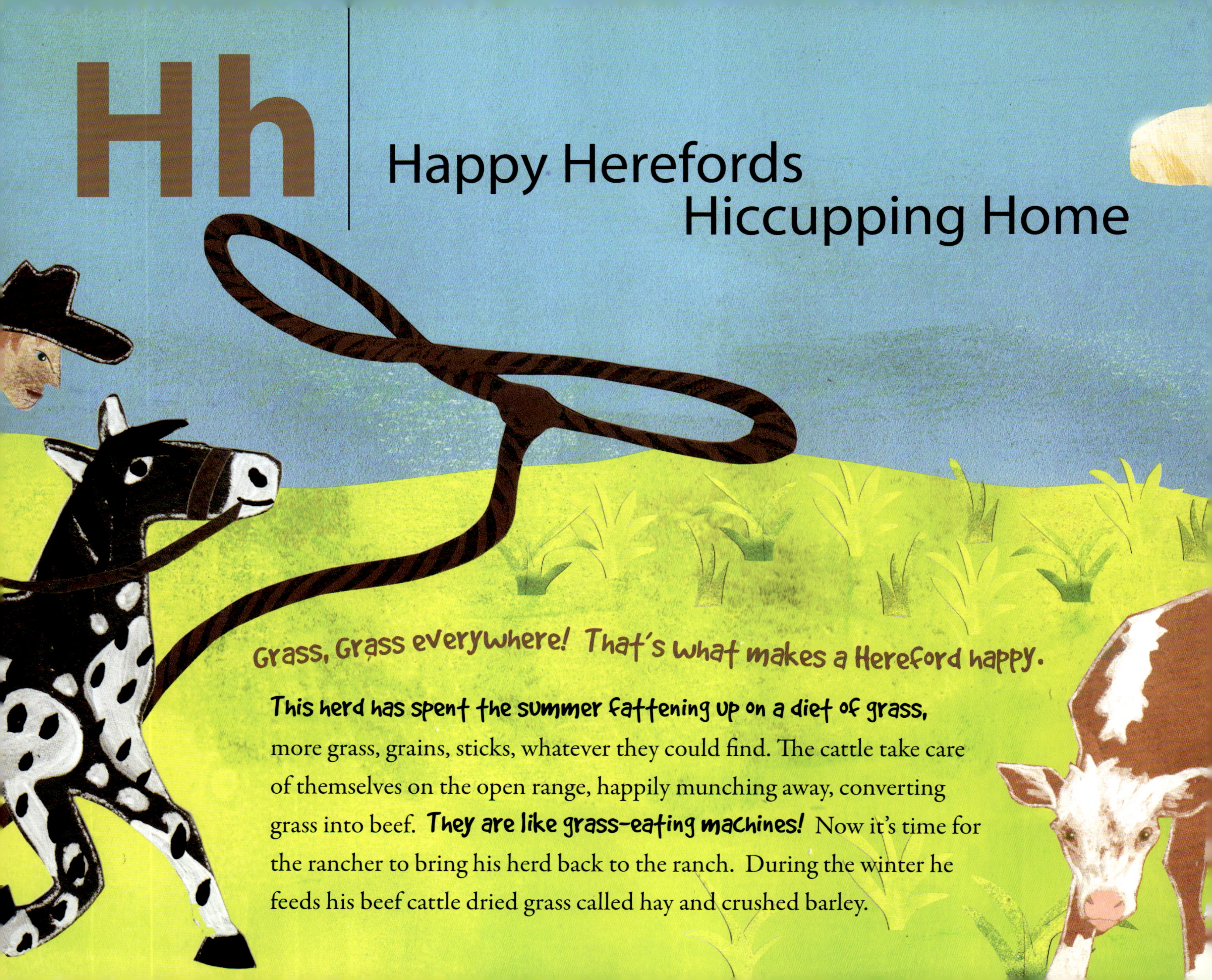

Hh

Happy Herefords Hiccupping Home

Grass, Grass everywhere! That's what makes a Hereford happy.

This herd has spent the summer fattening up on a diet of grass, more grass, grains, sticks, whatever they could find. The cattle take care of themselves on the open range, happily munching away, converting grass into beef. **They are like grass-eating machines!** Now it's time for the rancher to bring his herd back to the ranch. During the winter he feeds his beef cattle dried grass called hay and crushed barley.

A cow spends all day eating and chewing her cud. That's because she is a ruminant. While most animals like us only have one stomach to fill, a ruminant has four. Food is stored in one part called the rumen. When this is full, the cow lies down, **hiccups-up** portions of food, re-chews and re-swallows sending it to the other three stomachs to be digested. **That's chewing the cud.**

Cows have lots of names. Only mother cows should be called cows. A young female is a heifer. Males are called bulls or steers. Together they are called cattle. **A group of cattle is a herd.**

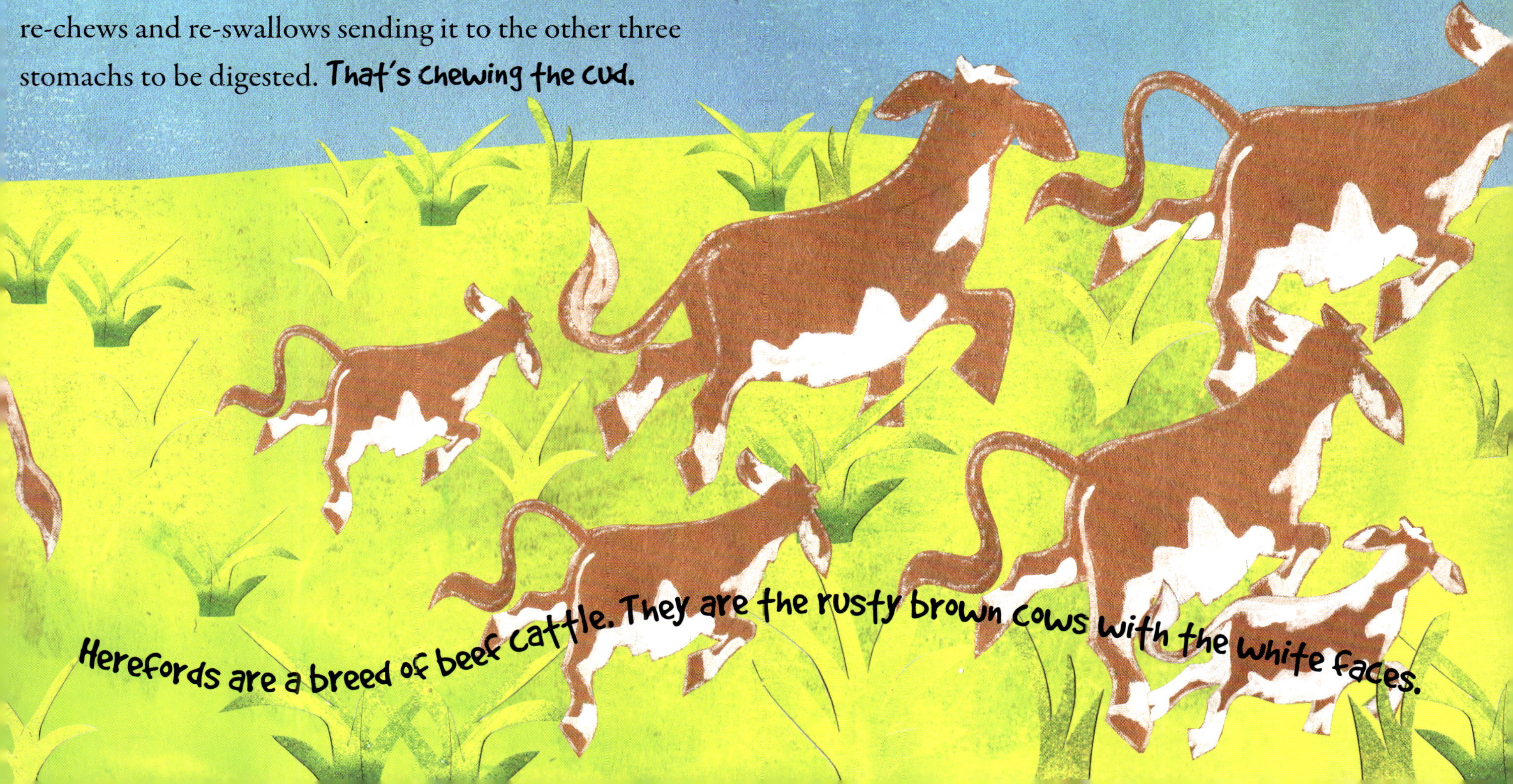

Herefords are a breed of beef cattle. They are the rusty brown cows with the white faces.

Ii

Icy Ice Cream

Frosty, creamy, smooth and sweet – ice cream is my favourite treat!

Feel the icy ice cream tingle your tongue, just like fresh snowflakes. So good and so simple, ice cream is made by mixing milk or cream with flavours and sweeteners and slowly cooling it down until it freezes. Vanilla, chocolate, strawberry, cookies and cream, pumpkin pie – **what's your favourite flavour?**

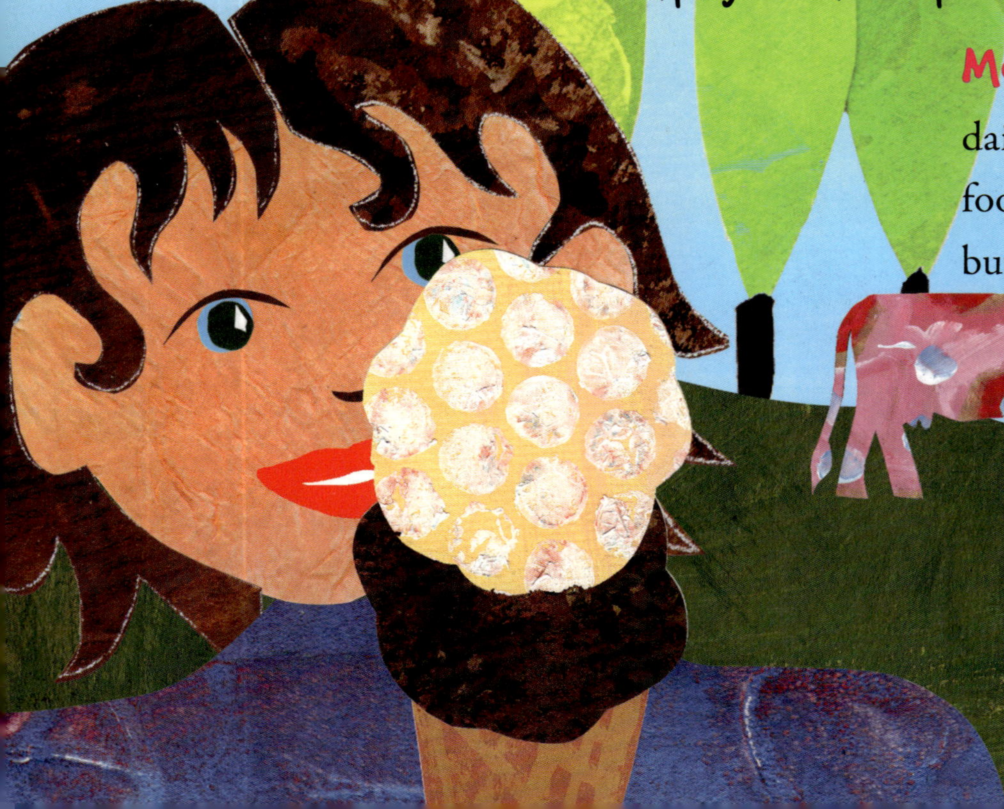

Most of the milk we drink comes from dairy cows. We use milk to make lots of good foods like yogurt, sour cream, whipping cream, butter and cheese. Ice cream too.

Do you want to have strong bones and muscles? Drink lots of milk. It's full of calcium and protein.

Jj

Juggling, Jiggly Jams and Jellies

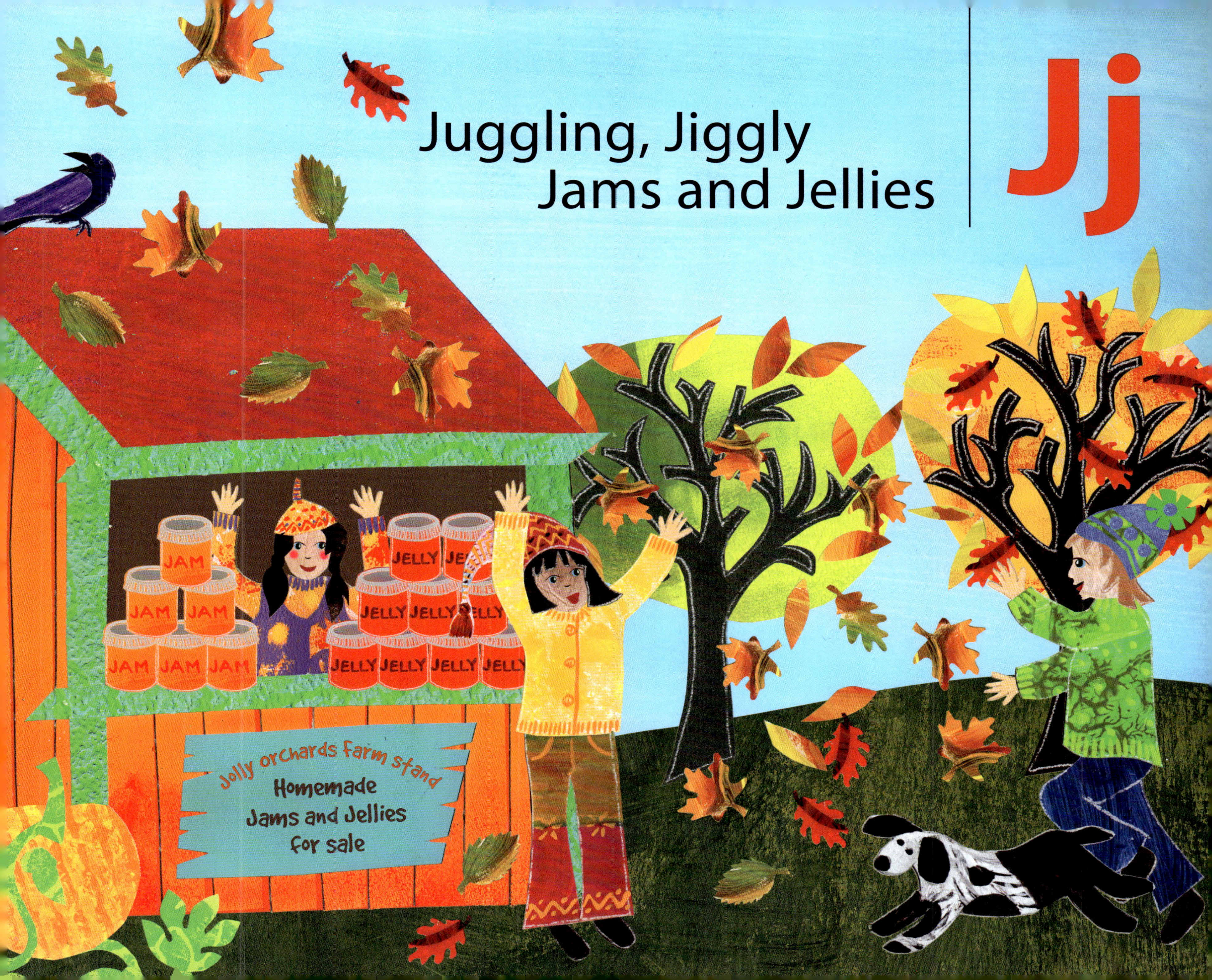

Kk

King-sized Kohlrabi

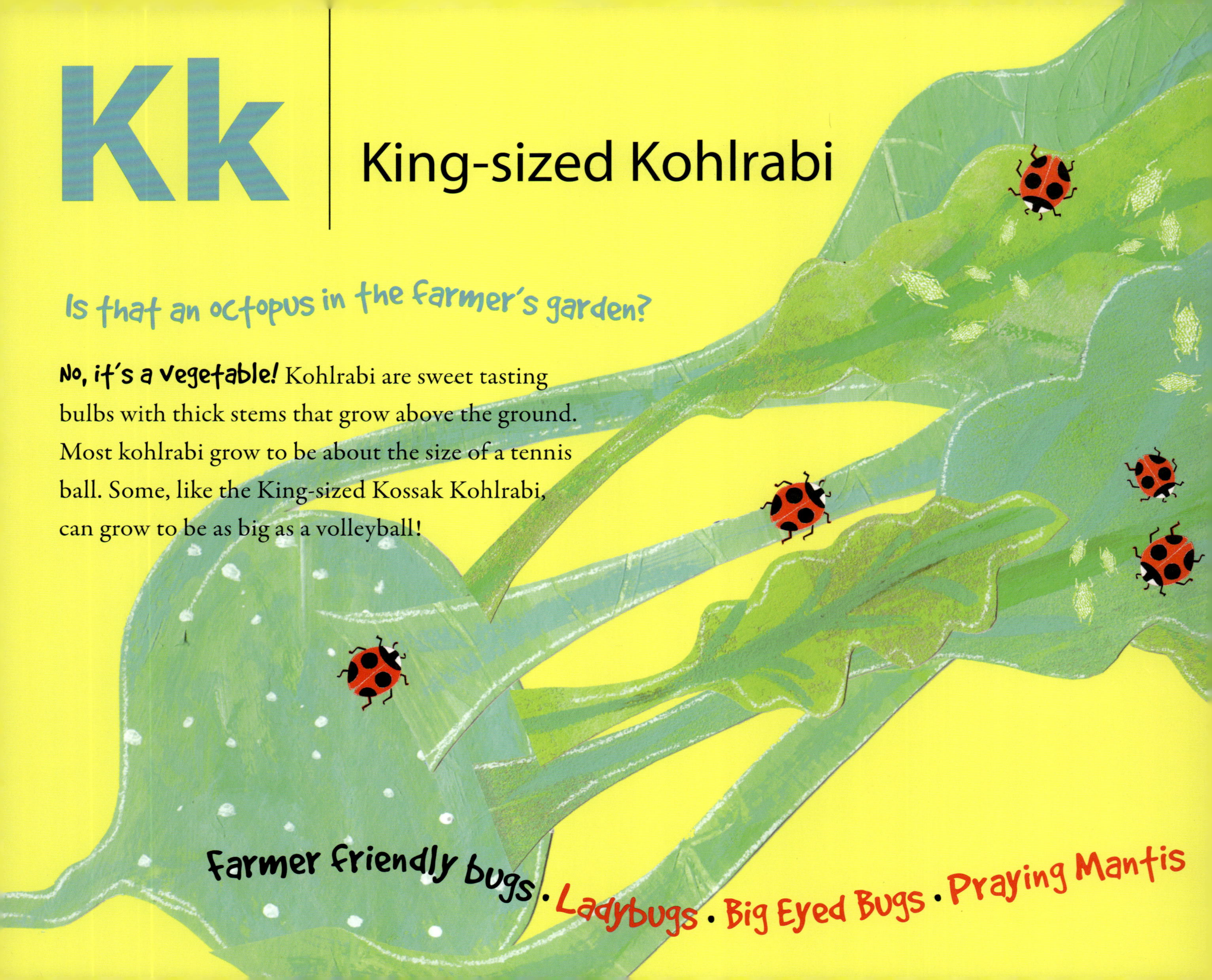

Is that an octopus in the farmer's garden?

No, it's a vegetable! Kohlrabi are sweet tasting bulbs with thick stems that grow above the ground. Most kohlrabi grow to be about the size of a tennis ball. Some, like the King-sized Kossak Kohlrabi, can grow to be as big as a volleyball!

Farmer friendly bugs · Ladybugs · Big Eyed Bugs · Praying Mantis

Ladybug's Lune

Ll

Look out APHIDS! Here comes ladybug and she's hungry!

Ladybugs are always hungry and will spend all day munching on their favourite snack, juicy green aphids. During her lifetime of about 1 year one little ladybug may eat as many as 5,000 aphids. No wonder farmers love ladybugs and use them as a natural way to keep aphids from harming their crops.

Ladybug Lore

- Ladybugs, also called ladybirds, are a type of beetle.
- Not all ladybugs are **ladies**. Some are **lads**.
- Most ladybugs are red or orange with black spots, but some have no spots at all.
- Ladybugs produce a bad smelling chemical that turns other bugs off eating them.
- Ladybugs hibernate for the winter.

Hover Flies • Green Lacewings • Spiders • Soldier Beetles • Damsel Bugs

Mm

Making Merry in the Mud and Muck

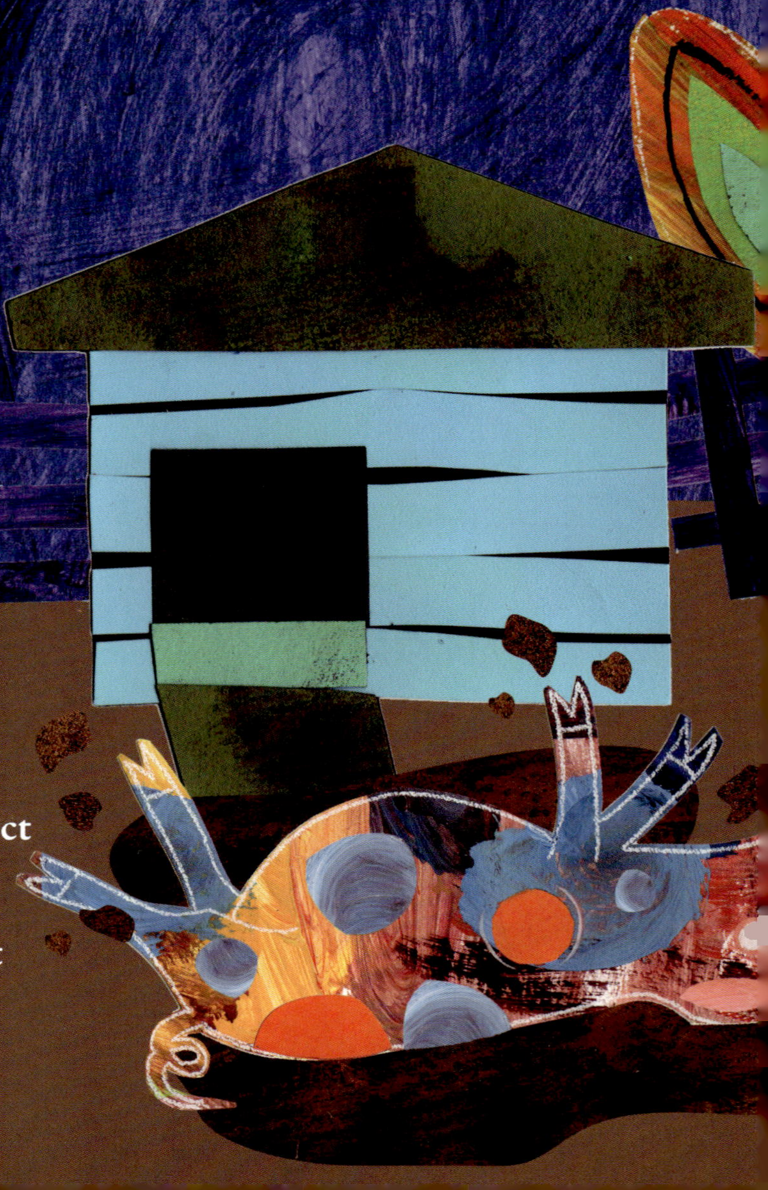

Pigs are misunderstood. Many people think pigs are dirty animals because they roll in mud. Pigs need to roll in wet mud to cool down. The mud also protects the pig's sensitive skin from insect bites and sunburn. Pigs are some of the cleanest animals in the barnyard and will get upset if their sty or bed is dirty. A pig will eat and sleep as far away as he can from his manure pile. So, next time you see a muddy pig don't call him dirty!

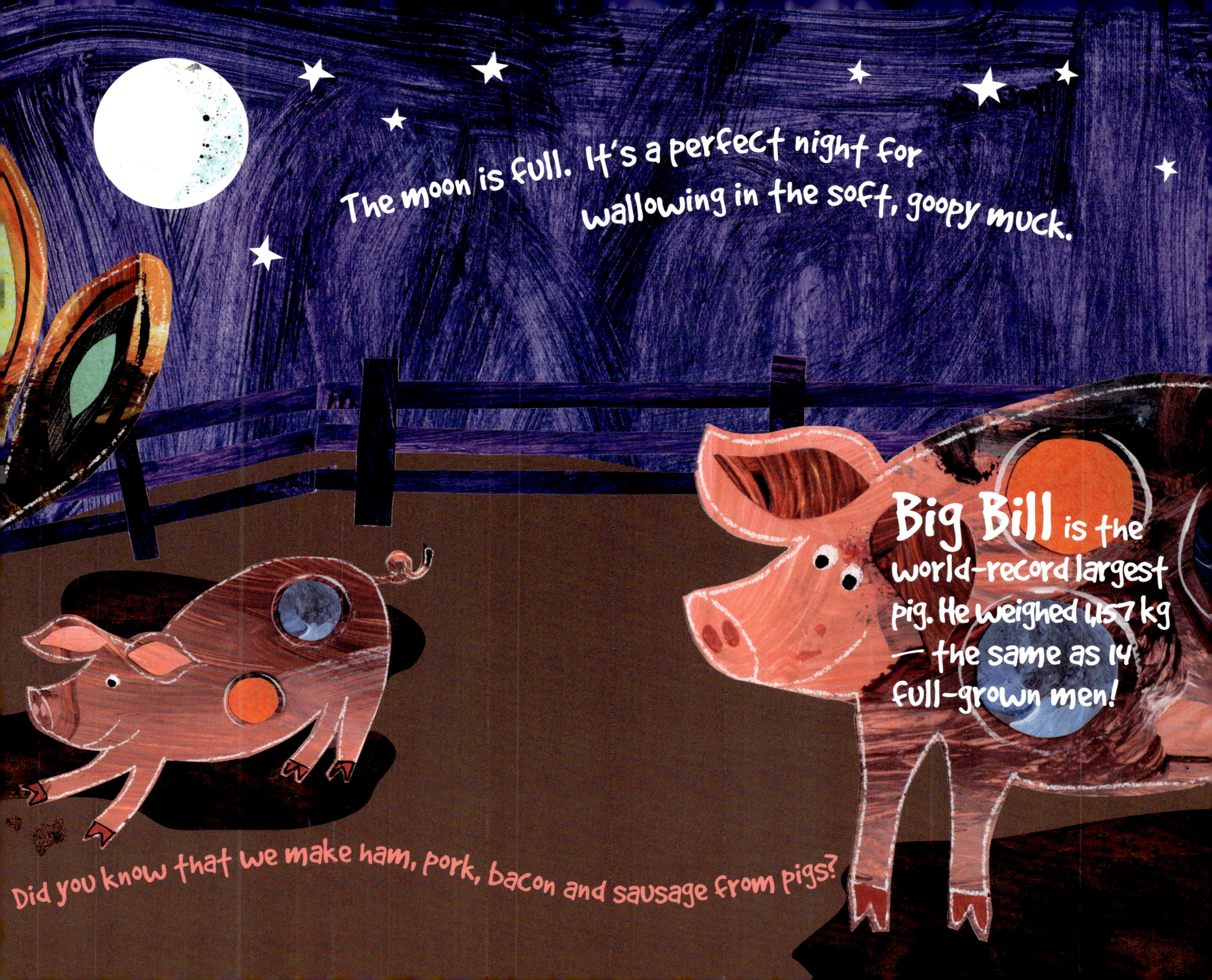

The moon is full. It's a perfect night for wallowing in the soft, goopy muck.

Big Bill is the world-record largest pig. He weighed 1,157 kg — the same as 14 full-grown men!

Did you know that we make ham, pork, bacon and sausage from pigs?

Nn

Nibbling Nectar

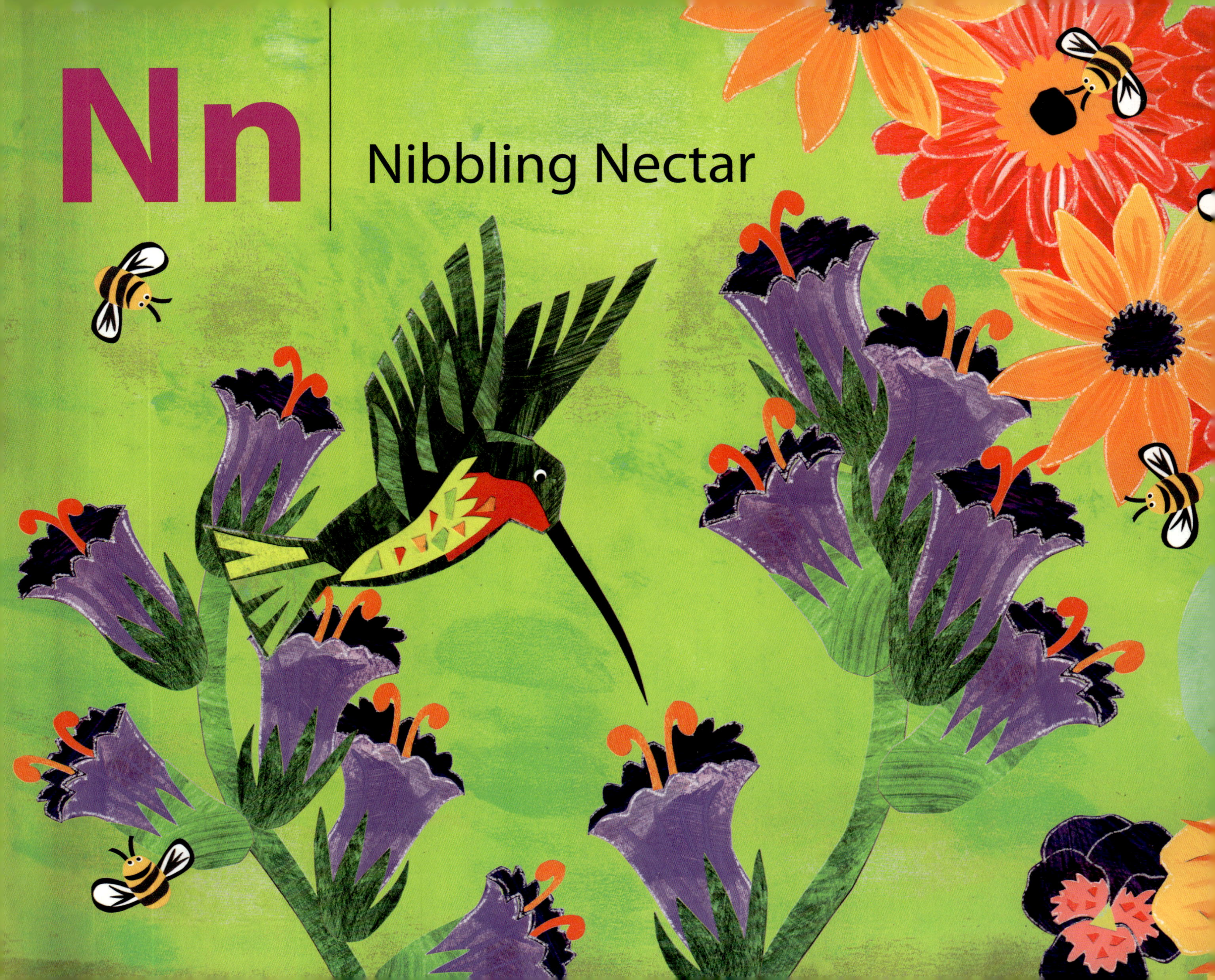

The hummingbird nuzzles his long beak into the funnel-shaped flower. What is he nibbling on?

Like the butterfly, the hummingbird is feeding on the sugary nectar within the flower. The sticky pollen and nectar from the flower clings to their bodies and is carried to the next flower they visit. This is called pollination and it helps plants to reproduce.

Pollinators are attracted to flowers by their colour, fragrance and shape. A nice wide nasturtium petal is the perfect resting spot for a butterfly.

Bees are star pollinators.
Birds and bats pollinate flowers too and some plants such as grains, trees and grasses even use the wind to pollinate.

Oo Oh! Overalls in the Orchard

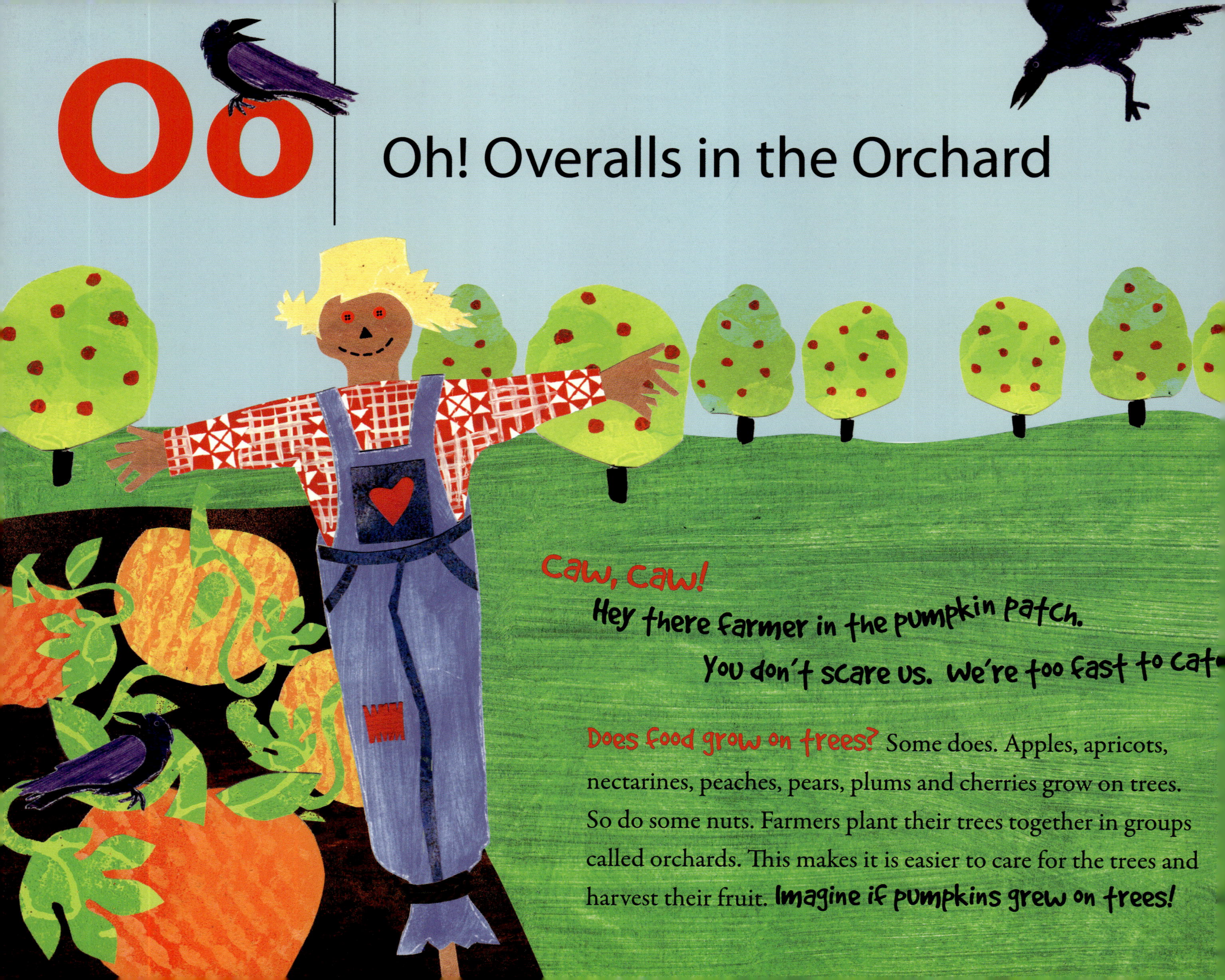

Caw, caw!
Hey there farmer in the pumpkin patch.
You don't scare us. We're too fast to cat

Does food grow on trees? Some does. Apples, apricots, nectarines, peaches, pears, plums and cherries grow on trees. So do some nuts. Farmers plant their trees together in groups called orchards. This makes it is easier to care for the trees and harvest their fruit. **Imagine if pumpkins grew on trees!**

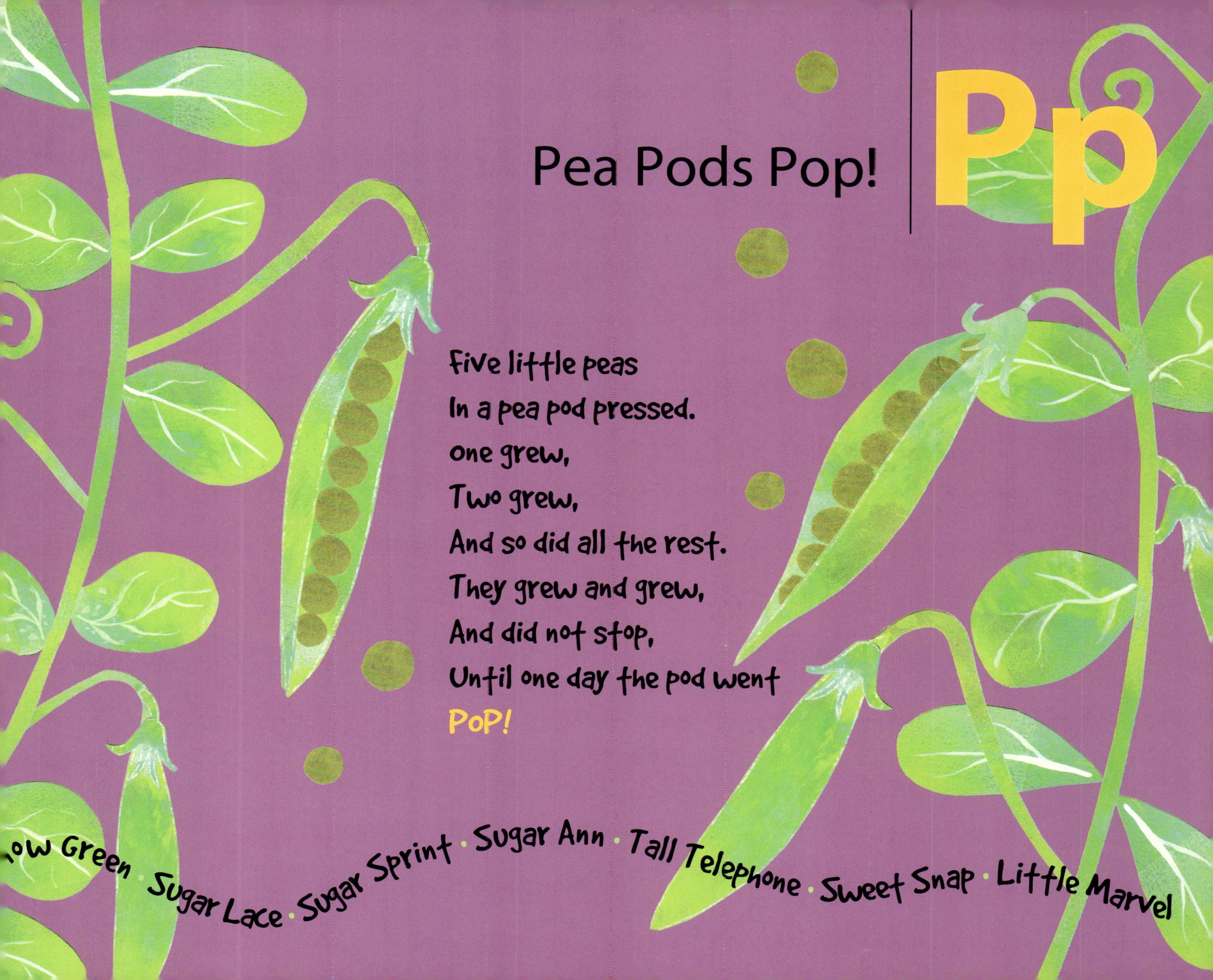

Pp

Pea Pods Pop!

Five little peas
In a pea pod pressed.
One grew,
Two grew,
And so did all the rest.
They grew and grew,
And did not stop,
Until one day the pod went
POP!

ow Green · Sugar Lace · Sugar Sprint · Sugar Ann · Tall Telephone · Sweet Snap · Little Marvel

Qq

Quietly Queuing for the Queen

All is quiet in the hive as the queen bee waits for her workers to arrive.

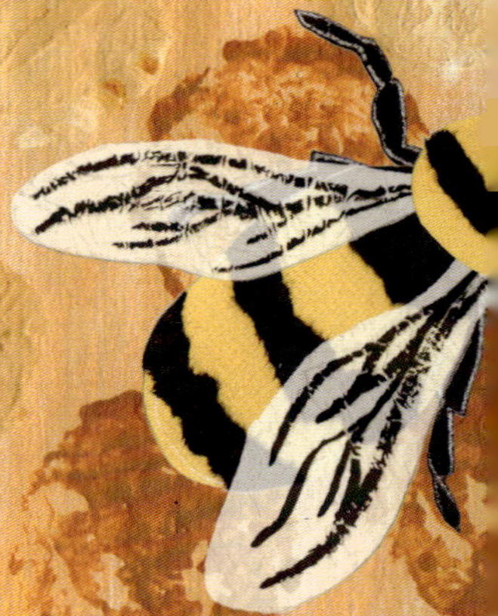

The queen is the largest bee and is the mother of all the bees in the colony. The male bees are called drones. Their only job is to stay in the hive and mate with the queen. Her daughters, the worker bees, do all the work. They leave the nest to gather sweet nectar and pollen to feed their queen and her new larvae. They also make honey from the nectar they have collected. Only the female bees have stingers. They guard the hive and protect their queen.

The beekeeper waits too. His bee farm is called an apiary (a-pee-air-ee) and he provides a place for the colony to live. He waits until the worker bees have converted the collected nectar into honey and stored it in their honeycombs. The beekeeper harvests only the extra honey. **He will do his job quietly and quickly so as not to disturb the bees.**

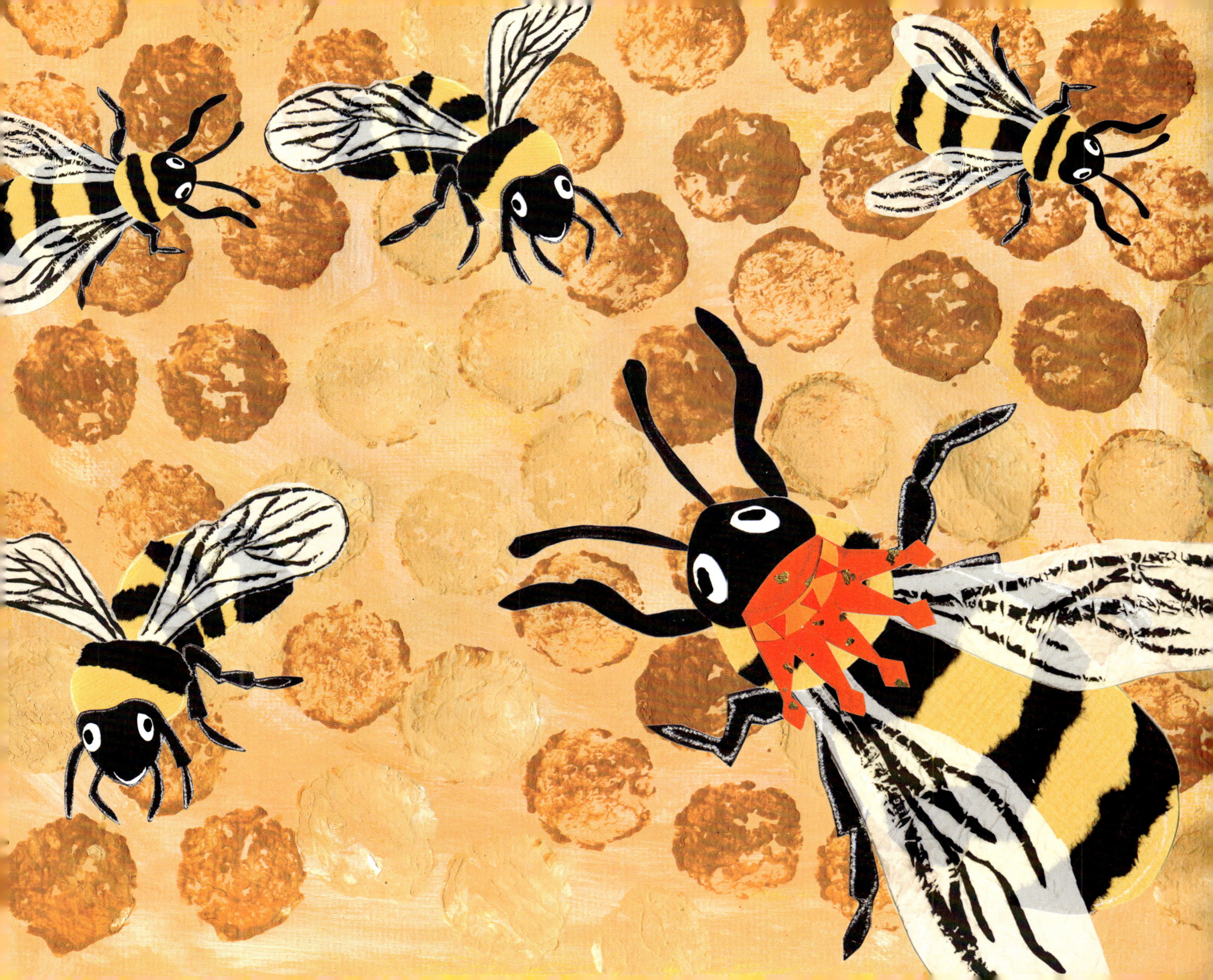

Rr

Reliable Red Rooster

The rooster rises with the sun every day on the farm. What a racket he makes!

The rooster doesn't just crow in the morning. He's very noisy and will crow at any time of the day, all day long. That's because a rooster crows to let the hens know when he's found something good to eat, or to warn them of trouble in the barnyard. He will also crow to let other roosters in the neighbourhood know who's in charge.

Hens are much quieter. They cluck when they are startled or when they lay an egg.

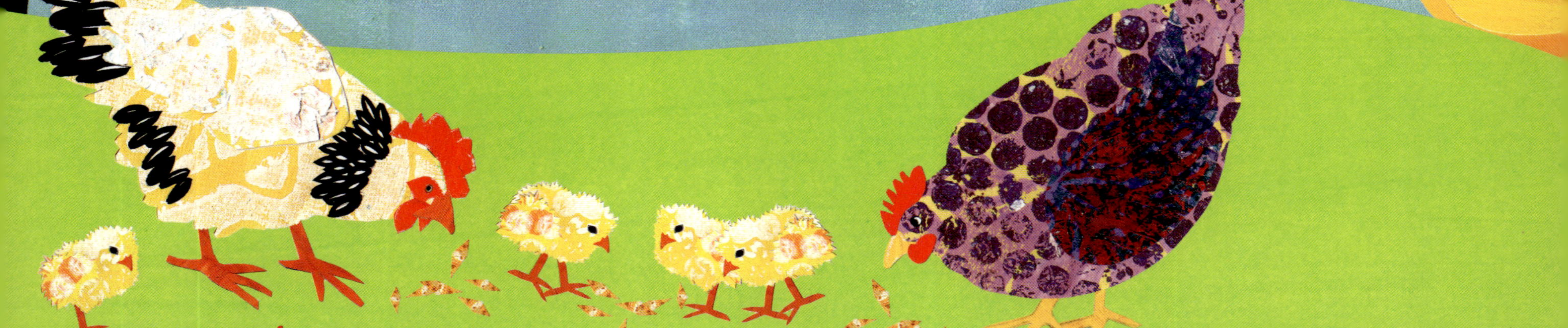

Bardrock • Bantam • Sebright • Silkie • Buff orpington • Jersey Giant • Leghorn

Five Fowl Facts

The chicken is the closest living relative to the Tyrannosaurus Rex.

Chickens don't have teeth. They swallow bits of grit and gravel to help grind up hard foods like grain in their gizzards.

3 There are more chickens than people in the world.

4 If there is no rooster in a flock a hen will take over, stop laying eggs and start crowing.

5 A chicken can run up to 14.5 km per hour.

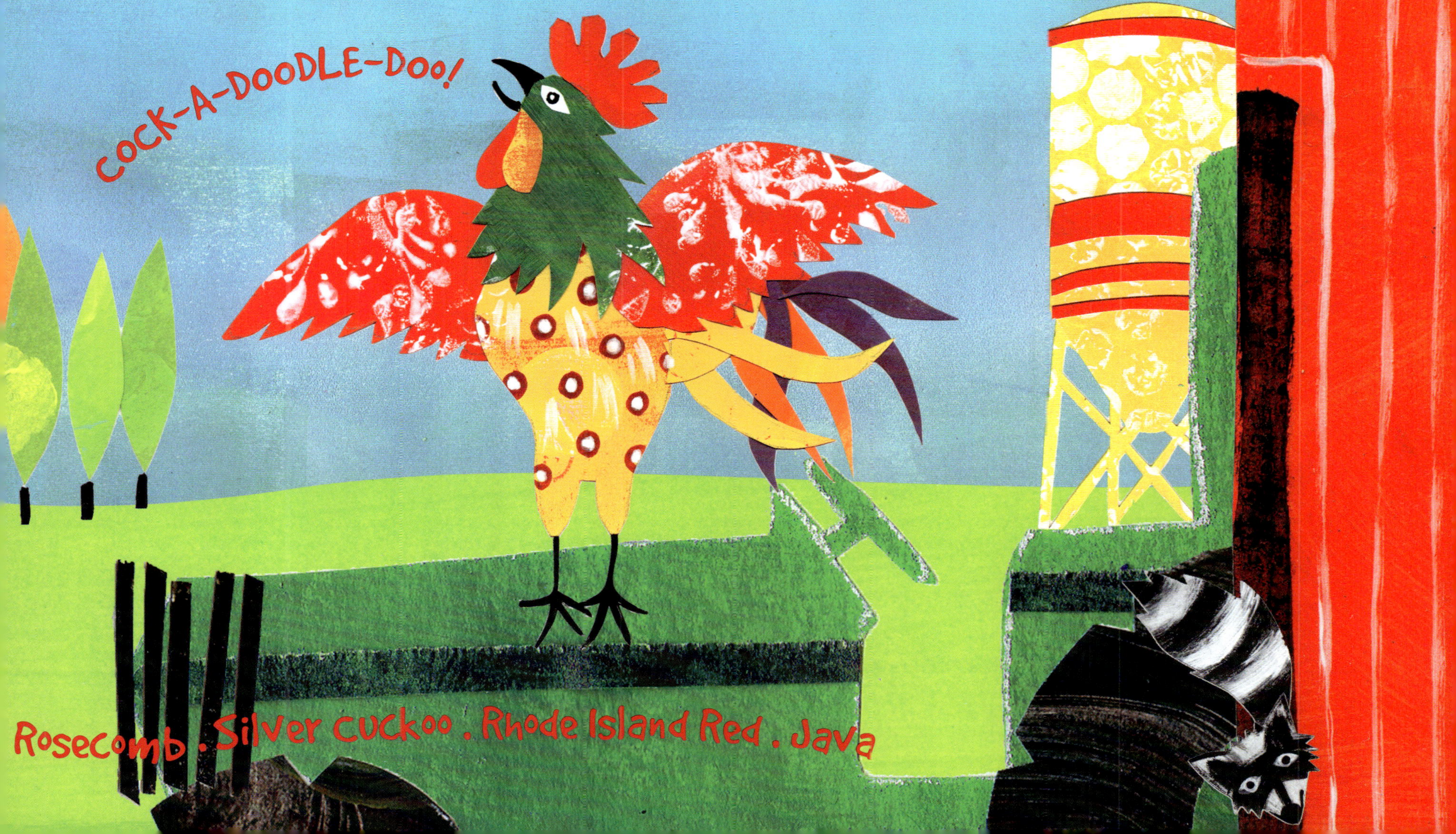

Rosecomb . Silver Cuckoo . Rhode Island Red . Java

Ss

Stink, Stank, Stunk

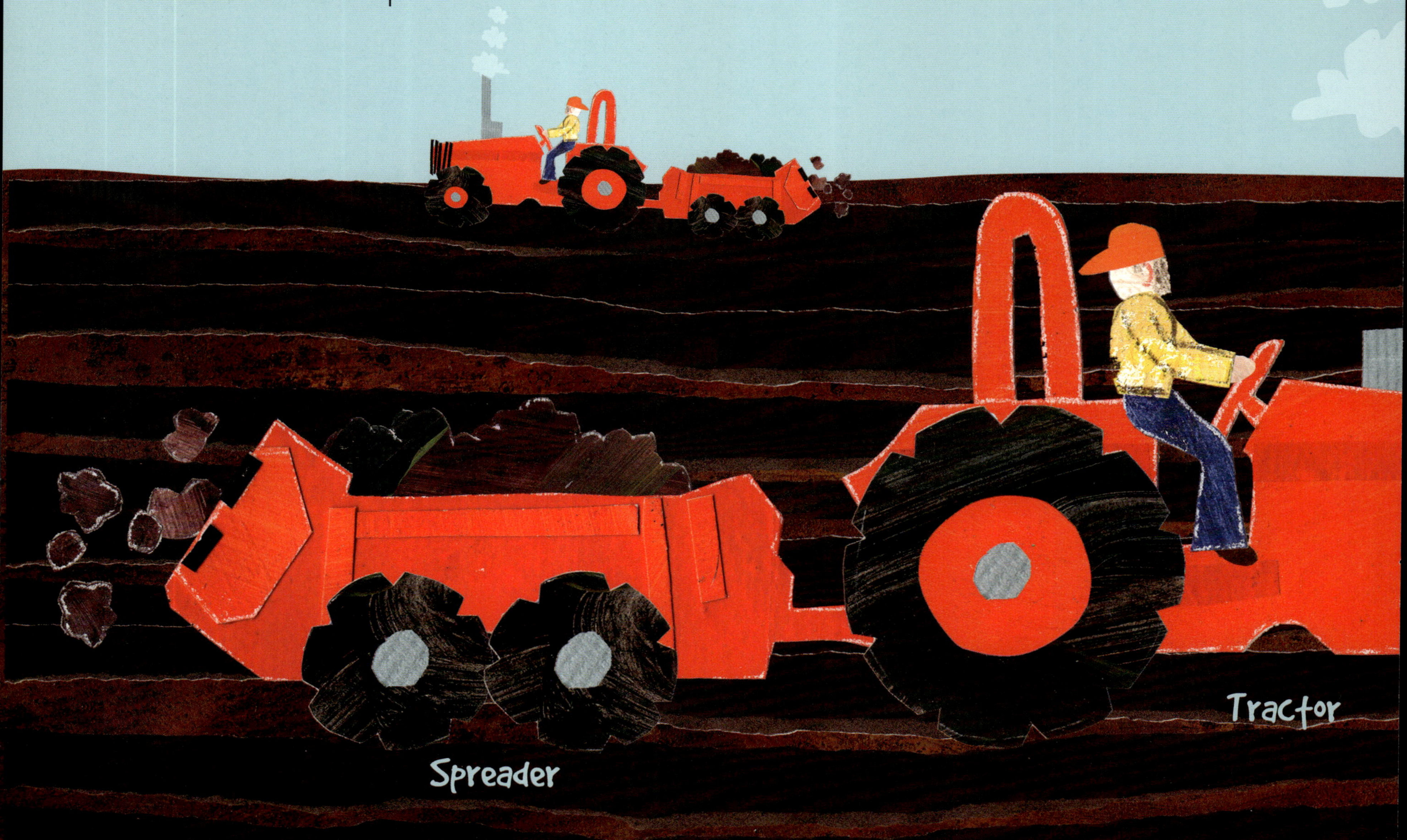

The farmer uses a spreader to spread manure on her fields. It stinks! To the farmer it's a good smell. It's food for her soil and her crops.

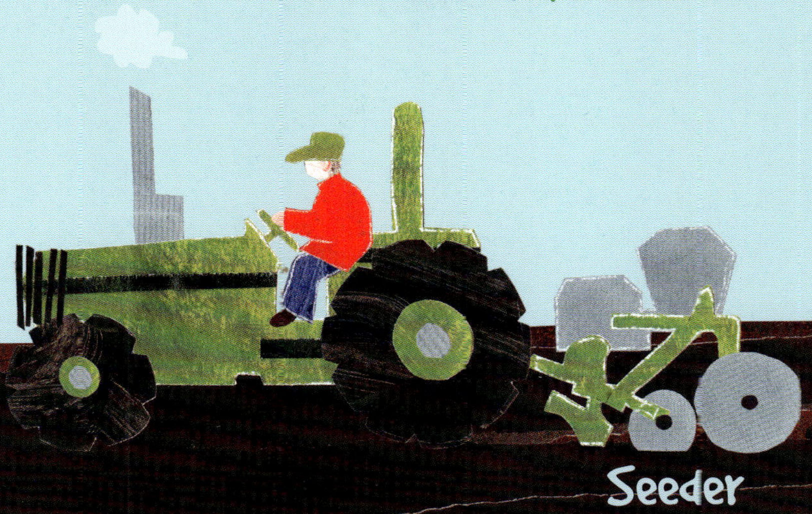

Soil has a secret ingredient called humus. Humus is rich dark earth made from rotting vegetables and animal waste. At home we put food scraps in our compost pile to make humus for our garden. The farmer takes manure from her animals and piles it up to make a huge compost pile.

Worms, insects, snails and small rodents help out by creating tunnels that allow air to enter and decompose the pile. The farmer adds the nutrient-rich composted manure to the soil to help her crops grow.

The largest worm ever found was 7 meters long. That's longer than a tractor!

Tt

Tip Top Tasty Tomato

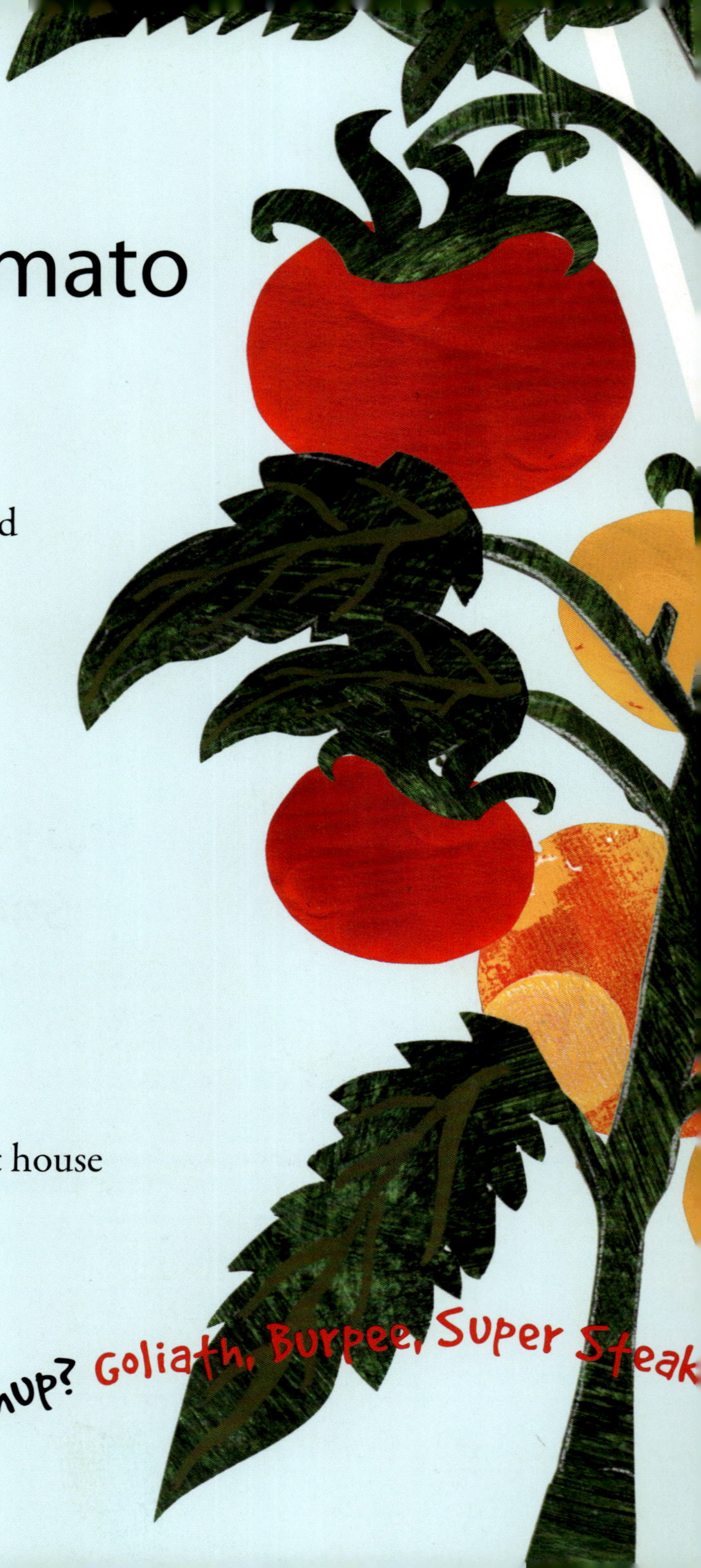

It's an easy life for a Hot House Tomato, a Sweet Bell Pepper and a Long English Cucumber. They have everything they need to grow inside their toasty greenhouse and they are safe from harsh weather and pesky insects.

Is a tomato a fruit or a vegetable? A vegetable is the edible stem, leaves or roots of a plant. A fruit is the edible part of the plant that contains the seeds. Since we eat the part with the seeds a tomato is a fruit!

These tomato plants like it so much in their hot house that they may grow up to 10 metres long.

Guess which of these tomatoes is used to make ketchup? Goliath, Burpee, Super Steak

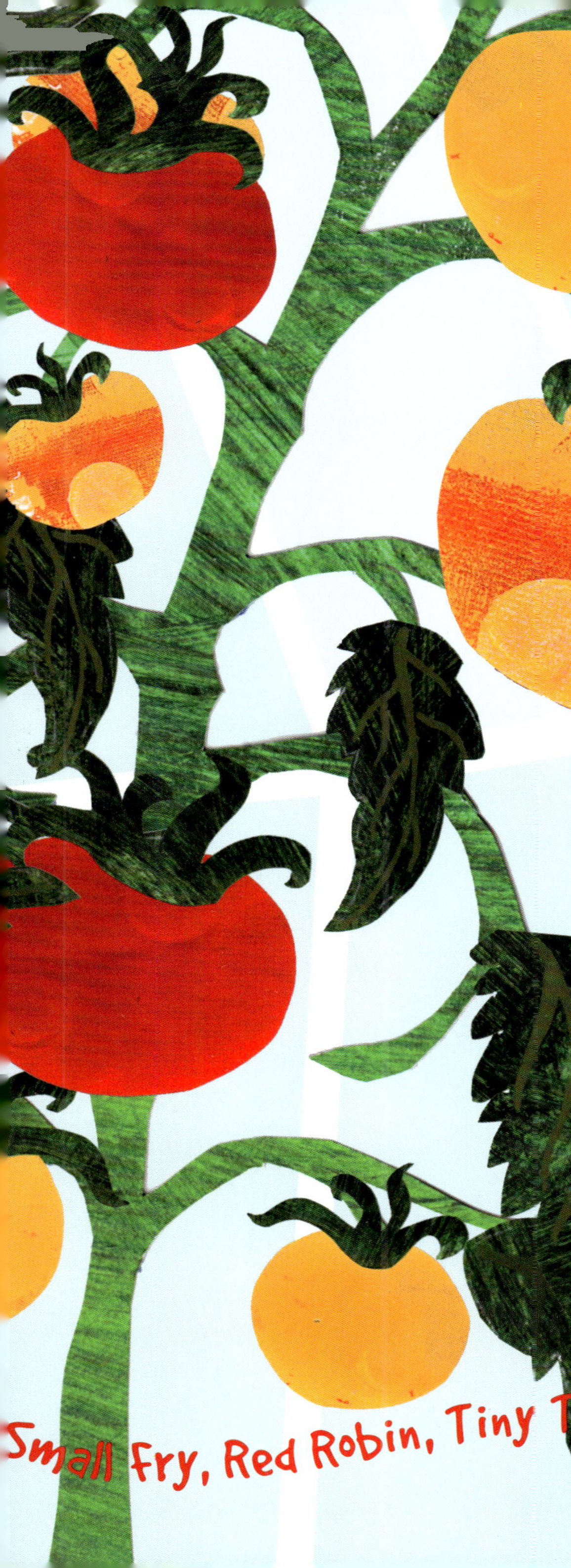

I'm a Big Red Tomato

Growing on a vine,
A big red tomato
Looking oh, so fine.
Now you can make good things with me –
Soup, juice, pizza to name just three.
I'm a big red tomato
Growing on a vine.
Grow, grow, grow.

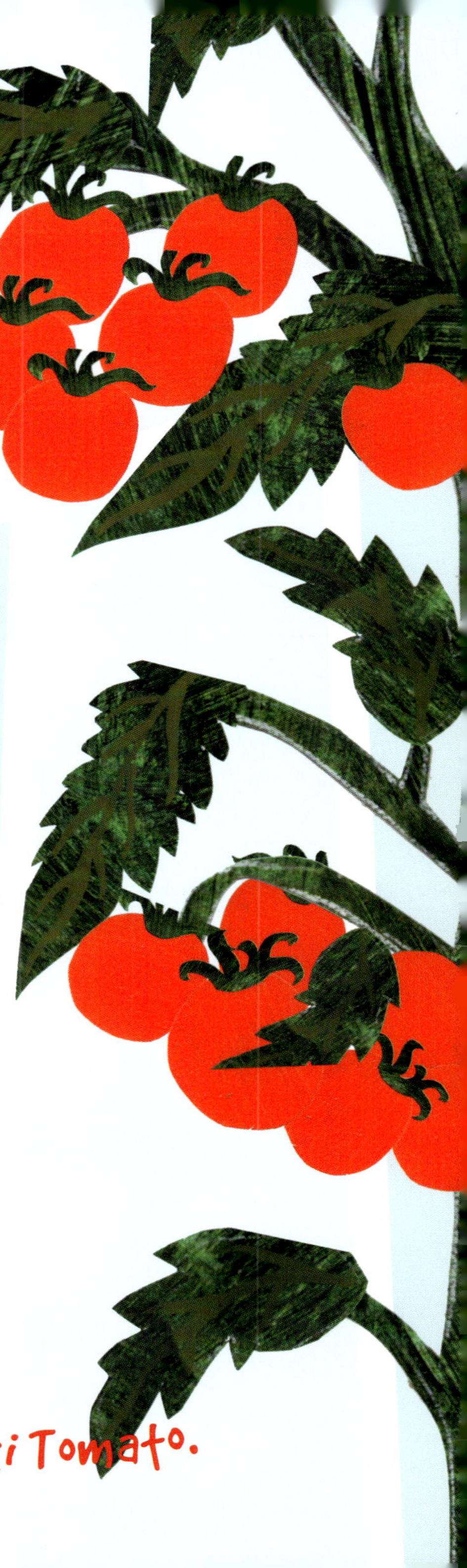

Small Fry, Red Robin, Tiny Tim, Banana Legs, Bonny Best, Heinz or Taxi Tomato.

Uu

Udders Under Umbrellas

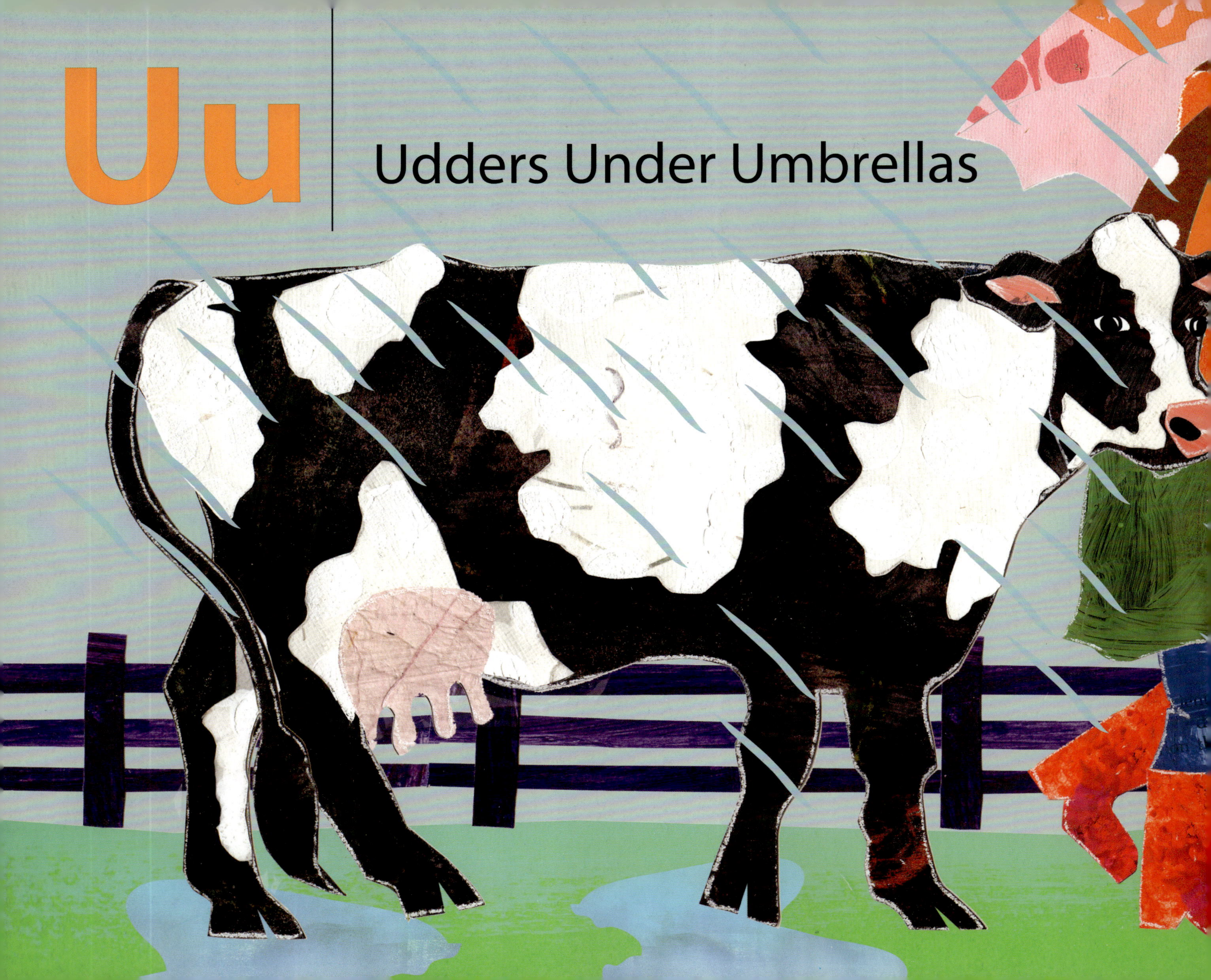

Everyone wakes up early for first milking, even on rainy days.

Twice a day, in the morning and the evening, the dairy cow follows us to the milking barn to give us her milk. Like the other black and white spotted cows on this dairy farm she's a Holstein.

The farmer feeds his dairy cows a mixture of hay and grain. The cows use the energy from their feed to make milk. The cows make lots of milk, more than their calves need. One cow can make enough milk every day to fill almost 100 glasses of milk.

Making milk is thirsty work. A dairy cow will drink about a bathtub full of water each day.

Every cow has four teats, one for each part of her udder.

Vv

Vegetable Voyage

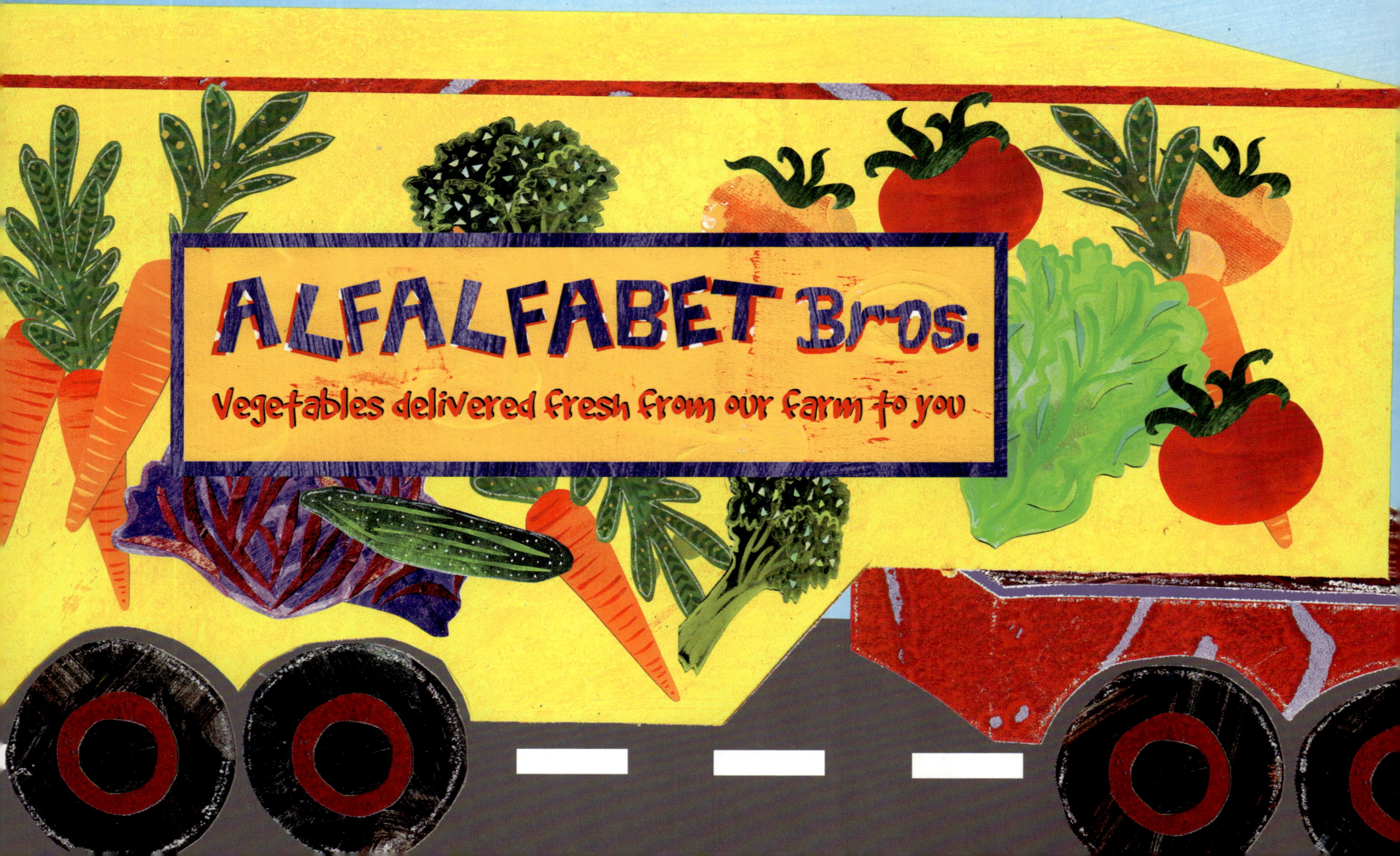

Have you ever wondered what vegetables would talk about if they could speak?

"Are we there yet?" the baby broccolini whined. *"Better be soon,"* the tomato replied. *"One more bump and I'll be bruised for sure!"*

"I don't know why you're complaining," moaned the lettuce. *"It seems like ages since we left the farm and my leaves are starting to wilt."*

"We're cold!" cried the mini cucumbers. *"We liked it better in the hot house."*

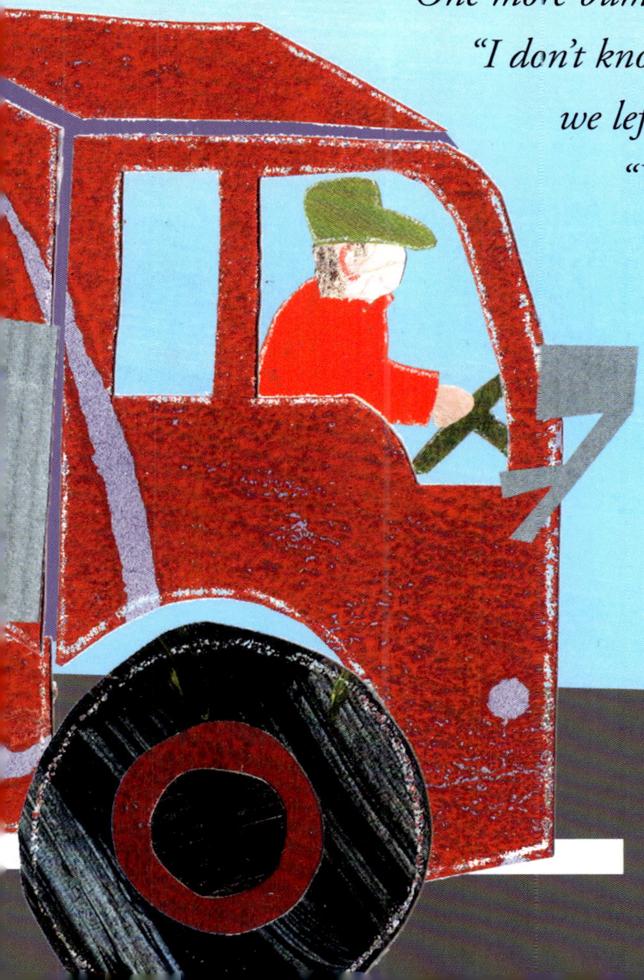

"Wait a minute!" bellowed the cabbage. *"First stop is the farmers' market then the rest of us will continue on for delivery to the supermarket. You've all been grown just for this journey,"* he scolded. *"Sit back and enjoy the trip. It will be over before you're really ripe!"*

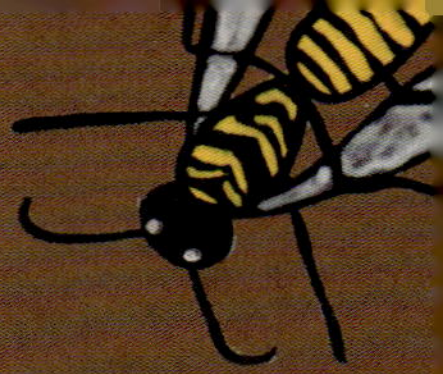

Ww

Woolly Bears Worry Watermelons

How to Take Care of a Woolly Bear Caterpillar

Woolly bear caterpillars come in lots of colours but most are black with an orange stripe in the middle. The best time to find one is in the fall when they are crawling about in search of a sheltered space to spend the winter. First, fill the bottom of a plastic container with a damp cloth and some dry leaves. Poke a few air holes in the lid so that your bear can breath. Next, put your woolly bear in his new winter home and keep it in a cold place like the balcony or porch. **Let your bear sleep.**

In the spring your bear will wake up hungry so find him some fresh dandelions (his favourite food) and damp soil. After feeding a bit, he will spin his silk cocoon and pupate. Soon, a Tiger Moth will magically emerge. That's called metamorphosis (met-ah-mor-fuh-siss). Release your moth that night so it can return to nature and repeat the life cycle.

Now the moth helps farmers by pollinating their crops.

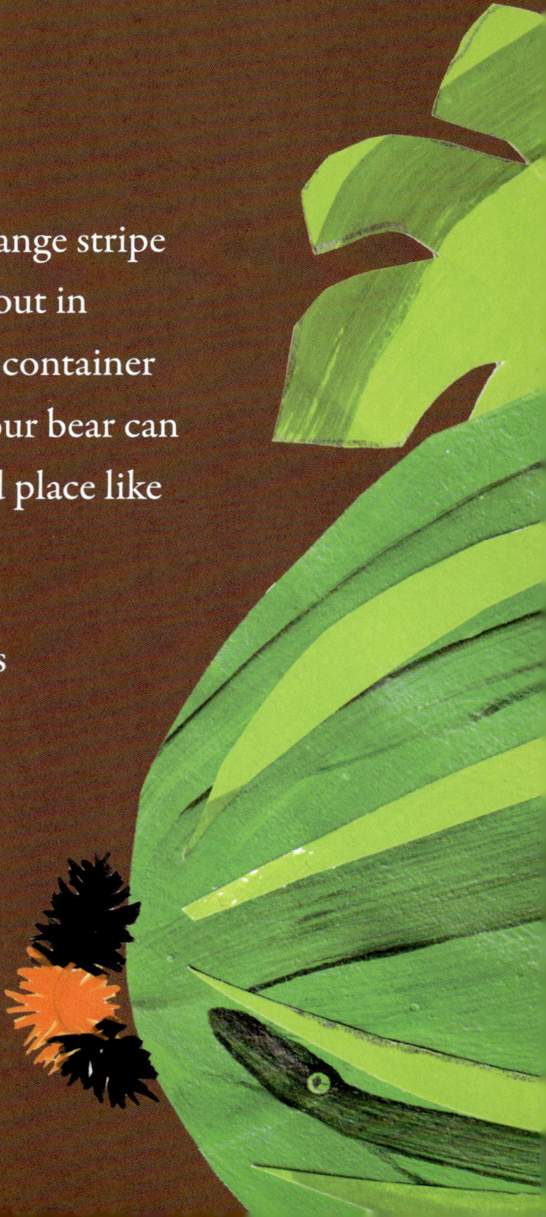

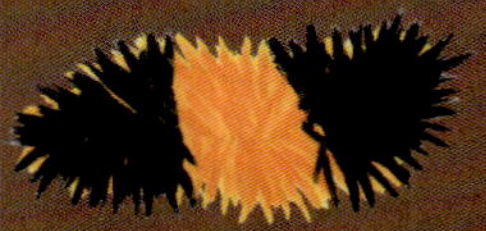

Do you think the watermelon is worried
that the waltzing woolly bears might fall off?

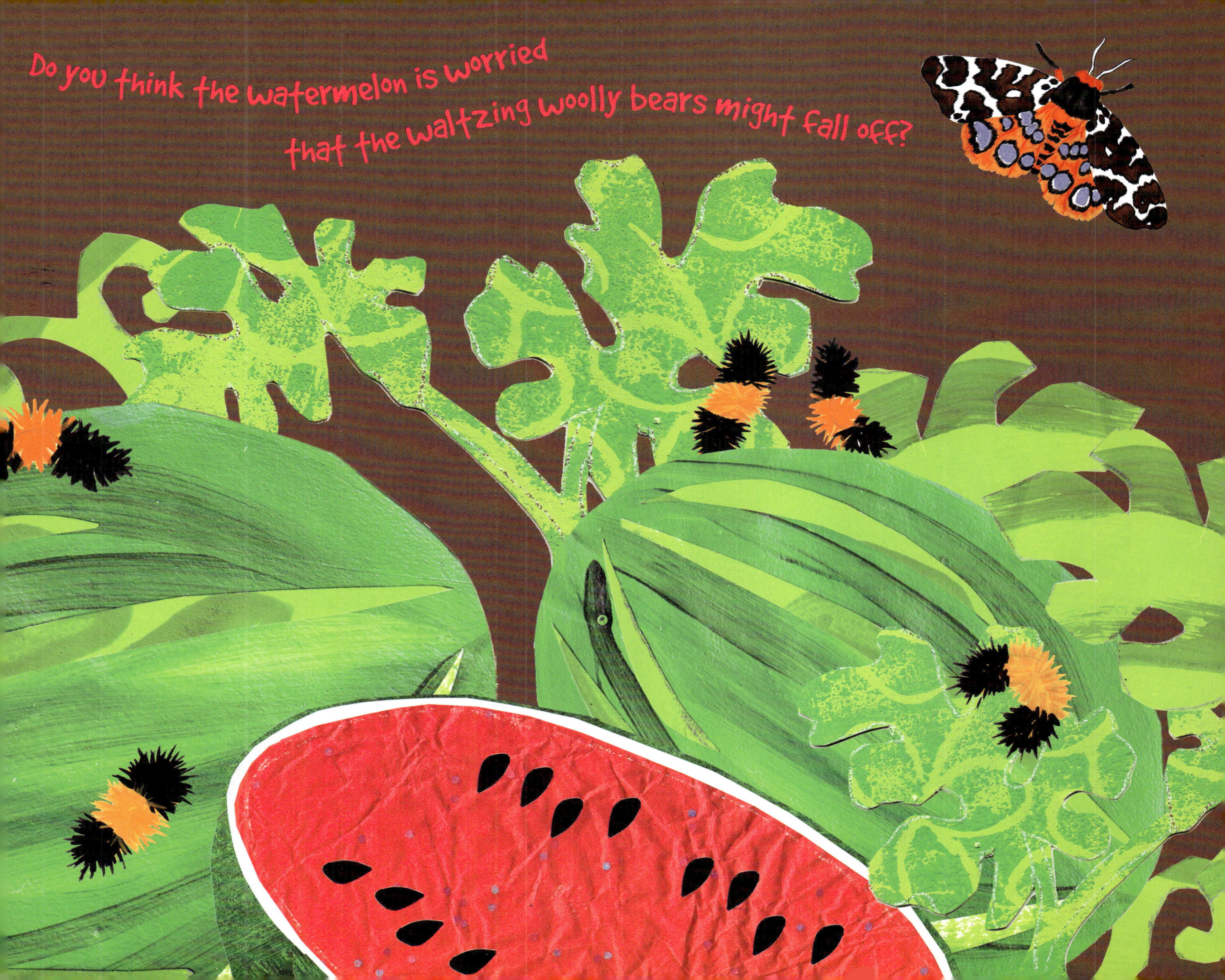

XxYy

X-Large Eggs with Yummy Yellow Yolks

Chickens come in different sizes and so do their eggs. The smallest eggs are called Peewees and the larger ones are Jumbo and Extra-Large.

Most of the eggs we eat come from chickens called layers. Ducks, geese and quail are raised for their eggs too. Of course ostriches lay the largest eggs. Eating one ostrich egg is the same as eating almost 24 chicken eggs! **That's one big fried egg!**

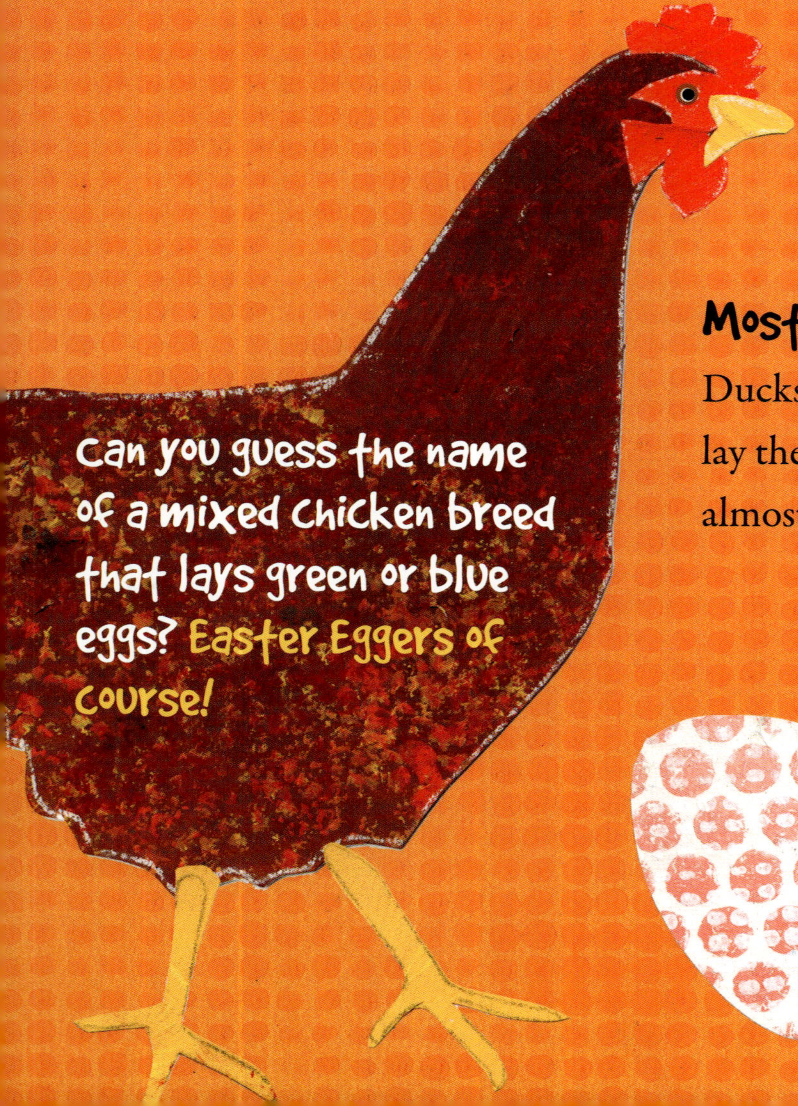

Can you guess the name of a mixed chicken breed that lays green or blue eggs? Easter Eggers of course!

What happens when you tell an egg a joke? It cracks up!

Did you know that not all chicken eggs are white?

Some breeds of chickens lay coloured eggs. Some eggs are even speckled. The White Leghorn breed lays white eggs. Rhode Island Reds and Silver Cuckoo hens lay brown eggs. A Yokohama is a white chicken with an elegant long tail that lays cream-coloured eggs.

A fun way to find out if a hen will lay coloured eggs is to check her ears! Hens with white earlobes lay white eggs and hens with red earlobes lay coloured eggs.

The most number of yolks ever found in one egg was nine.

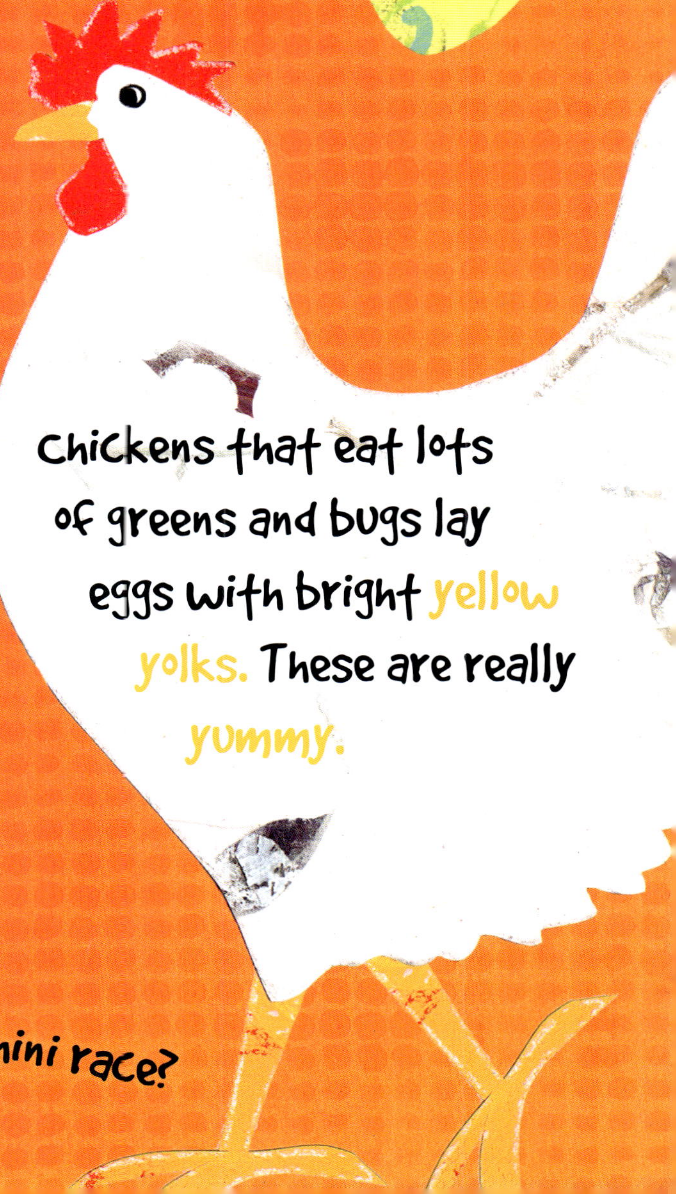

Chickens that eat lots of greens and bugs lay eggs with bright yellow yolks. These are really yummy.

Have you ever seen a zucchini race?

Zz

Zoom Zoom Zucchini

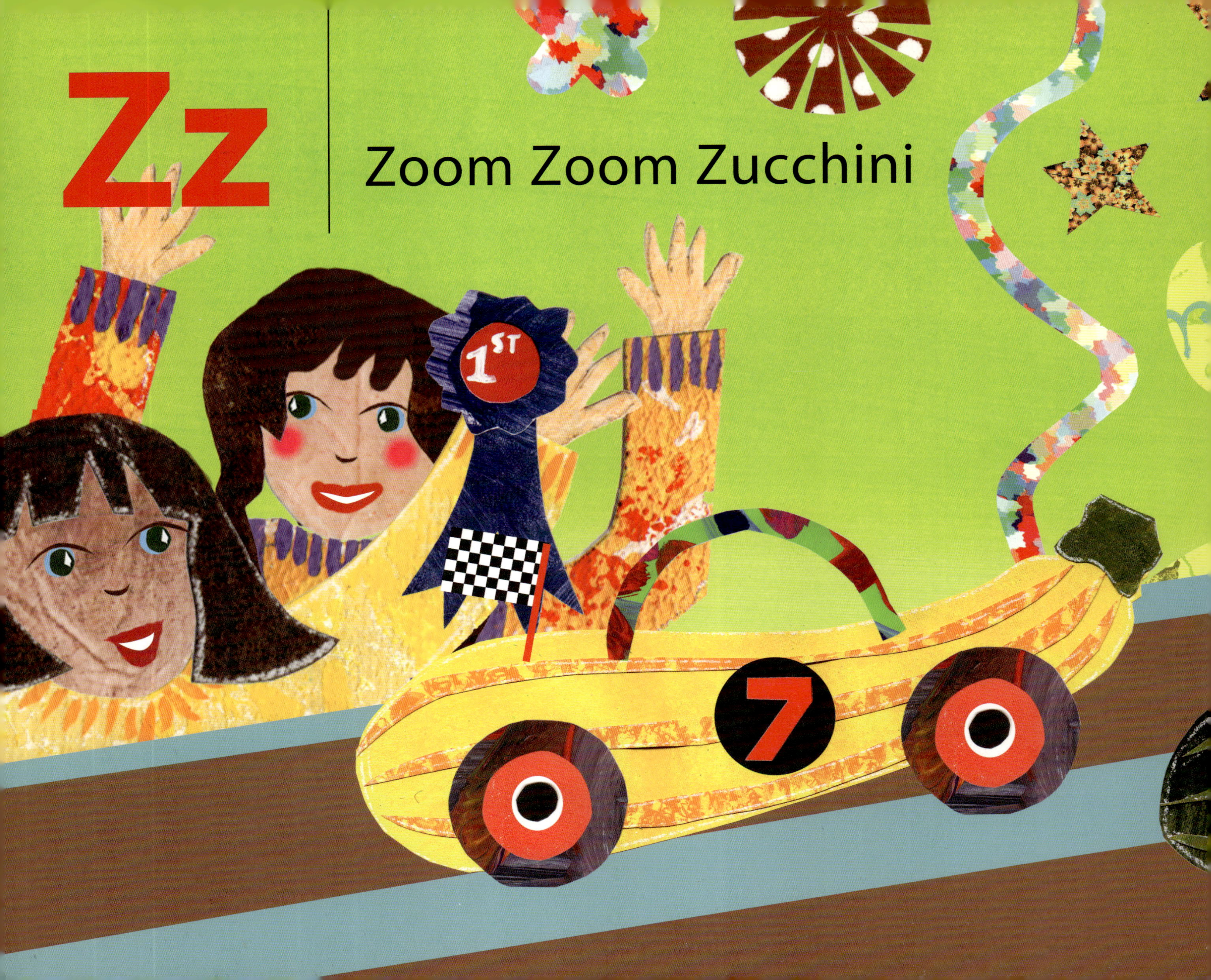

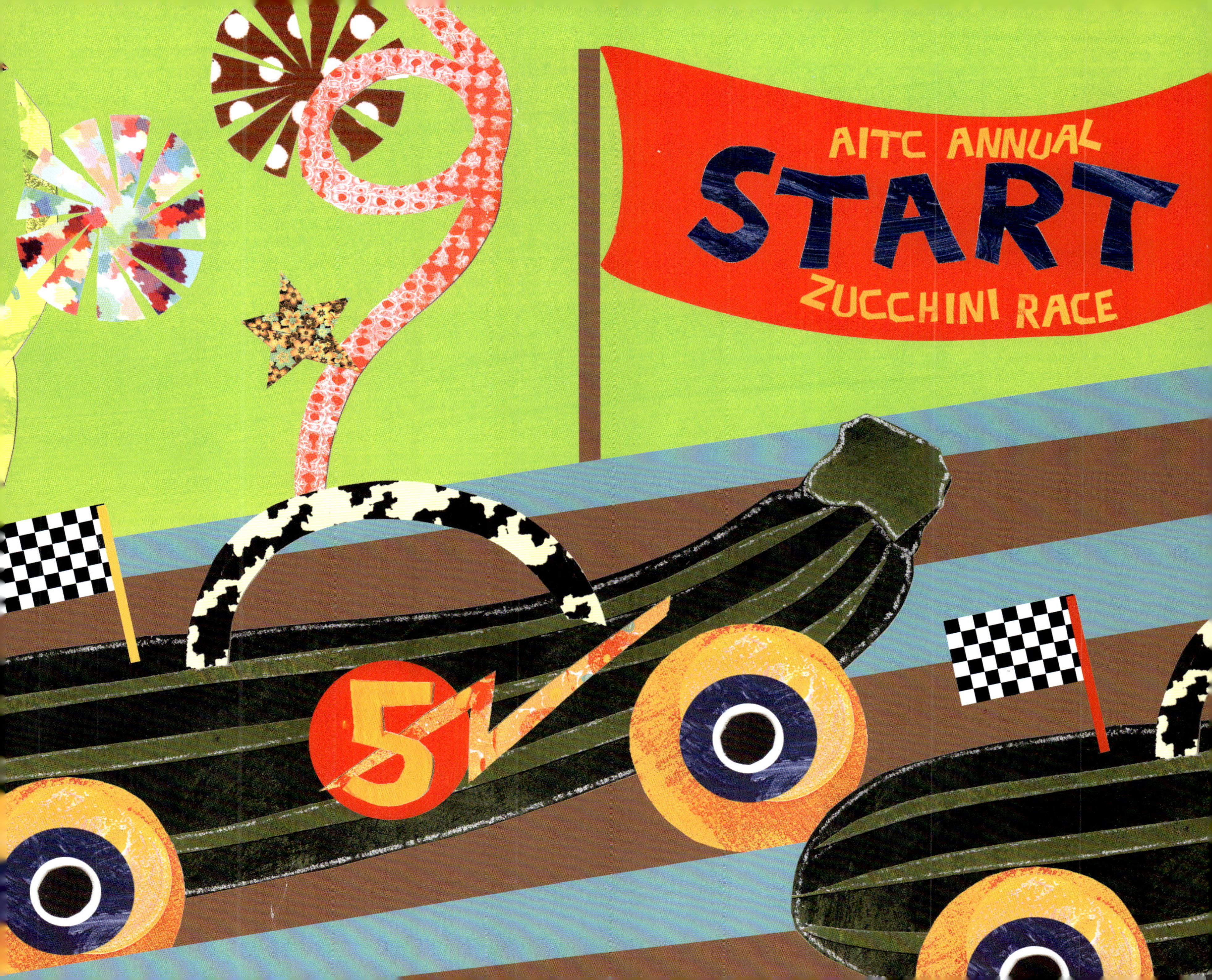
AITC ANNUAL
START
ZUCCHINI RACE
5

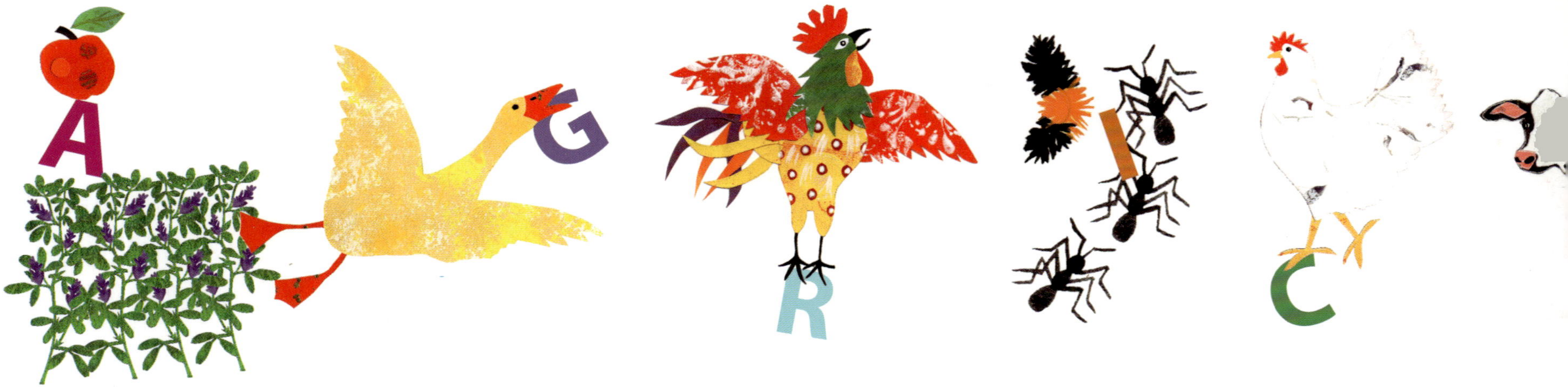

dairy aphid caterpillar berries alfalfa carrot manure

farmer geese honey kohlrabi muck harvest

bee jelly ewe crops dinner egg milk flock greenhouse

horse dig apples grain fruit calf ladybug apricot

heifer chicken lettuce beef humus mud breed jam

moth asparagus

manure bull field beans market earth grow lamb

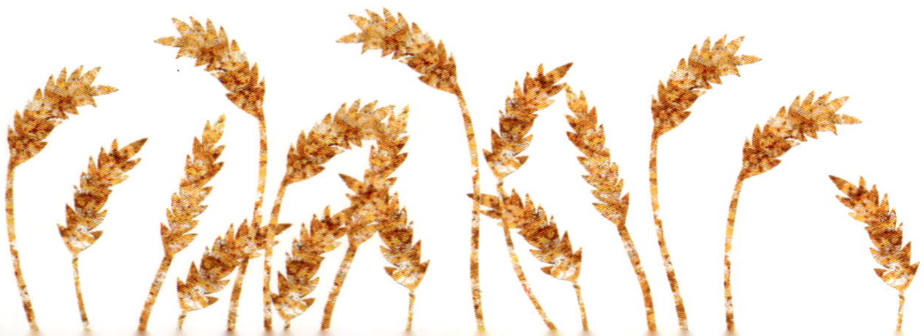

Can you find these wonderful wor

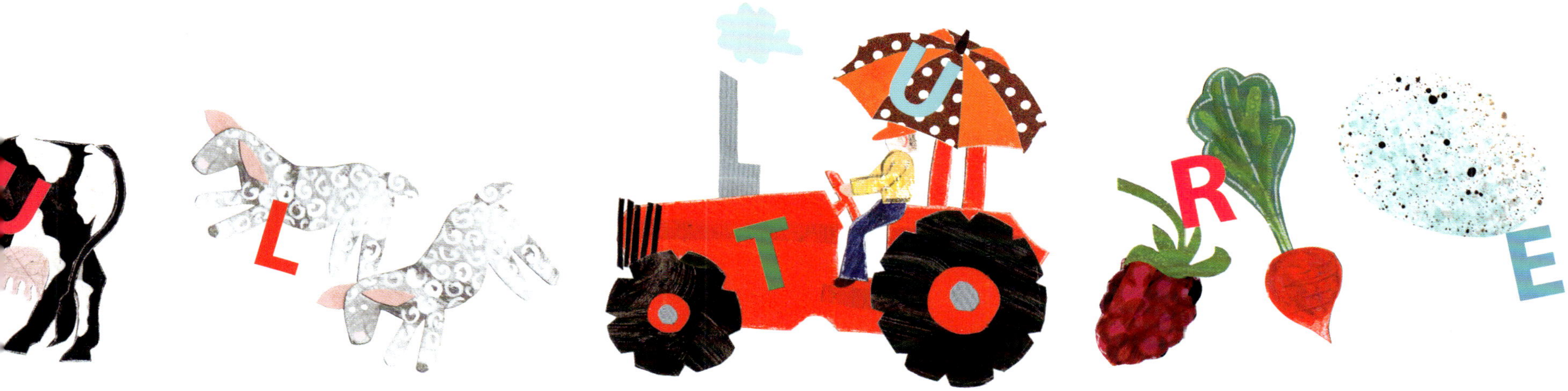

range rooster wool overalls underground sprouts

queen pollen

pig vegetable wheat nectar zucchini

trees roots

seeder orchard udder

pear tuber

spuds

nutrients hay ruminant

stalks watermelon

pea oats

water spring tomato

rainy

tractor ram barn soil

yolks

pumpkin potato

pollinate

ripe stink ranch hen sheep

worm

om agriculture in Alfalfabet?

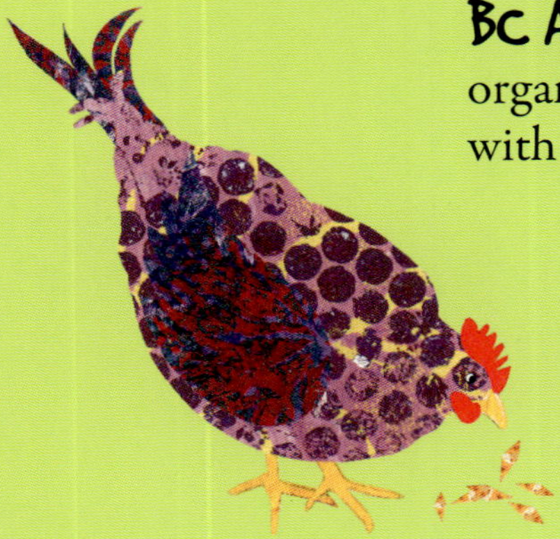

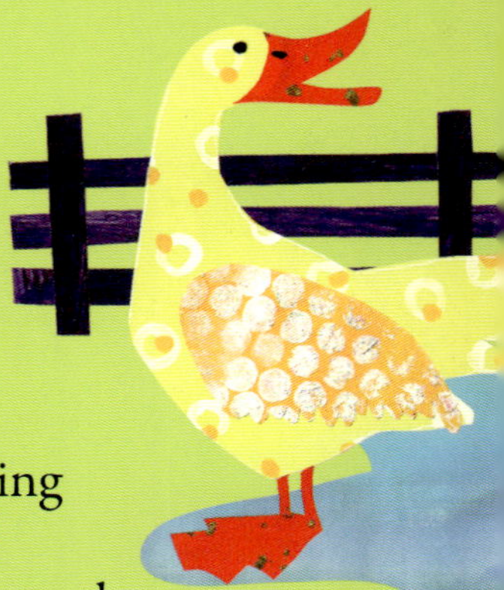

BC Agriculture in the Classroom Foundation (BCAITC) is a non-profit organization that through its various teaching resources and programs works with educators to bring British Columbia's agriculture to their students.

At BCAITC we believe that learning about agriculture is not only learning about food. It is also learning about the special people who work with the environment to provide our food and the hundreds of products that we use and enjoy every day. We believe that having a good understanding of agriculture enables students to make better food choices. It also leads to an awareness of the role we play in the sustainability of agriculture in our communities.

In 'Alfalfabet' agriculture and literacy come together to invite new and emerging readers to discover the wonderful words from agriculture. Through language and pictures new readers will discover many new sights, sounds, smells and flavours from agriculture and in turn learn how agriculture enriches and nourishes their own lives and that of their community.

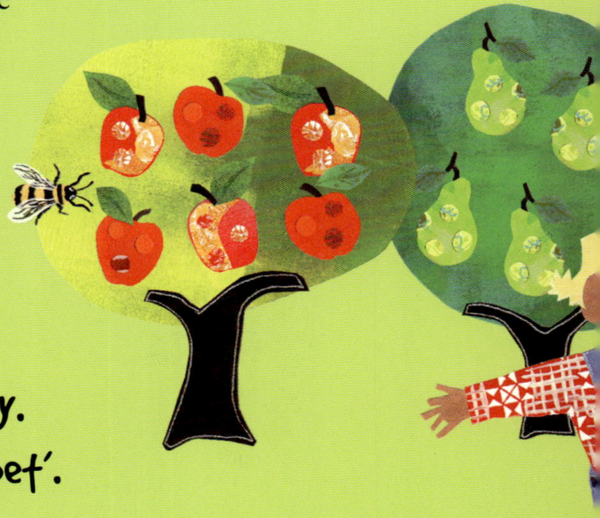

BCAITC offers a wealth of resources and programs for teachers and their students. We invite you to visit our website to learn more about how you can bring agriculture into your students' lives.

Thank you for inviting us into your classroom and library.
We hope that you and your students will enjoy 'Alfalfabet'.

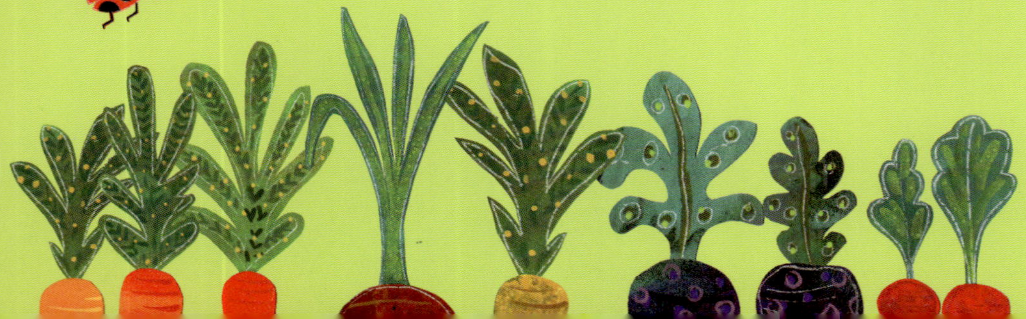

To learn more about our school programs and teaching resources visit:

aitc.ca/bc

British Columbia Agriculture in the Classroom Foundation

For Sebastian, Julia, Kayla and Brenna – our number one readers and vegetable eaters.

First published in hardcover by BC Agriculture in the Classroom Foundation in 2009

Library and Archives Canada Cataloguing in Publication

Watterson, Carol, 1960-
Alfalfabet A to Z : the wonderful words from agriculture / written by Carol Watterson ; illustrated by Michela Sorrentino.

"British Columbia Agriculture in the Classroom Foundation".
ISBN 978-0-9812317-0-9

1. Agriculture--Juvenile literature. 2. English language--Alphabet--Juvenile literature. 3. Alphabet books. I. Sorrentino, Michela, 1962- II. British Columbia Agriculture in the Classroom Foundation III. Title.

PE1155.W39 2009 j630 C2009-901830-6

This book has been printed on 100lb Matte stock with 10% post consumer waste.
The illustrations were prepared using collage with hand printed papers and acrylics.
Cover and interior design by Michela Sorrentino, hermanisorrentino.com

Printed and bound in Canada by Friesens

The authors would like to thank the teachers at Lord Roberts Annex for their input and enthusiasm.
Special thanks to Lindsay Babineau and BCAITC for making this book possible.

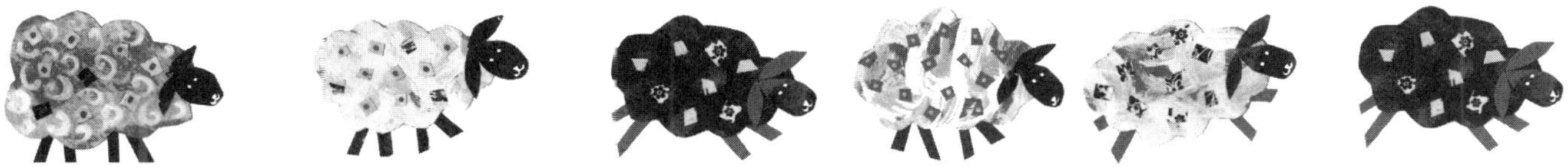

For additional information, please contact:
BC Agriculture in the Classroom Foundation
Abbotsford Agriculture Centre
1767 Angus Campbell Road, Abbotsford, BC V3G 2M3

visit our website at: aitc.ca/bc